BETRAYAL AND OTHER ACTS OF SUBVERSION

BETRAYAL AND OTHER ACTS OF SUBVERSION

FEMINISM, SEXUAL POLITICS, ASIAN AMERICAN WOMEN'S LITERATURE

Leslie Bow

PRINCETON UNIVERSITY PRESS   PRINCETON AND OXFORD

Library of Congress Cataloging-in-Publication Data

Bow, Leslie, 1962–
Betrayal and other acts of subversion : feminism, sexual politics,
Asian American women's literature / Leslie Bow.
p.   cm.
Includes bibliographical references and index.
ISBN 0-691-07092-X (alk. paper)
ISBN 0-691-07093-8 (pbk. : alk. paper)
1. American literature—Asian American authors—History and
criticism. 2. American literature—Women authors—History and
criticism. 3. Feminism and literature—United States. 4. Women
and literature—United States. 5. Asian American women in literature.
6. Asian Americans in literature. 7. Sex role in literature. I. Title
PS153.A84 B69   2000
810.9′9287′08995—dc21   00-058488

This book has been composed in Sabon

Printed on acid-free paper. ∞

www.pup.princeton.edu

Printed in the United States of America

10 9 8 7 6 5 4 3 2 1

10 9 8 7 6 5 4 3 2 1
(Pbk.)

Acknowledgment goes to the following publishers for permission to reprint previously published material: "The Gendered Subject of Human Rights: Asian American Literature as Postcolonial Intervention." *Cultural Critique* (Winter 1999): 37–78. "Le Ly Hayslip's Bad (Girl) Karma: Sexuality, National Allegory, and the Politics of Neutrality" published in *Prose Studies*, vol. 17, no. 1, pp. 141–60 by Frank Cass Publishers, London. "Cultural Conflict/Feminist Resolution in Amy Tan's *The Joy Luck Club*." In *New Visions in Asian American Studies: Diversity, Community, and Power* ed. Franklin Eng, Judy Yung, Stephen Fugita, and Elaine Kim, Washington State University Press, 1994. 235–47. "The Illusion of the Middle Way: Liberal Feminism and Biculturalism in *Fifth Chinese Daughter*." In *Bearing Dreams, Shaping Visions: Asian Pacific American Perspectives* ed. Linda A. Revilla, Gail M. Nomura, Shawn Wong, and Shirley Hune, Washington State University Press, 1993. 161–75.

To Russ and Julian

Contents

Acknowledgments

THIS PROJECT could not have been completed without the support and inspiration of mentors, friends, colleagues, and family members. I am indebted to Akasha Hull, Helene Moglen, and José David Saldívar, whose guidance and commitment brought this project to fruition and whose scholarship serves as a model for my own. I want to thank Nora Okja Keller and Laura Hyun Yi Kang for their inspiration and friendship at the University of California, Santa Cruz. Renny Christopher, Ellen Hart, Ekua Omosupe, and Miriam Wallace all offered me valuable feedback and encouragement. I am most grateful to Elena Tajima Creef, whose unequivocal support is equaled only by the shining example of her own work in Asian American Studies.

My heartfelt thanks goes to C. Lok Chua, Tassie Gwilliam, Wendy Hesford, Daniel Kim, Elaine Kim, Wendy Kozol, Josephine Lee, Robert Lee, Frank Palmeri, Sangeeta Ray, Malini Johar Schueller, Mihoko Suzuki, Lindsey Tucker, Sau-ling Wong, and Robyn Wiegman, who graciously read and commented on parts of the manuscript in its various manifestations. Your astute feedback has sustained and motivated me throughout the writing process. I wish to thank Peter Bellis, Shari Benstock, Suzanne Oboler, and Sandra Pouchet Paquette for their support and collegiality. To those who make up the Humanities Colloquium at the University of Miami, especially David Glimp and Michael Rothberg, your commitment to intellectual life provided necessary nourishment and engagement. To Janice Okoomian, Susette Min, and Lynn Ink: your work challenged me to give my best. I cannot thank Thomas LeBien at Princeton University Press enough for his professionalism at a crucial stage of this manuscript's production. The artist Hu°o°ng graciously assented to the reproduction of her painting, "Students," to adorn this book's cover. I am grateful to Wendy Law-Yone, Fiona Cheong, and Jade Snow Wong for their willingness to talk with me about their work.

To my parents, Willie and Sue Mae Bow: without your sacrifices and love this work would not have been possible. Julian Ty continually entertained and delightfully diverted me in the course of this project.

Most of all, Russ Castronovo stimulated and challenged this work and I am grateful for his energy, faith, and love.

This book was completed with the generous fellowship support of the Office of the President of the University of California, the Center for Cultural Studies and Oakes College at the University of California, Santa

Cruz, and the James Knight Junior Faculty Fellowship at the University of Miami. I would also like to acknowledge grant support from the Dean of the College and Dean of the Faculty at Brown University; the Board of Literature and the Feminist Studies Organized Research Activity at the University of California, Santa Cruz; and the Max Orovitz Summer Research Awards at the University of Miami.

Leslie Bow
Miami, Florida

BETRAYAL AND OTHER ACTS OF SUBVERSION

One

Introduction

THEORIZING GENDERED CONSTRUCTIONS
OF ETHNIC AND NATIONAL COLLECTIVITY

Notes on the Notorious

A betrayal is a breach of trust. Its threat lies precisely in its rupturing the invisible cohesion of community. The charge of women's betrayal, of infidelity, has been represented as intrinsic to feminine nature; women have long been invested with both fickleness and the power to beguile. As agents and embodiments of inconstancy, women bear the blame for the dissolution of bonds between men. Allegations of feminine perfidy thus offer ready instances for understanding both the homosocial nature of collective associations, including ethnic and national ties, and the role of women in securing and maintaining these associations. As symbolic boundary markers for ethnic and national affiliations, women embody ethnic authenticity, patriotism, and class solidarity—and their repudiation. For Asian American women, these symbolic boundary markers are especially fraught.

Betrayal and Other Acts of Subversion examines Asian American women's putative betrayals to bring to light the very terms of collective identification, subjectivity, and belonging. This book investigates implicit and explicit charges of disloyalty in Asian American women's writing in order to explore the gendered nature of literary rhetoric. How are Americanized gender norms deployed to understand, for example, the terms of U.S. citizenship, Asian ethnic solidarity, or postcolonial nationalisms? In examining the gendered discourse of political appeal in literature, this study reveals how mechanisms of affiliation are constituted and analyzes the stakes of their maintenance, particularly for women who transgress borders drawn by multiple loyalties. In doing so, I suggest that "betrayal" can constitute subversion of another kind, a subversion of repressive authority that depends on upholding strict borders between groups and individuals.

I begin with two exemplary female "traitors," the first charged with undoing a popular icon, and the second with betraying a nation. Both examples highlight the connection between gender and regulation at work in Asian American women's literature.

It might be said that performance artist Yoko Ono's most significant cultural "happening" or Fluxus[1] event was the successful seduction of John Lennon in a London art gallery using the unlikely tools of a ladder, a magnifying glass, and the word "yes." Initiated by Lennon's interest in her *Ceiling Painting* (aka *Yes*), which required the viewer to climb a ladder in order to inspect the single, affirmative word attached to the ceiling, Lennon and Ono's connection was consolidated the moment she handed him a card that said, simply, "BREATHE." In 1966, Lennon was, for all intents and purposes, happily married to both wife Cynthia and to the other three lads who made up the Beatles. That a strange little Japanese artist could steal a married man from his wife, allegedly break up the Beatles, and transform Britain's greatest "magical song-maker and radical rocker" into a sibylline peace activist and later, househusband, was a series of events perhaps only slightly more remarkable than Ono's own transformation years later from reviled foreigner to shrewd American businesswoman and grieving widow—an accepted, if not much beloved, fixture in American popular culture.[2] Anointed "the High Priestess of the Happening," poet-composer-sculptor-performer Ono quickly became "a kind of psychic lightning-conductor for other people's hostility," particularly in the British press (Michael Bracewell cited in Simon Grant, "Ono! It's Her Again," *The Guardian*, 5 Feb. 1997, sec. 2, col. 3: 12). The hatred leveled at her was not so much due to her association with the avant-garde, although mainstream rock fans no doubt found incomprehensible Ono's attempts to eke profundity out of apparently nonsensical instructions or scripts ("Use your blood to paint . . . Paint until you die," "Stir inside of your brains with a penis" [Ono 1970, n.p.]) designed to "induce music of the mind in people." Lennon's remark, "they're dying for us to fall apart, for God knows what reason," was perhaps disingenuous for the very obviousness of that reason: the press and public were interested in Ono's downfall because of what was perceived to be her undue, corrupting influence on John, a *premeditated* engineering of Lennon's abandonment of his male comrades.[3]

Ono's notoriety was thus intrinsically tied to her perceived talent at both sexual and psychological seduction, an ability made all the more mysterious by her apparent lack of physical attractiveness ("I don't think she's ugly," a bewildered Lennon opined. "I think she's beautiful," cited in Cott and Doudna 1982, 38). Hers was a political seduction as well—a seduction away from bourgeois modes of perception and from the separation of art from everyday life, both tenets associated with the Fluxus movement. She would later note, however, that the "circus like atmosphere" after their meeting signaled an end to "the quiet kind of conceptual games" that made up her art (cited in Haskell and Hanhardt 1991, 12). Later artistic involvements with Lennon were neither quiet nor simply conceptual, garnering the attention of the FBI and the Immigration and Naturalization Service (INS), who watched their antiwar involvements with an eye to deportation.[4] Earlier countercultural performances staged by the couple shocked bourgeois norms with an overtly challenging sexuality; as Lennon noted regarding their 1969 piece, *Bed-in* (aka *Bed Peace*) in the Amsterdam Hilton, "the press came, expecting to see us fuckin' in bed. They'd all heard John and Yoko were going to fuck in front of the press for peace." The phalanx of reporters who showed up were therefore relieved to see only a couple in bed in pajamas saying, "Peace, brother" (Cott and Doudna 1982,108). *Bed-in* was intended to convey the symbolic union of men and women, East and West. Yet contrary to her intent, Ono's public reception revealed that their coupling had been taken another way; it was the West's corruption by the East abetted by the distaff's controlling influence, a perception later reinforced by her feminist phase as epitomized by the statement, "Woman is the Nigger of the World."

Reaction to Ono reveals more than the fact that women often take the blame for men's choices, including infidelity; it demonstrates the powerful mythmaking surrounding an Asian female public figure whose notoriety lay in an imagined seductive power. Ono's "foreignness" was an intrinsic part of that notoriety although explicit references to her outsider status might often remain veiled; a memo to Beatles Fan Club members on the eve of the Lennon/Ono wedding urged in its pseudo-liberalism, "we should at least give Yoko the same chance we are going to be giving Linda and that Maureen and Patti got! I know this news is shocking, but I suppose if it will make John happy, we should all be very enthused too" (cited in Cott and Doudna 1982,36).[5] But the marriage did not represent a betrayal of John's female fans as much as it did a betrayal of man's allegiance to other men; perceptions of Yoko's difference potentially enhanced belief in the siren's mysterious ability to break homosocial allegiance.

In connecting female sexuality and racial difference to seduction and betrayal, Ono's example resonates with the conviction of another ethnic Japanese woman, first in the courts of public opinion, and later in U.S. federal court. While a young Yoko Ono experienced unaccustomed wartime deprivation outside Tokyo during World War II, nisei Iva Toguri d'Aquino was working as a disc jockey for Radio Tokyo's popular English-language propaganda and entertainment program, "Zero Hour," written and produced by a number of Allied POWs being held in Japan. In 1949, d'Aquino was convicted of one count of treason against the

United States as the infamous radio personality, Tokyo Rose. D'Aquino's alleged treason carried specifically gendered resonance: the accusation that she undermined Allied morale by broadcasting misinformation about Pacific losses was made more insidious by reports of her methods, namely, interspersing her record introductions with hints of women's infidelity back home. As one of the journalists who "broke" the Tokyo Rose story after the war melodramatically reported, "She would play nostalgic music, which they loved, and then inform them their wives and sweethearts were carrying on with 4F's and highly paid war-workers while they were giving their sweat, blood and lives in the heat, muck, rain and jungles of the Pacific." "Well, boys," Tokyo Rose was alleged to have said. "I'll be signing off for tonight. I'm going to get my loving tonight. How about you?" But as subsequent investigation bore out, Iva Toguri d'Aquino was merely in the wrong place at the wrong time; there was no English-speaking female radio announcer broadcasting under the name "Tokyo Rose" in the Pacific; moreover, the two witnesses whose testimony sealed a single treason conviction later recanted long after d'Aquino had served her six-year sentence. In fact, the Office of War Information had concluded prior to Japanese surrender, "There is no Tokyo Rose; the name is strictly a GI invention." Nonetheless, reports of Rose's seductive, American-accented, poisonous female voice were mythic constructions attributed to numerous exotic sources—among them, a beautiful Eurasian, the wife of the last Japanese ambassador to Washington, General Tojo's mistress, a hula dancer born in Maui, a Canadian nisei, and a white woman from St. Louis.[6]

D'Aquino's conviction is noteworthy not only for the role the postwar press played in agitating for her prosecution and exerting pressure on the attorney general to go forward with the case in spite of what was previously acknowledged to be flimsy evidence. More significant is that during the trial the "Tokyo Rose" fantasy was powerful enough to trump points of the defense that were at odds with popular belief, specifically that Iva Toguri d'Aquino neither looked nor, more important, sounded remotely like a sexy Asian Mata Hari. The two reporters who later claimed to have solicited Tokyo Rose's "confession" in the form of an interview in which d'Aquino testified she was "the one and only Tokyo Rose" were surprised and no doubt disappointed by her physical appearance; one noted that she "was a pleasant-looking girl, but by no stretch of the imagination a siren" while the other was considerably less charitable, describing her as "unattractive, even for a Japanese woman."[7] D'Aquino later acknowledged their deflated hopes, conceding, "It should have been Ava Gardner, but instead it was me" (Duus 1979, 21). As the prisoner of war in charge of "Zero Hour," Australian Major Charles Cousens testified that he had chosen d'Aquino as a disc jockey precisely because her "comedy voice" would help undermine his captors' efforts at effective propaganda; he wanted "a gin-fog voice, anything but femininely seductive," a voice suitable for broadcasting largely innocuous radio program content described as "hokum" and "corn" mixed with popular music (Weyl 1950, 386).

The mystique surrounding Rose, the femme fatale with an insinuating insider's knowledge of troop movements in the Pacific, was thus a powerful counter to the reality of Iva Toguri d'Aquino's goofy, teasing broadcasts ("Like that? Well, be good and we'll have an even better one directly . . . Please to listening!" [Kutler 1980, 453]). The sexual aura surrounding the legend granted d'Aquino a celebrity equal to General Tojo's and out of proportion to her wartime involvement.[8] One reporter asked American GIs in the United State and Japan what they thought should be done to "Tokyo Rose"; while some of the answers "were unprintable," others responded, simply, " 'I'd sure like a date with her' " (C. Lee 1947, 90). Popular understanding of "Rose's" crime—inciting soldiers with images of the cuckold's humiliation—exaggerated fears about the loss of military-as-sexual potency, an effect that was not, in the end, operative in the nineteen words for which d'Aquino was actually convicted ("Orphans of the Pacific, you are really orphans now. With all your ships sunk, how will you get home?"). For d'Aquino, promoting anxiety over women's infidelity easily metamorphosed into the charge of her own national infidelity. The story of Tokyo Rose speaks to a belief in the power of sexual alliances to disrupt other collective alliances, specifically, loyalty to nation and comrades-in-arms.

Feminine power is often perceived to be located in the capacity to both maintain and disrupt loyalties; the perfidy of both Ono's and d'Aquino's supposed seductions lay in their ability to corrupt men's identification with other men, undermining allegiance to the group or to the nation. Western public response to these figures also speaks to associations between female power and racial difference, associations that produced consequences for these Japanese/American women who, once accused of betrayal, became victims of the charge. I begin with the examples of Ono and d'Aquino because their inscription within American popular culture reveals to different degrees the underlying function of an accusation of betrayal: a means of determining cultural alliance, it is intended to deauthenticate some affiliations while reconsolidating others. The charge of betrayal, of disloyalty, exposes the competitive structure of overlapping group affiliations by signaling a transgression of solidarity. Ono's and d'Aquino's cases work somewhat differently: while both were seen as active catalysts inciting infidelity and subject to FBI inquiries on the basis of wartime involvement with the media, d'Aquino's case was tried by the state as well as in the court of public opinion. D'Aquino was branded a traitor in the legal sense while Ono's condemnation on the basis of her antiwar activism paled in comparison to her vilification for the more politically innocuous seduction of an international cultural icon. Ono's example is less directly a confrontation with American nationalism than D'Aquino's, but her calumniation speaks to particularly American, racially motivated anxiety about incorporating difference. Although the FBI viewed Lennon as a potential threat to national security and his Englishness would mark him as "equally" an outsider, his alien status could be redeemed by American rock 'n' roll. In contrast, distaste for Ono's racially marked inscrutability and her allegiance to an incomprehensible avant-garde was later compounded by rumors of a financial ruthlessness coded in the United States as quintessentially Japanese by the 1980s.

Accusations of disloyalty clearly serve to regulate female sexuality but, as significantly, they police and uphold the identifications necessary for affiliation and connection. These two contextualized instances highlight the ways in which representations of seduction and betrayal consolidate alliances formed across, in these cases, national boundaries. The "love to hate her" aura of Ono and the infamy of Tokyo Rose speak to the racial vilification that appears as a predicate of national cohesion; femininity's association with inconstancy imbues this racialization with moral force. Such a discursive overlayering has specific consequences for Asian American women: How do they negotiate a process of racialization that represents sexuality as disruptive to nationalism and ethnic solidarity as homosocial bonds? In shifting to the more quotidian scenes that populate literature—scenes that do not reflect the scandal of Ono's or Toguri's stories but are nonetheless marked as scandalous—I want to analyze the charge of cultural betrayal as it comes to regulate group belonging. To be cast as a traitor, as beyond the pale of an at times unspoken collective, is to confront the fact that such affiliations have terms of admission, that they are neither natural nor, at times, uncoerced. The flashes of consciousness in the literary vignettes that follow precipitate an awareness of the way sexual identity overlaps ethnicity and national affiliation—and may appear to challenge it. With the recognition that disloyalty to group ties becomes sexualized through charges of infidelity, this study looks at the ways in which expressions of sexuality both signify and interrogate political alliance and ethnic collectivity.

Embodiment and the Rhetoric of Allegiance

"Every cultural change is signified through and on the body," Shirley Geok-lin Lim notes. "My Westernization took place in my body" (Lim 1996, 89). In making this connection, Lim highlights a specific interaction confronted by and commented on by Asian American women across ethnic boundaries. For example, Eleanor Wong Telemaque's *It's Crazy to Stay Chinese in Minnesota* depicts its seventeen-year-old Chinese American heroine pondering her sexuality in her attic bedroom amid leftover charity furniture, piles of movie magazines, and a hidden diary "filled with exclamation marks." The daughter of an ardent Chinese nationalist turned midwestern restaurant owner, Ching is critically scrutinizing her breasts in front of the mirror when she is startled by a knock on the door: "What are you doing, Ching?" her aunt demands. Ching dives for her bathrobe and innocently lies, "I'm studying Chinese. I have learned how to write the characters for filial piety" (Telemaque 1978, 41).

The exchange characterizes the disjunction between Ching's desires and ethnic expectation. Pressures of filial piety find expression in her father's hope that she will one day save China from the Communists; her own wish is less ambitious—she wants to find a boyfriend and lose her virginity. Ching's lament, "I don't want to be Chinese, I want to be American!" (105), positions these identities as a contradiction. In the course of the novel, the concerns she aligns with Americanization—boys and sex—become increasingly at odds with her parents' expectations for a Chinese daughter, one who is dutiful in respect to parents, docile in regard to marriage, and loyal to a country she has never seen. For Ching, control of her own body becomes the means by which she expresses resistance to her parents; losing her "hated hymen" comes to symbolize severing "the umbilical cord" that ties her, in her view, to ethnic belonging. The scene dramatizes dual affiliation as a matter of gender role expectation, with sexuality serving as the mediator between opposing cultural dictates. As the image reflected back by the bedroom mirror and the image her parents hold become increasingly discordant, Ching's body becomes the site of struggle between duty and desire, ethnic loyalty and Americanization.

It is thus in *Bombay Talkie*, a novel about an Indian American woman's return "home" to Bombay, that Ameena Meer's Sabah initially takes pleasure in her (hetero)sexual appearance given the responses her miniskirt elicits on a San Francisco street from a group of Indian men. Their public appreciation graphs national resonance onto her bodily display: " 'Did you see that girl?' one says in Hindi. 'Hey,' shouts the other, 'Miss America!' " (Meer 1994, 8). Sabah's choice of self-presentation is made ambivalent down the street, when she encounters the stares of her fellow diasporic countrywomen:

> Farther down the road, there's a group of their women, in salwar kameezes, their heads covered with scarves. Sabah cringes as they turn to look at her. She's embarrassed. She knows them well. She feels like the paper doll who's had the wrong outfit put over her body. (Meer 1994, 5)

As these gazes regulate Sabah's sense of self, her connection to the nation—her ability to signify "Miss America"—is measured according to her seemingly self-directed sexuality. It is this connection that becomes destabilized in the body's public display. Similarly, Ginu Kamani's short story, "Ciphers" in *Junglee Girl*, portrays the narrator's return to India for the first time since childhood and her encounter with a fellow Gujarati woman on a Bombay train, an encounter that turns into a guessing game about the narrator's ethnic identity as the curious onlooker struggles to locate her, despite—or perhaps because of—her short hair and Western dress. The narrator speculates that it is not the superficiality of attire that betrays origins; she thinks, "even in a sari, or other traditional Indian clothes, something in my eyes, and the set of my mouth, would give me away, would mark me as other, outsider oblique" (Kamani 1995, 7). The narrator senses the disapproving woman's fear, a fear of difference not based on the unconventionality of her hair and dress, but on the overtness of her desire:

> It doesn't matter anymore what identity I was born into. . . . What matters is that I am *sexual*. . . . Being sexual has reshaped my knowledge, my feelings, my very breath. *That* is what fools you; that is what you turn away from in *yourself* when you turn away from me. (11–12)

Whether expressed as desire between women or as a woman's relationship to her own body, displaying specific attitudes toward eroticism trump ethnic markers.[9] In commenting on his daughter's posture and stride, giveaways to her American acculturation, Jeanne Wakatsuki Houston's father challenges in *Farewell to Manzanar*, "How come your daughter is seventeen years old and if you put a sack over her face you couldn't tell she was Japanese from anybody else on the street?" (Houston and Houston 1973, 126). Feminine sexuality becomes the sign of acculturation in the public sphere.

What becomes clear is also that ethnic and national affiliation are determined in part by conflicts over how sexuality is performed, potentially situating the female body as a register of international and domestic political struggle, as a site of national divisions and loyalties. This book thus explores the ways in which Asian American women's ethnic and national identities are represented through gender issues—through contestations over women's roles, feminist solidarity, and expressions of feminine sexuality. Encompassing discussions of both cultural nationalism, broadly defined as Asian ethnic or racial alliance in the United States, as well as nationalism conventionally defined via citizenship, *Betrayal and Other Acts of Subversion* nuances the interactions evident in these vignettes, the competition between national loyalty and sexual expression or alliance, between ethnic and gender communal identification. In doing so, it dialogues with current academic emphasis on globalization and transnationalism, the "imagined" nature of national communities, and postmodern theories of racial identity that privilege fluid movements among geographic locations, identities, and political affiliations. Complicating this emphasis on border shuttling, my interest lies in the ways that subjects are increasingly governed by the rhetoric of allegiance. As Asian American women's literature reveals, negotiating multiple affiliations becomes fraught as the language of betrayal comes to regulate fidelity and communal belonging. This work examines one pervasive figuration, that of feminine sexuality and feminism marking ethnic or national betrayal, particularly as sexuality mediates between progress and tradition, modernity and the "Old World," the United States and Asia. Sexuality becomes a gauge of progress, a gauge that informs the interface between Westernization and modernization.

Oppositions between cultural nationalist and feminist concerns have been clearly manifested in domestic American coalition politics as evidenced by the initial mutual exclusivity of the women's and civil rights movements. But the conflictual nature of multiple identifications is also reflected internationally; on the exclusivity of nationalist sentiment, V. Spike Peterson notes, "[I]intergroup hostility is institutionalized to the extent that identification with a single, essentialized group—the nation—is promoted at the expense of multiple, fluid identifications and trans-group solidarities" (Peterson 1996, 7). Moreover, Third World feminists have documented the often antagonistic relationship between feminism and nationalism as feminism becomes positioned as an imported Western corruption of the indigenous traditions on which anti-imperialist movements have been founded. However, my emphasis here is not on representative social movements, but on the political resonance of imagined relations of affiliation as they serve distinct social purposes. My focus on the interstices of overlapping collectivities is not an attempt to privilege "in-betweeness" or, to invoke Gloria Anzaldúa, borderlands as a potentially radical site (Anzaldúa 1987). Rather, I suggest that the language of betrayal signals the artifice of naturalized racial, ethnic, or national belonging; the charge does not simply contest the authenticity of one's identity or commitment whether in regard to alliances characterized by biological inevitability or those politically chosen, but instead becomes a potent *rhetorical* figuration deployed to signal how affiliations are formed and then consolidated. Asian American women writers not only mediate sexuality's construction as a determiner of loyalty but manipulate that construction as a tool of political persuasion, reconceptualizing "disloyalty" as resistance to repressive authority. If women have reason to be, in terms Adrienne Rich has borrowed, "disloyal to civilization," then this betrayal of racism, patriarchy, or a repressive state constitutes a form of creative activism for Asian American women.[10]

This inquiry engages the rhetoric of betrayal to draw a connection between Asian immigrant writing that uses sexuality to articulate the terms of citizenship and national belonging, and American literature on Asia that expresses the individual's relationship to the state through a similar gendered discourse as part of its geopolitical critique. In what follows I attempt to situate Asian American women not as cultural informants who write to affirm a preestablished sociological reality of ethnic experience, but as agents who craft rhetoric for their own political purposes.

"To Plant a Flag on Water"

Painting to Let the Evening Light Go Through

Hang a bottle behind a canvas.
Place the canvas where the west light
comes in.
The painting will exist when the bottle
creates a shadow on the canvas, or it does
not have to exist.
The bottle may contain liquor, water,
grasshoppers, ants or singing insects, or
it does not have to contain.
    (*Yoko Ono*, 1970)

For Asian Americans the question of nationalism often appears in the form of the paradox of being simultaneously "American born and foreign": "What a crazy riddle," thinks Faye about Korean American identity in *Clay Walls*, "to be yet not to be" (R. Kim 1986, 299). That Asian Americans across ethnic groups are represented as perpetual outsiders is a compelling justification for that coalitional identity. Defined as an "enemy alien" in the country of her birth, poet Janice Mirikitani writes after Japanese American internment,

I do not know the face of this country
it is inhabited by strangers
who call me obscene names.

Jap. Go home.
Where is home?
  (Mirikitani 1987, 7)

The speaker's question defines the border between inclusion and exclusion, enfranchisement and disenfranchisement, home and displacement: Is the barbed wire of the internment camp designed to keep her in or out? As the logic of racial exclusion freezes her into the position of perpetual alien, the speaker internalizes relocation as rootlessness: "Where is home?" she asks. "Who lives within me?" The poem signals the difficulty of reincorporating the national division produced by the war into a subject who must contain national antagonisms. Mitsuye Yamada's "The Question of Loyalty" reflects a similar exploration in its depiction of an issei's dilemma when confronted with the loyalty oath required of interned Japanese Americans:

If I sign this
What will I be?
I am doubly loyal
to my American children
also to my own people.
How can double mean nothing?
   (Yamada 1982, 30)

Political loyalties are positioned as mutually exclusive; their multiplicity renders them suspect. Yet Nellie Wong's poem, "Where is My Country," articulates a contrasting dynamic as her body becomes positioned as a fluid and shifting map expressive of various ethnic affiliations:

Where is my country?

Salted in Mexico
where a policeman speaks to me in Spanish?
In the voice of a Chinese grocer
who asks if I am Filipino?

Channeled in the white businessman
who discovers that I do not sound Chinese?
Garbled in a white woman
who tells me I speak perfect English?
Webbed in another
who tells me I speak with an accent?

Where is my country?
Where does it lie?
   (N. Wong 1984, n.p)

As ethnic specificity becomes subsumed within the larger category of racial difference, part of the answer to the speaker's question lies in her recognition that as a Chinese American her life is linked to those for whom she is mistaken. The compensation for the speaker's multiply signified, ethnic-as-national affiliation is kinship with others whose own ethnic difference is so easily transposed onto her body. Giselle Fong's poem, "Corrosion," reflects on the "they-all-look-alike" syndrome reflective of Asian racial formation in the United States as the speaker is quizzed, "Are you Chinese, Japanese, Korean, Filipino, Hawaiian? Do you eat lice? Do you know Bruce? / Oh AAAAH So, Sukiyaki!" (G. Fong 1990, 117). Fong's poem exposes the parallel between the racial stereotype and racial erasure, the paradox of prejudice, which "renders its victims simultaneously invisible and over-exposed" (Mukherjee 1981, 36). Ethnic homogenization is linked to the project of racial exclusion at the same time that it has the potential to contribute to pan-ethnic alliances.

These potent explorations of belonging and exclusion speak to the process of Asian racialization in the United States and to concepts of national affiliation that exceed both conventionally static definitions of citizenship and linear models of immigrant acculturation, and, as I discuss later, postmodern theories of identity. It is thus that critic Susan Koshy's argument about the inadequacy of "old" sociological patterns of acculturation associated with early Asian immigration resonates with literary representations expressive, not of a progressive embeddedness within national culture, but deterritorialized notions of home. Cynthia Kadohata's appropriation of the Japanese term *ukiyo*, the floating world, to convey family cohesion in the face of cultural and class disenfranchisement is a case in point. This emphasis on fluid national identification also implicitly challenges what has been situated as a master narrative in Asian American Studies, the opposition between cultural nationalism and assimilation. Lisa Lowe notes that the "trope that opposes nativism and assimilationism can be itself a 'colonialist' figureused to displace the challenges of heterogeneity, or subalterneity, by casting them as assimilationist or anti-cultural nationalist" (Lowe 1991, 76). Both "old" sociological models of acculturation and the master narrative that opposes ethnic solidarity to assimilation posit political affiliation as a linear, finite process, the former in its presumption of acculturation as a temporal movement and the latter in its attempt to fix an essential, normative politicized ethnic identity. Contestation between these "old" social science models of minority group interaction with the dominant culture and models of global migrations have, as Sau-ling Wong has noted, attained the status of a paradigm shift in Asian American Studies, a shift she characterizes as one away from domestic to diasporic or denationalizing perspectives (Sau-ling Wong, 1995a). Both Koshy's and Lowe's conceptualizations resonate with postmodern theories of identity and self-location as they shed light on the complex and ongoing processes of allegiance.

Reflecting Anzaldúa's borderlands, where those with multiple identifications refuse the fixity of self-location, the move away from "old" models of acculturation attempts to reconceptualize static definitions of identification and change. But this move is also the result of the critic's choice to privilege individual agency over the disciplining forces of power. Who controls the shifting and potentially multiple identifications, associations, and allegiances that govern self-conception? In emphasizing the charge of betrayal in boundary maintanance, in demarcating authenticity or patriotism, I suggest that any recognition of the fluid nature of identities and identifications must also acknowledge the role of the nation-state in defining the limits of "home,"a point that may become lost in projecting the downfall of the state in its successfully maintaining allegiances in the era of globalization. For example, in drawing a distinction between immigrant and transnational paradigms within Asian American Studies, Koshy suggests that what renders obsolete finite immigration and assimilation patterns are the complex, nonstatic Asian migrations currently taking place in the era of transnational capital: "The earlier patterns of Asian immigrant experiences created more bounded immigrant communities where differentiations were experienced most keenly in separation from the dominant culture, from the home country, or across gender and generational divisions" (Koshy 1996, 339). Koshy's assumption that the assimilatory process loses power in the current era of global economic transformationmakes plausible her conclusion that "becoming American does not necessarily involve a loss of the home culture, or a choice between ethnicity or mainstreaming as in earlier patterns of immigration to this country" (335).

This assumption echoes characterizations of transnational diasporas as global communities linked by technological advancements in communication, characterizations that celebrate, in anthropologist James Clifford's words, a "to-and-fro made possible by modern technologies of transport, communication, and labor migration" that "reduce distances, and facilitate two-way traffic, legal and illegal, between the world's places" (Clifford 1997, 247). Such portrayals reflect a belief in the globalization of culture, explicitly or implicitly challenging presumptions of American cultural and economic hegemony in favor of a two-way exchange or what Arjun Appadurai calls the indigenization of culture (Appadurai 1994). But the question remains: Has the American assimilative process lost its former power? Can one ignore the significant role of the American state in specifying the privileges bestowed by legal citizenship or defining and delimiting the "voluntary" identifications of individuals?

Koshy takes Asian American literary criticism to the task for failing to produce theories of literature adequate to understanding "the effects of transnational forces on Asian American ethnicity" in "newer" literary texts (Koshy 1996, 331). But, as I suggest in this study, her emphasis may be misplaced. It seems less important to account for the accuracy of a sociological model as it applies to something that might be called the literature of globalization, than to understand how loyalties are nurtured or attenuated. What gets overlooked in the debate—domestic or transnational, finite or fluid acculturation—is an understanding of the very structure of allegiance. To represent maintaining diasporic loyalties as a

resistant stance against a bullying America may merely romanticize individual agency. Such a move may discount the disciplining power through
which civil and state institutions enforce allegiances and identifications, a
power that Asian American women's literature eloquently interrogates.
Moreover, it may also elide the pressures that ethnic groups themselves
assert over individuals in the process of upholding group boundaries and
self-definitions.

The vignettes I have highlighted here all speak to deterritorialized concepts of home. Certainly writers have rarely portrayed the acculturation
process according to the finalities associated with sociological models of
inevitable assimilation, indicating that such models were never adequate
to describe the complexities of immigrant experience. However, I would
argue that drawing a distinction between "old" domestic and "new"
transnational paradigms is also illusory given that both patterns of migration are driven by responses to capital. In times of global economic restructuring it is clear that affiliations become *more* rather than less
codified, suggesting that commodities may move more freely across national borders than do subjects.[11] The more significant issue may not concern the accuracy of specific paradigms—domestic or diasporic—but
more appropriately the degree to which one can resist the hegemonic
pressures of American culture both "at home" and abroad. At a moment
in which scholars in the humanities find globalization to be a compelling
analytic framework to celebrate or expose as a guise for neocolonialism,[12] economists provide cautions about overstating the porousness of
national borders and the degree of world market globalization. In response to dire warnings about the erosion of state power in light of globalization, Hirst and Thompson note:

> The state may have less control over ideas, but it remains a controller of its
> borders and the movement of people across them. Apart from a 'club-class' of
> internationally mobile, highly skilled professionals, and the desperate, poor
> migrants and refugees who will suffer almost any hardship to leave intolerable
> conditions, the bulk of the world's populations now cannot easily move. . . . In
> the absence of labour mobility states will retain powers over their peoples, they
> define who is and is not a citizen, who may and may not receive welfare. (Hirst
> and Thompson 1995, 420)[13]

Thus, with economic restructuring affiliations become subject to greater
pressures of repudiation and substantiation both from within the "private" realm of voluntary group identification and the coercive regulation of identities enforced by the state. Gender becomes foregrounded in
this regulation as the domestic space takes on greater significance in reproducing "voluntary" affiliations if the powers of the state in eliciting
such affiliations become compromised (Peterson 1996).

In regard to Asian Americans, an effort to consolidate communal loyalties underlies the master narrative that opposes ethnic cultural nationalism and assimilation; it is a figuration that attempts to fix identification toward a specific purpose, in this case, toward a normative ethnic (and ultimately gendered) identity that symbolizes commitment and resistance through an odd mixture of asserting American nativism and ethnic particularism. This narrative associated with the "old" immigrant paradigm within Asian American Studies is thus not displaced but put in dialectical tension with transnational, global theoretical models of diaspora as both come to express cultural negotiation in terms of connection and disassociation. Such expressions serve to expose the stakes on which affiliations are created and upheld; thus, in commenting on the uneasy displacement of "American" in Asian American Studies Wong writes, "By definition, a world where most travel requires passports and visas is not ready for 'world citizenship,' a phrase that to me means as much as, or as little as, 'just a human being,'" a point that reflects the reservations of economists to overemphasizing the dilution of national influences (Sau-ling Wong 1995, 19). Crucial to the study of a literature expressive of transformation, loss, transition, or migrancy, then, is the recognition that cultural movements are often charted through the *rhetoric of allegiance.*

The "crisis" of nationality in Asian American literary texts across historical time periods and ethnicities often appears as the question of reconfiguring loyalties and alliances: "The sea swallows everything. It is impossible to plant a flag on water," a Korean ship's captain passing as Japanese tells Haesu in *Clay Walls.* "Not so on land. Men plant their flags in the ground and begin the battle. We are born to our nationality by fate" (R. Kim 1986, 77). The captain's "choice" to pass is coerced by the history of Japan's colonization of Korea, but it nonetheless represents to the protagonist Haesu a complicity with the repressive state for personal gain. The captain's justification of his passing, his assertion of the need to be free of encumbering alliances and "unresolveable commitments," initially offends her Korean nationalism. Yet the captain's example provides the catalyst for a revision of her own loyalties as she comes to feel suspended between a homeland under Japanese colonial rule and American racism. In a larger sense, the captain's desire to seek a space in which national loyalties become fluid and shifting speaks to a dual tension in the formation of Asian American identity. While the sea signifies a place in which the self can be remade, its possibilities are not free-floating; it is often *necessary* to plant a flag in water. However much literature may express the desire for a deterritorialized concept of home, articulating belonging in terms of suspension or liminality, literature also indicates

the overdetermined stakes for sustaining liminality or multiple allegiances. For women who are controlled in the interest of demarcating
identities or situated at the point where alliances are ruptured, the stakes
are often higher.[14]

Immanuel Wallerstein notes that establishing boundaries through
affiliation (and exclusion) lies at the basis of defining culture: "[C]ulture
is a way of summarizing the ways in which groups distinguish themselves
from other groups. It represents what is shared within the group, and
presumably simultaneously not shared (or not entirely shared) outside it"
(Wallerstein 1991, 158–59). This definition resonates with now axio-
matic postmodern recognitions of the "imagined" nature of affiliations
such as nationalism as well as the mutually constitutive nature of race,
class, and gender (Anderson 1990). These recognitions were not revolu-
tionary to Asian American Studies; the very designation "Asian American" early on acknowledged a politically defined coalitional identity
rather than a naturalized one. But the awareness that these general theories of subject construction bear significance for the study of race enables
the field's resituation into larger national and potentially global discourses beyond a purely pluralistic concept of minority inclusion. In focusing on the ways in which subjects are constituted through exclusion
and differentiation, two avenues of inquiry appear: analyzing the role
that Asian racial difference plays in the construction of American national identity, and correlating the historical treatment of Asians in the
United States to changing tides of American diplomacy in Asia to investigate domestic "Asianness" as a symptom of global diplomatic and economic relationships. Lisa Lowe's *Immigrant Acts* links both avenues of
analysis by foregrounding two sites, which locate individuals in relation
to nation: the legal/judicial system expressive of theoretical national enfranchisement promising equal political representation through citizenship, and the terrain of culture where "the individual invents lived relationship with the national collective" as he or she becomes "immersed in
the repertoire of American memories, events, and narratives" (Lowe
1996, 2). In suggesting that the American citizen has been defined in opposition to the Asian immigrant, Lowe uncovers the ways in which Asian
immigrants "have been fundamental to the construction of the nation as
a simulacrum of inclusiveness" (5). As Asian subjects in the United States
are constructed partly as a response to American economic and military
interests in Asia, she suggests, legal definitions of belonging are likewise
constituted by various projections of Asian difference.

Historically based and materialist, Lowe's field-defining argument follows in a tradition of scholarship on race that highlights the mutually
constitutive relations of the margin to the center in terms of psychological

projection; her analysis locates what has been repressed—in this case, the disenfranchised Asian—as central to national unity. It has been variously argued that American identity has been constructed in opposition to a perceived Other most often embodied by African American and Native American figures. Toni Morrison's *Playing in the Dark*, the most prominent of these, suggests that Africanness "provided the staging ground and arena for the elaboration of the quintessential American identity," reflecting Frantz Fanon's recognition of the dependent construction of whiteness to blackness (Morrison 1993). In contrast and complement, Michael Rogin notes that "American literature, as critics from D. H. Lawrence to Richard Slotkin have argued, established national identity in the struggle between Indians, and whites" (Rogin 1992), a point that Carroll Smith-Rosenberg echoes in her exploration of white women's role in the construction of Europeans as the "true Americans" against the American Indian in the eighteenth-century.[15] The work of these Americanists epitomizes the significant body of scholarship concerned with difference as a constitutive element in national construction, the ways in which American homogeneity depend on the projection of internal difference, a point echoed in colonial critique as in Homi Bhabha's recognition that "the production of discriminatory identities . . . secure[s] the 'pure' and original identity of [colonial] authority" (Bhabha 1994, 112). Such work reveals the consequences of placing populations in juxtaposition and competition, necessarily exposing the vilification and violence that attend the demands of homogenization that bolster political fictions of unity. It unmasks the exclusions at the heart of modern political theory, exclusions enabled by the ideal, as Iris Marion Young puts it, "Citizenship for everyone, and everyone the same qua citizen" (Young 1990, 114). This scholarship foregrounds the role of discursivity in securing the nationalist imaginary and justifying terms of American belonging based on an absent present racial hierarchy.

But the racial dynamics theorized in this scholarship vis-à-vis the nation may obscure the fact that "minority" groups invoke similar demands for homogenization and exclusion as predicates of their own group cohesion. The same dynamics these American Studies scholars uncover, as Lowe's work acknowledges, may apply to the construction of differences within ethnic groups themselves. In shifting the frame of reference from portrayals of a national Other to the cultural productions of those very Others, my aim is similar to these Americanists in its exploration of the ways group solidarity, not only domestic American but Asian national as well, is secured by those who appear to stand outside that solidarity. Intragroup cohesion is made possible, in other words, by those who are seen to have betrayed it.

In making this shift, this study suggests that not all forms of minority discourse contest national narratives; I investigate the ways in which Asian American texts may also serve the purposes of nationalism. It is generally recognized that literary representations of people of color *by* people of color exceed the reflexive, abject portrayals of racial subjects historically reflected in dominant cultural texts; the challenge they represent to these portrayals resists given narratives on race, which is why, Toni Morrison writes, the Africanist figure as a "metaphorical shortcut" is not open to her as an African American writer (Morrison 1993, x). More complexly, Lowe notes that as the sedimented contradictions between citizenship as the democratic promise of inclusion and the material realities of racial hierarchy erupt in Asian American cultural productions, they become contestatory sites of American national culture. But I also want to suggest that Asian American literary texts may also replicate normative American values (and apply them to Asia); in this, the "subversion" of my title thus takes on a multiple meanings by situating Asian American literature within and against national narratives.

The Americanist work on race discussed above suggests a tension between postmodernism and the activist intent of feminist and Ethnic Studies scholarship that helps define the dual reading strategies of my project. In suggesting that marginal groups come to delineate domestic national interests, these critics establish a theoretical basis for the centrality of the oppressed that does not merely respond to a desire for pluralist inclusion. The dialectical tension present in these arguments resonates with Eve Kosofsky Sedgwick's conception of a "universalizing" model of approaching the homo/heterosexual opposition in queer theory distinct from what she calls a "minoritizing" model now associated with Gay and Lesbian Studies. It might be said that the latter model merely adds sexuality to "the more traditionally visible cruxes of gender, class, and race" by situating gays and lesbians as minority subjects with important stakes in the distinction between gay and straight. In contrast, privileging the universalizing model within her analysis, Sedgwick argues that the homo/heterosexual distinction has primary importance for "all modern Western identity and social organization (and not merely for homosexual identity and culture)" (Sedgwick 1990, 11). Highlighting the deconstructive nature of her argument, she notes,

> The analytic move [the argument] makes is to demonstrate that categories presented in a culture as symmetrical binary oppositions—heterosexual/homosexual, in this case—actually subsist in a more unsettled and dynamic tacit relation according to which, first, term B is not symmetrical with but subordinated to term A; but, second, the ontologically valorized term A actually depends for its meaning on the simultaneous subsumption and exclusion of term B; hence,

third, the question of priority between the supposed central and the supposed marginal category of each dyad is irresolvably unstable, an instability caused by the fact that term B is constituted as at once internal and external to term A. (Sedgwick 1990, 9–10)

The decision to choose a minoritizing or universalizing viewpoint in dealing with "minor" literatures reflects the political stakes confronted by feminist theorists. Does one favor a deconstructive stance that dismantles gender as a category of difference or a stance located in identity politics that maintains the concept of gender difference and works from and within it?[16]

Transposed to an Asian American context, the theoretical dilemma initiates this division: on the one hand, a deconstructivist reading of East-West would unmask the interdependent nature of global relations, and the inclusion-exclusion binarism that exposes how normative conceptions of American identity are produced. On the other hand, emphasizing a "minoritizing" stance establishes a constituency of subjects actively mediating their experiences within categories of class, race, gender, or nationality as well as establishing a commonality of experience about which something can be said. This latter model formed the basis of Asian American Studies; but while the necessity of asserting the visibility of another marginalized canon continues to be pressing as racial hierarchies become increasingly solidified, this assertion may also run the risk of including Asians within the history of race relations in a way that does not alter the American landscape, thereby failing to skirt the dangers of a reductive pluralism. As feminist theorists have cautioned, the addition of women's experiences to history should not preclude an ideological examination of the systemic nature of differentiation (Scott 1992). In order to question the apparent exclusivity of these reading strategies for Asian American Studies, I want to turn briefly to literature itself.

Perhaps ironically but no less aptly given her infamous public persona, I take as an epigraph to this section, Yoko Ono's "Painting to Let the Evening Light Go Through." The "poem" illuminates politically invested deconstructive critical practice in suggesting that the painting/subject's content can only exist through a trick of Western light, that its actual content is subordinate to the shadow it casts. In this the poem implies that the subject's interiority is arbitrary, immaterial to its representation: "[the bottle] does not have to contain." Moreover, it suggests that the shadow cast, the representation imposed from the West, *is* the content and that its existence is both temporal and contingent. Meant to be a metaphysical meditation, the piece nonetheless carries racial resonance akin to her sculpture, *Play it by Trust*, a white chessboard in which black as a contrasting color has been removed to render competitive play based on visual differentiation impossible. Other works explore that interior/exterior distinction in ways that resonate with postmodern readings of race. In *Bag Piece* (1965), Ono and a male assistant enter a huge black bag, remove their clothes, take a "nap," redress in the bag, and exit both the bag and the stage. She notes, "When you are in the bag, you can see outside. But when you are outside, you can only see the outline of the bag. It is very easy for us to clearly see outside and say 'listen. I'm here—you can see what I am.' But, of course, the other person can only see your outline" (Haskell and Hanhardt 1991, 72). In playing with notions of visual epistemology as well as the sexual titillation of voyeurism, *Bag Piece* questions the limits of reading surface. Like Ono's "Painting," it suggests that what is seen is never wholly embodied, but accessible only contingently through certain positionalities and times—and to extrapolate, only within certain configurations of power. Such is the political import of David Henry Hwang's *M. Butterfly*, which, in the manner of Jean Genet's *The Blacks*, exposes the mutuality of race, gender, and national subject positions.

A twist on the story of Madame Butterfly's tragic East-West romance between Gallimard, a befuddled Frenchman, and his lover, Song, a cross-dressing Chinese spy, Hwang's play also evokes the limitations of a purely deconstructivist, or in Sedgwick's terms, universalist, model of analysis for a "minority" constituency. In conceiving *M. Butterfly*, Hwang was less interested in a "real" woman than the idea of the perfect woman; thus for both Hwang and his character's "play" to work, there can be no space for an Asian female subject outside her Orientalist construction. In witnessing the entry of Comrade Chin, a Chinese woman, Gallimard, preferring Song's camp rendition of Oriental femininity, recoils:

GALLIMARD (To Song): No! Why does she have to come in?
SONG: Rene, be sensible. How can they understand the story without her? (Hwang 1988, 47)

The fiction of the play depends on the simultaneous presence of Oriental femininity and the absence of the Asian woman. Gallimard's Butterfly fantasy cannot be challenged by the appearance of a "real" woman; however, we must entertain the idea of authentic femininity against Song's transvestism in order to "understand the story." What must remain offstage is the recognition that Asian femininity is no less an artifice for Asian women than it is for Song; the play only works if we as spectators occupy the position of Gallimard, in the words of poet Frank O'Hara, willing to believe that there is real pleasure in loving a shadow and caressing a disguise. The political significance of the play lies in its exposing the mutually constitutive nature of social identity, in blurring the division between the material and the discursive.

But the absence of the "real" woman in M. *Butterfly* also suggests a pragmatic limitation to Sedgwick's universalist questioning of humanity's division into unequal categories of identity. For better or worse, speaking from specific subject positions carries increasing urgency as coalition politics are one of the few avenues though which citizens can be heard within American democracy. It is in recognition of this commitment to the goals of identity politics—however now maligned a term—that I invoke a category such as "Asian American women" even while acknowledging the insupportability of any naturalized concept of such a constituency, a point I address in the afterword. The tension Sedgwick recognizes, has been otherwise characterized as a divide between postmodern and materialist feminism, a divide that Judith Butler interrogates. In questioning the distinction between subjectivity and the body, she notes that discourse produces and regulates the very intelligibility and materiality of the body (Butler 1993). It is thus necessary to both invoke the Asian female subject and to uncover the discursive conditions of her speech and identity. The activist potential in "universalizing" or poststructuralist models of interpretation must be weighed against the "minoritizing" necessity of speaking about "real" women, about active subjects both determined by and capable of refiguring oppressive social structures.

My emphasis on rhetoric arises from this dual imperative. Following Foucault's concept of the enabling, yet disciplining power of discourse to construct our notions of truth, of the material, I analyze the language and tropes in Asian American literature that construct as well as reflect the specific political realities of, for example, the emerging Cold War, domestic multiculturalism, human rights under globalization. These linguistic interventions are particularly American productions that are instrumentally informed by their authors' position as Asian and American women. Nonetheless, the world in which these textual productions circulate is itself a rhetorically produced field, a point that bears critical scrutiny as this field governs literature's reception, context, and persuasive appeal; as Foucault notes, "[I]n any society, there are manifold relations of power which permeate, characterise and constitute the social body, and these relations of power cannot themselves be established, consolidated nor implemented without the production, accumulation, circulation and functioning of a discourse" (Foucault 1980, 93). Most of the works addressed in these chapters have an implicit but more often explicit activist intent and investment. In analyzing this investment, I try to avoid presuming, as Wendy Hesford and Wendy Kozol caution, "a reality that exists independent of representation . . . wherein resistance remains the uninterrogated site of the real," a point I return to in the afterword (Hesford and Kozol, forthcoming).

It is precisely this postmodern recognition of the discursivity of the material that theorists have found potentially liberating. Recent modes of theorizing race and gender delink identity from biological determinism and humanist notions of the subject. The very concept of "minority-hood," Immanuel Wallerstein notes, is not necessarily numerically based on population but refers to degrees of social power (Wallerstein 1995, 83). Henry Louis Gates Jr.'s discussion of race as "a trope of ultimate, irreducible difference" (Gates, 1986, 5) complements what sociologists Michael Omi and Howard Winant posit as the process of racial formation or the ways in which "widely disparate circumstances of individual and group racial identities, and of the racial institutions and social practices with which these identities are intertwined, are formed and transformed over time" (Omi and Winant 1986, 69). In a similar vein, anthropologist Michael Fischer positions ethnicity as "something reinvented and reinterpreted in each generation by each individual . . . not something that is simply passed on from generation to generation" (Fischer, 1986, 195). The "postessentialist" shift in theorizing race also foregrounds the subject's political orientation over identity, a shift reflected in, for example, bell hooks's distinction between "being" a feminist and advocating feminism: academics no longer speak of identities but of identifications (hooks 1989, 182). These postmodern theories of subjectivity open a space for challenging naturalized conceptions of identity. My emphasis on the trope of betrayal takes this shift as its point of departure, but it is also intended as a caution against downplaying the consequences of claiming multiple positionalities, shifting affiliations.

In theorizing identity away from biological inevitability, these changes emphasize the historical production of categories of difference and so stress the subject's agency in reforming and reconfiguring those categories: W. E. B. Du Bois's characterization of race as "two souls warring in one dark body" is rewritten from debilitating internal conflict to a potentially radical site for social revision. In "straddling the walls between abysses" or mediating allegiances to groups that characterize the facets of her identity as a lesbian Chicana writer, for example, Gloria Anzaldúa asserts, "Who, me confused? Ambivalent? Not so. Only your labels split me" (Anzaldúa 1983, 205). Trinh Minh-ha echoes Anzaldúa's concept of "the borderlands" as a subversive positionality:

> Since the self, like the work you produce, is not so much a core as a process, one finds oneself, in the context of cultural hybridity, always pushing one's questioning of oneself to the limit of what one is and what one is not. When am I Vietnamese? When am I American? When am I Asian and when am I Asian-American or Asian-European? Which language should I speak, which is closest to myself, and when is that language more adequate than another? By working

on one's limits, one has the potential to modify them. Fragmentation is therefore a way of living at the borders. (Cited in interview with Pratibha Parmar,
"Woman, Native Other," *Feminist Review* 36 [Autumn, 1990]: 72)

"Living at the borders," like metaphors of travel, migrancy, or the floating world, exemplifies the theoretical shift toward conceptualizing
identity as fluid, shifting, continually negotiated and contextualized. In
stressing the division between biology and cultural construction in the
formation of an empowering Black consciousness Stuart Hall thus writes,
"[I]t is not because of their skins, that they are Black in their heads" (Hall
1991, 20). The relationship among identity, performativity, and discursivity has also figured prominently in feminist theory, emphasizing, to
paraphrase Hall, that is not because of their bodies that they are women
in their heads.

What *Betrayal and Other Acts of Subversion* stresses, however, is that
for subjects marked by race, gender, and nationality, negotiating what
Maxine Hong Kingston's narrator in *The Woman Warrior* calls "boundaries not delineated in space" is potentially more fraught than these modes
of theorizing difference imply. As Anzaldúa recognizes, "to live in the
Borderlands" is to recuperate the self's fragmentation, but it is also a
space of surveillance and violence (Anzaldúa 1987). While postmodern
theories of marginalized identity seek to allow for the subject's intervention in potentially determining constructions of race and gender, they can
also imply that identity formation takes place in a value-free space; more
attention is devoted to furthering the concept that one can "shuttle between identities" than to analyzing how one goes about it or what it
means to make that attempt. Thus, my interest lies in how, despite the
demystification of socially constructed categories, the subject's struggle
for self-definition is yet contained within ideological structures; in the
theoretical emphasis on employing without avowing difference, discussions about how the subject negotiates contradictory positionings are
often elided. In regard to Asian American women, what can become
erased is the specificity of the intersection between gender and race, how
it is often figured as the competition between collective alliances. Kwame
Anthony Appiah and Henry Louis Gates Jr.'s comment, "Ethnic and national identities operate in the lives of individuals by connecting them
with some people, dividing them from others," downplays the conflictual
nature of that process of connection and division (Gates and Appiah
1992, 627). They mildly observe, "[I]mportant events occur in the landscape of identity when race and gender compete for and combine in a
single body" (628). These "important events" bear greater consequences
for those who embody the site of competition, Asian American women
and other women of color.

Negotiating "Boundaries Not Delineated in Space"

For Asian American women as for other women of color, one upshot of multiple subject positioning is the often competitive relationship between feminism and cultural nationalism. The "either-or" view that one's primary identity must be based either in peoplehood or in sisterhood sets up a mutually antagonistic opposition. As Trinh Minh-ha writes, it is "convincing to reject feminism as a whitewashed notion and a betrayal of roots values, or vice versa, to consider the promotion of ethnic identity treacherous to that of female identity or feminism" (Trinh 1989, 106). For many women at the beginning of the women's movement, ethnic identification was not only seen as exclusive of feminism, but in competition with it and a matter of setting priorities: "Essentially," stated one Asian American woman interviewed for a study on Asian American feminism, "I think I'm more Asian American than feminist" (cited in Cheng 1984, 11). Katheryn Fong reported on this either-or figuration during a 1974 conference on women in which an Asian American woman pronounced, " 'If I am forced to choose to fight against racism or sexism, my first battle must be to fight racism'" (cited in K. Fong 1978, n.p). The chorus of boos that this statement sustained from the feminist audience convinced Fong that "the priorities of the 'women's movement' were not my priorities." For other women of color confronted with the opposition between cultural nationalism and feminism, the choice to prioritize the struggle against racism is clear. During the crisis at the second Wounded Knee, the question of sexism seemed trivial to Lakota activist Mary Crow Dog:

> At one time a white volunteer nurse berated us for doing the slave work while the men got all the glory. We were betraying the cause of womankind, was the way she put it. We told her that her kind of women's lib was a white, middle-class thing, and that at this critical stage we had other priorities. Once our men had gotten their rights and their balls back, we might start arguing with them about who should do the dishes. But not before. (Crow Dog 1990, 131)

The absence or presence of "our men's balls" is often positioned as a crucial determiner of a women of color's feminist activism. In her research on the development of Chicana feminism, Alma M. Garcia writes, "[M]any Chicano males were convinced that Chicana feminism was a divisive ideology incompatible with Chicano cultural nationalism" (Garcia 1990, 424). And in her discussion on the emergence of Chinese American women's social activism, Judy Yung notes that while the Chinese American newspaper *Chung Sai Yat Po* supported progressive gender reforms in China, it questioned the suffrage movement in the United States

and white women's voting rights when Chinese men denied naturalization were thus denied the right to vote (Yung 1990, 201). Feminism is
often portrayed as irreconcilable to cultural nationalism through its association with the dominant culture: "When I first became a feminist,"
Michele Wallace writes, "my Black friends used to cast pitying eyes upon
me and say, 'That's whitey's thing'" (Wallace 1982, 10). Marta Cotera
notes that for Chicanas expressing feminism is sometimes taken as evidence of assimilating to the ideology of an "alien" culture that "actively
seeks our cultural domination" (cited in Garcia 1990, 424).

The association between assimilation and feminism in the domestic
context mirrors attempts to discredit feminism as a Western import in
postcolonial nationalist movements where women's issues are represented as diluting anti-imperialist interests.[17] This competitive construction is highlighted in the work of international feminist scholars who note
that nationalist movements' appeal to indigenous traditions often sets
women up as either custodians of cultural authenticity or as most vulnerable to corruption by foreign influences.[18] As Geraldine Heng points out,
this conflictual relationship is often tied to an ambivalence about modernization in the developing world:

> The ease with which, historically, the 'modern' and the 'Western' have been
> conflated and offered as synonymous, interchangeable counters in both nation-
> alist and Orientalist discourse have meant that a nationalists' accusation of
> modern and /or foreign—that is to say, Western—provenance or influence,
> when directed at a social movement, has been sufficient for the movement's
> delegitimization. (Heng 1997, 33)

These representations of feminism as a foreign ideology link internal ethnic dynamics in the United States to international dynamics of Third
World nation formation, ethnic cultural nationalism to nationalism.[19]
The subordination of feminist to cultural nationalist or nationalist concerns reflects the belief that promoting group interests is predicated on
competition; more specifically, as Peterson notes, patriarchal control of
women as social reproducers of group identifications often precludes
"women's identification with *women* as a group in favor of their identification with the (territorial, class, ethnic, race) group of which they are
a member and which is based on male-defined needs" (Peterson 1995, 6).
One issue within feminist analysis then becomes how to locate gender
among other numerous and competing affiliations, whether to situate
women's alliances with one another as merely another collective identity
open to them or whether in fact gender difference can itself be read as a
means of producing, solidifying, or transforming territorial, class, ethnic,
or racial allegiances. Following my discussion of recent Americanist
scholarship, I argue that it is the latter that poses a significant frame for

reading Asian American women's literature, particularly in light of the fact that, as Third World feminists have noted, women are made to serve as boundary markers among ethnic, national, and religious collectives (Kandyoti 1994).

This dynamic underlies Elaine Kim's analysis of the antagonisms between Asian American and feminist concerns. Kim links such antagonisms to increased autonomy and opportunities for Asian American women created by social upheavals upon immigration:

> Contemporary Asian American discourse reflects tensions between nationalist and feminist concerns that are rooted in Asian American social realities. At times, what has been detrimental to men in the ethnopolitical territory they have defined has been of comparative benefit to the women. (E. Kim 1990, 73).

Kim notes that this increase in women's opportunities did not have a reciprocal effect on men: "Relative and limited increases in options for Asian women in American society have been made possible largely because Asian patriarchy was pushed aside or subsumed by an American patriarchy that did not, because of racism, extend its promise to Asian American men" (75). Kim's statement points to an important, if controversial, interaction between sexism and racism. While Asians often suffered class demotion due to the effects of racism in this country, Asian women benefited by the diminishment of traditional Asian patriarchal authority. This implies that the gender position of Asian women improved upon immigration as a direct result of disruption to the social fabric of the family—women's working outside the home, for example—if improvement is measured by the standard of increased autonomy. Kim's analysis dovetails with potentially conflictual relationships between feminism and nationalism in Asian postcolonial contexts where feminism—at least when expressed in terms of women's rights or as an increase in women's involvement in the public sphere—is equated with Westernization.

Part of the backlash to this sociohistorical reality, Kim suggests, is that the recovery of masculine authority comes at the expense of women: "Deprived of the rewards of patriarchal legitimacy, some Asian men have responded by attempting to reassert male authority over the cultural domain and over women by subordinating feminism to nationalist concerns." This masculine reassertion has been most publicly fostered by Chinese American writer Frank Chin, whose work draws a connection between assimilation and feminism in order to characterize Asian American women as racial traitors, as "Jade Snow Wong Pocahontas yellow." Such sentiments expressed over the course of twenty years are well known to Asian American scholars and writers, perhaps giving immoderate notoriety to Chin's manifesto-type pronouncements over his other creative work. Paralleling debates in African American literature over feminist representations of black men, Chin charges that Kingston and other Chinese American writers have sold out to white feminism by falsifying Chinese history in order to pander to American publishers who "went crazy for Chinese women dumping on Chinese men." In Chin's taxonomy, expressing feminism becomes a bid for honorary whiteness (Chin 1991, 27). As he figures Chinese American cultural pride as the aggressive remasculation of a people rendered metaphorically impotent by racism, sexual domination of white women becomes symbolic of Chinese (male) enfranchisement: "And while your chained dog barked, Joy /A hundred years of Chinamen / In public / Took turns / At a piece of / White ass. // Father's home" (Chin 1978, 133). The debate over Chinese American representation and authenticity has become central to discussions of Asian American literature to the point of obscuring the complex dynamic that underlies it. I have noted elsewhere that as this debate comes to impact the discipline of Asian American Studies, it complicates feminist critical positioning in the field.[20]

To emphasize the trope of betrayal as it resonates with the opposition between cultural nationalism and feminism might seem to grant undue weight to a crusade often individualized as Chin's, and to authorize its terms as a singular framework for debates within Asian American literature. But the underlying tensions—if not the substance and ultimate trajectory—of these attempts to regulate ethnicity are worth scrutiny, perhaps using another lens. As in his insistence on "real" and "fake" Chinese American, basic to Chin's charge of ethnic feminist betrayal is an effort to establish an essential ethnic identity based on masculinist notions of resistant consciousness determined by simple oppositions—nationalist or assimilationist, Asian-identified or white-identified. This attempt to fix collective allegiance by dictating the terms of community testifies to the belief that coalitional uniformity is a necessary precondition to asserting social power and that this assertion is most appropriately expressed through masculinist rhetoric. Rather than dismiss the constructed antagonism between ethnic and gender loyalties as unadulterated misogyny, this work looks at the ways that oppositional definitions of community produce moments of narrative conflict that expose the very terms of communal belonging. I suggest that accusations of betrayal enable an understanding of the processes by which identifications (and thus identities themselves) emerge through contestation with competing group affiliations.

As Asian American women's writing comments on these processes, it exposes the socially constructed and politically invested nature of affiliations. Gender, I suggest, offers ready tropes of difference (whether through discourses of maternality, sentimentality or inconstancy, for example) that serve to produce ethnic, racial, or national cohesion but also enable certain types of activist appeal. For example, how can associations between gender and assimilability enacted within women's literature be read as a meditation on American national enfranchisement? Just as masculinity offered a rhetoric through which racial groups asserted presence and citizenship in the civil rights era, other gendered terms can likewise be deployed to describe specific relationships to the state or to expose the very homosociality that underwrites political group cohesion. As literature by Asian American women shows, such deployments both draw on and exceed representations of women's ethnic or national betrayal.

Asian American literary texts engaged with postcolonial Third World critique and those situated as immigrant literature situate overlapping collective affiliations as significant for understanding the production of identities with and against state interests. For example, how does feminine sexuality come to regulate, mediate, or control racial difference in the U.S.? In *Farewell to Manzanar*, a reflection on Japanese American internment, Jeanne Wakatsuki Houston notes, "I knew intuitively that one resource I had to overcome the war-distorted limitations of my race would be my femininity" (Houston and Houston 1973, 117). Her comment reveals the unconscious negotiation of overlapping, often competitive prescriptions of race and gender. Her initial belief that participating in such gender-defined activities as baton twirling and homecoming would inscribe her as American suggests one link in the interaction between race and gender: that the accession to a feminine role colludes with racial acceptability. This conjoining is similarly reflected in Bharati Mukherjee's portrayal of an obnoxious yuppie whose taste for adventure finds expression in his relationship with his Filipina girlfriend. "There's a difference between exotic and foreign," he explains. "Exotic means you know how to use your foreignness, or you make yourself a little foreign in order to appear exotic. Real foreign is a little scary, believe me" (Mukherjee 1988, 81). Feminine sexuality here intercedes in "foreignness" to transform the fearful and unknown into the benign and alluring. The perceived association between gender and assimilability produces this consequence: femininity appears to domesticate racial difference. What, then, does Asian American women's literature confirm or expose about this collusion?

Chapter 2 investigates the ways in which women's commitment to nation comes to be expressed through feminine performativity as signifier of political fidelity. The chapter explores what Lauren Berlant calls the "fantasy of a national democracy . . . based on principles of abstract personhood" and the theoretical implications of racialized and gendered notions of citizenship (Berlant 1997, 18). The fact that likeness is a requisite for civic participation (Lowe 1994) indicates that national inclusion demands an identification with patriarchal nationalism; I argue that gender role conformity ironically enables this identification. In *Farewell to Manzanar*, for example, hyperfeminine masquerade becomes a means of demonstrating loyalty in a postwar era when "real foreign" was "a little scary." Similarly, Mukherjee's first-person essay, "Love Me or Leave Me," expresses national identification through desire for a sexually potent white woman. In situating women's place in the nation as simultaneously one of gendered embodiment and racial erasure, the chapter contends that "privatized" issues of sexuality and identification carry national resonance and mark the notion of equal, homogeneous citizenship as a political fiction.

While feminism is often associated with cultural critique in its indictment of the patriarchal status quo, feminist texts do not necessarily counter national narratives in their interaction with racial discourses. Chapter 3 examines two popular Chinese American "feminist" texts that portray American culture as inherently *less* oppressive to women than their ethnic cultures; these narratives implicitly or explicitly link acculturation with increased women's autonomy. In suggesting that liberal feminist narratives work to normalize ethnic difference by producing intelligible racial subjects, chapter 3 argues that such works consolidate First World/Third World distinctions through the inscription of subjects easily interpolated within the rubric of individual equality. By extolling ideas of women's opportunity, for example, Jade Snow Wong's *Fifth Chinese Daughter*, an autobiography seeking to "contribute in bringing better understanding of the Chinese people so that in the Western world they would be recognized for their achievements," produces an image of the good Chinese as capitalist entrepreneur that could be exported to Asia during the Cold War. In Amy Tan's *The Joy Luck Club*, feminist generational transmission implicitly supports the link between development and American acculturation through ideas of progressive self-betterment for each successive generation of women.

Such narrative plot structures complicate Lowe's point that "the demand that the immigrant subject 'develop' into an identification with the dominant forms of the nation gives rise to *contradictory* articulations that interrupt the demands for identity and identification, that voice *antagonisms* to the universalizing narratives of both pluralism and development and that open Asian American culture as an alternative site to the American economic, political, and national cultural spheres" (Lowe 1996, 29, emphasis mine). The mutually reinforcing interaction between race and gender discourses endemic to certain feminist plot structures does not necessarily articulate antagonism to American ideology but can service national agendas. They suggest, for example, that advocating gender equality supports the need for contained collective oppositionality, a collectivity easily reconciled to a national rhetoric on tolerating or celebrating individual difference. Multiculturalism is the other side of liberal feminism, both serving to produce, in Lowe's terms, the "simulacrum of inclusiveness" (Lowe 1996, 5).

Texts with an immigrant focus serve to validate First World conceptions about the Third World if they mark the connection between economic liberalism and "privatized" issues of self-fulfillment as a logical and inevitable result of Westernized modernization. Chapters 4 and 5 show that viewing nationalism and ethnicity as collective affiliations similarly contested and substantiated through the rhetoric of gendered loyalty erodes the presumed difference between American and Third World feminist treatments of sexuality—and between Asian American immigrant and Asian postcolonial literature. As theorists of Third World feminism have pointed out, an initial difference between Third and First World feminist treatments of sexuality was that the latter primarily addressed issues of male domination and questions of self-fulfillment or autonomy rather than engaging economic or national politics.[21] Rather than substantiating or refuting either take on this difference, I suggest that Asian American representations of feminine sexuality invoke gendered discourses such as liberal feminism, maternality, or the psychologizing of women's battery that are familiar to a post-women's movement American readership in order to critique postcolonial Asian politics. These methods of rhetorical appeal characterize Asian American literature's American investment even as it envisions solutions to unresolved political conflicts on a global level.

The rhetoric of exclusion and belonging establishes a parallel between depictions of women's positioning in the patriarchal family and the national collective. Gender represents a potential disenfranchisement from the family as one arena of collective identification, a condition referred to as the "outward tendency in females." As Maxine Hong Kingston's narrator notes, "Females desert families . . . I was getting straight A's for the good of my future husband's family, not my own" (Kingston 1989, 47). "We were in the family but not of it," Su-ling Wong writes about women's place within Confucian tradition (Su-ling Wong 1952, 90). That gender represents a condition of impending "exile" raises questions about women's loyalty to the family collective echoing Virginia Woolf's famous dictum on women's ambivalent allegiance to patriarchal nationalism: "[A]s a woman, I have no country. As a woman I want no country. As a woman my country is the whole world" (Woolf 1938, 197). Woolf's assertion of women's transcendent global citizenship counters the obvious ways in which women or other feminine figures have been yoked to the promotion of nationalist imaginaries. Such representations signal women's place in nationalist movements as largely symbolic: women can represent nation but women are often denied the agency *as women* to express nationalist solidarity.

Reflecting the concerns of chapter 2, chapters 4 and 5 thus uncover the dynamics through which women's commitment to nation and political fidelity are measured through sexual alliances. The trope of betrayal thus narrates an individual's relationship to the state as literature exposes how charges of sexual disloyalty serve the purposes of government (or counterinsurgent) control. Engaging Le Ly Hayslip's *When Heaven and Earth Changed Places: A Vietnamese Woman's Journey from War to Peace* in light of its activist agenda, chapter 4 argues that the autobiography relies on a gendered pacifism in order to advocate for United States/Vietnam reconciliation at a strategic moment in which Vietnam becomes open to Western investment. Hayslip's rendering of her experiences in the war zone as a kind of feminine picaresque, a *testimonio* of sexual trauma, resituates her from traitor to nationalist daughter with a healing message. Her advocation of a gendered neutrality appealing to maternal duty ultimately substantiates her activist agenda centered on humanitarian aid. As a "Third World" commentary, *When Heaven and Earth Changed Places* is not an indictment of Western neocolonialism; rather, it makes a sentimental plea for increased American involvement in Vietnam's modernization.

Chapter 5 investigates the politicism inherent in the concept of human rights as it is deployed in Wendy Law-Yone's *Irrawaddy Tango* and Fiona Cheong's *The Scent of the Gods*. In representing methods of government repression such as torture, forced confession, and detention without trial, the novels critique the nationalist agendas of Burma and Singapore by appealing to the female body's sovereignty and the sovereignty of the domestic space of the home. Yet the novels depend on the construction of female subjects of state reprisal: as women's sexual transgression is portrayed as nationalist betrayal, the literature links the regulation of women's sexuality to the repression of dissent in the interest of consolidating state power and the submersion of individual rights for the collective good.

These two chapters nuance theories that position Asian American identity as a reflection of U.S. diplomacy in Asia; both engage the inverse dynamic by invoking specifically American discourses such as women's rights as civil rights to intervene in postcolonial politics. These commentaries carry implicit Western agendas even as they advance ideals seemingly transcendent of American national interests. The discussion of the "universal" concept of human rights in chapter 5 highlights literature's appeal to a *trans*national means of governance predicated on the rights of the Enlightenment subject. Similarly, Hayslip's call to action relies on a gendered pacifism marked as a moral obligation to justice that transcends the duties attached to citizenship in spite of the fact that her activism is authorized by her position in the West. Such Asian American texts about Asia constitute not an elision of "America" but an enactment of its values and precepts, values that authorize a narrative appeal. These American investments do not specify a singular response to the historical conditions in which the texts were produced, namely, the movement toward increasing globalization. The texts discussed in chapters 4 and 5 do not echo warnings from the academic left that see economic globalization as either ungovernable or dictated by the West as a form of neocolonialism. Nor do they uncritically or explicitly advocate for participation in a world economy. Rather, these texts imply that Asian American literature engages global economic shifts through representations of postcolonial history without deflating the heterogeneity or specific immediacy of those responses.

Betrayal and Other Acts of Subversion suggests a means of bridging the apparent divide between immigrant and transnational disciplinary paradigms. For example, *Fifth Chinese Daughter* could be said to exemplify models of acculturation associated with the first wave of Asian immigrants to the United States. As I discuss in chapter 3, Jade Snow's entrepreneurial method of "claiming America" had implications beyond a domestic context in an era of political uncertainty and economic expansion, a point fully appreciated by the U.S. State Department. Wong's values were deliberately exported to Asia by the State Department to inaugurate the conditions necessary for a developing world sympathetic to American capitalism. In this mission, gender is not merely a rhetorical afterthought but structures Wong's means of persuading her American (and later, Asian) readers that change does not involve loss, that business opportunities are unfettered by minority status. To mark a literature as internationalist, transnational, or diasporic as opposed to immigrant or "multicultural" does not speak to how literary texts are situated within the ideological tension between Neo-Marxist critiques of global capital and validations of liberalism and free market exchange that underwrite its transnational flow. The investment, then, should lie not in boundary marking but in developing dialectical readings that expose ideological continuities between national sites.

The goal of my textual inquiry is not to replay what Amy Tan calls "the tired and presbyobic, bifocal lens of two themes: immigration and assimilation,"[22] but neither is it to dismiss a continually compelling lens in deference to current transnational paradigms. Rather, I want to emphasize the mutual dependency of discourses that draw a connection between Asian immigrant writing engaging gendered rhetoric and American literature on Asia that employs that same rhetoric as a tool of political persuasion. Foregrounding the dynamic between alliance and identity, this book looks at the ways in which Asian American women figure, mediate, and contest the articulation of ethnic, gender, and national affiliation in terms of competition. This focus renders ambivalent the assertion of Bharati Mukherjee's Jasmine: "For every gesture of loyalty there doesn't have to be a betrayal" (Mukherjee 1989, 201). To explore depictions of loyalty and betrayal as part of literature's commitment to social justice and change, this study thus theorizes the complex negotiation between feminine accommodation and feminist resistance to question any naturalized connection between oppositionality and marginality and to look at the ideological constructs that govern women's alliances.

The project is not intended to develop a canon of literature by Asian American women (even one that could be "separate but [and] equal")[23] although there are clear disciplinary stakes for doing so. Such a project would seem merely to enforce what Robyn Wiegman calls "a methodological propulsion toward increasingly territorialized interpretations of social and subjective being" (Wiegman 1995, 130) or what Gayatri Spivak terms "identitarianism," the ways in which "ethnicist academic agendas make a fetish of identity" (Spivak 1993, 63). As Fredric Jameson notes, "One cannot acknowledge the justice of the general poststructuralist assault on the so-called 'centered subject,' the old unified ego of bourgeois individualism, and then resuscitate this same ideological mirage of psychic unification on the collective level in the form of a doctrine of collective identity" (Jameson 1986, 78). Rather, in positing commonalities around one trope in particular, that of betrayal, my intent is to locate Asian American women's literature as a site where questions can be posed about the gendered relationship of the individual to the state, about the status of the subject defined by group affiliation, and about the exclusions that produce national unity. *Betrayal and Other Acts of Subversion* gives most extended treatment to texts produced by Japanese, South Asian, and Chinese American women in its domestic focus, and to Vietnamese, Burmese, and Singaporean American women in its postcolonial focus. In spite of this book's subtitle, "Asian American Women's Literature," I cannot hope to approach representativeness; but this is not, in effect, my goal. This study is self-consciously concerned with the ways in which unity is itself a mirage that can be solidified or reconstituted around imaginary lines of affiliation—and the ways in which women are made to suffer the fallout of such actions.

Accusations of ethnic or national betrayal are intended to contest authenticity or commitment; by exposing the tenuousness of racial, ethnic, or national belonging, such accusations signal the politically invested interests in which affiliations are formed and consolidated. These interests often remain invisible until one transgresses "boundaries not delineated in space." Gender is central to this process as it becomes positioned as a difference that secures group cohesion. Such a positioning can certainly come at the expense of women, as my discussion of Ono's and Toguri's "infidelity" reveals, but in exposing what remains veiled, the charge of betrayal can also betray normalizing processes of power. This book investigates the political uses of categories of identity as they are exposed in juxtaposition with other such categories in order to ask, "What relations do multiple affiliations create, and what are the stakes for individuals compelled to negotiate conflicts between them?" The following chapter explores these complex interactions between race and gender inscription in literature that portrays feminine sexuality as the resolution to a crisis of national citizenship.

Two

To Enjoy Being a Girl

SEXUALITY AND PARTIAL CITIZENSHIP

TA: What is your ambition? What do you want to
be?
LINDA: I want to be a success as a girl. Oh, it's nice
to have outside accomplishments like singing,
cooking or first aid. But the main thing is for a
woman to be successful in her gender.
(. . . sings contemplatively)

> When I have a brand new hair-do,
> With my eyelashes all in curl,
> I float as the clouds on air do—
> I enjoy being a girl!

(*Rodgers and Hammerstein*, Flower Drum
Song)

[T]he attention I first gained as a majorette went
hand in hand with a warm reception from the Boy
Scouts and their fathers, and from that point on
I knew intuitively that one resource I had to
overcome the war-distorted limitations of my race
would be my femininity.
(*Jeanne Wakatsuki Houston and
James D. Houston*, Farewell to Manzanar)

THE IMAGE that accompanies these lyrics in *Flower Drum Song* is nothing
if not camp. In portraying the Americanized Linda Low as the quintessential "female female," the film represents self-conscious Asian femininity
in the form of multiple images of Nancy Kwan striking poses before the
mirror in a towel that seems to defy the natural laws of physics. The song
attests to the pleasures of femininity: to coquetry, to gossip, and to dress-
up, all of which assume the air of heightened artificiality at the same time
that they confirm the essential frivolousness that lies the heart of female
nature. The image both relies on and reproduces a common belief: that
Asian women embody the hyperfeminine.

Cathy Song's poem, "Ikebana," ironizes the effort that goes into achieving "girlness" by paralleling gendered passivity and the aesthetic perfection of traditional Japanese flower arrangement.

> Reveal the nape of the neck,
> your beauty spot.
> Hold the arrangement.
> If your spine slacks
> and you feel faint,
> remember the hand-picked flower
> set in the front alcove,
> which, just this morning,
> you so skillfully wired into place.
> How poised it is!
> Petal and leaf
> curving like a fan,
> the stem snipped and wedged
> into the metal base—
> to appear like a spontaneous accident.
>   *(Song 1983, 42)*

A "how to" primer on womanly grace, the poem reveals the artificiality of femininity by exposing the self-consciousness that goes into demonstrating spontaneity, the deliberation necessary to convey naturalness in this particularly Eastern art form. This "oriental-as-ornamental" expectation translates into a belief in Asian women's hyperbolic femininity. Such an expectation makes plausible the cross-dressing premise of David Henry Hwang's *M. Butterfly*, a premise predicated on what Edward Said calls the Orientalist male power-fantasy: Oriental women "express unlimited sensuality, they are more or less stupid, and above all they are willing" (Said 1979, 27).

In explaining how the link between sexuality and racialization influences Asian American women's representation, Elaine Kim notes, "In the peculiarly American tangle of race and gender hierarchies, the objectification of Asian Americans as permanent political outsiders has been tightly plaited with our objectification as sexual deviants: Asian men have been coded as having no sexuality, while Asian women have nothing else" (E. Kim 1990, 69). Signifying "nothing else" but body provides the context for the conflation of body parts that functions as a synecdoche of Asian female identity. In Janice Mirikitani's poem, "The Question Is," the voice of a white male "rice lover," leers, "Is / it true / your cunt is slanted too?" (Mirikitani 1978, n.p.). The question reduces race and gender to an embodied essence: "cunt" comes to stand in for woman and "slant" for Asian as irreducible and indistinguishable markers of difference.

These attestations of, to echo *Flower Drum Song*, Asian women's "success" in their gender nonetheless render their citizenship suspect and have significantly impacted the history of their immigration to the United States. Their portrayal as having "nothing else" but sexuality defined their relationship to the American state: the conditions under which Asian women were granted permission to immigrate, first as prostitutes, then as picture brides, war brides, and now mail-order brides, reflects the centrality of sexuality as a determiner of inclusion. Historian Sucheng Chan writes that a "large majority of the pioneer Chinese female immigrants were poor girls who had been sold into prostitution. This fact had a profound impact on the subsequent history of Chinese women—who the state suspected of being prostitutes—from entering" (S. Chan 1991, 105).[1] Women's exclusion, or as poet Fay Chiang puts it, the fact that "america only let guys in," produced skewed gender demographics in Asian American populations that curtailed the development of community. Chandra Mohanty notes that the first exclusion law positioned morality as a condition of Asian women's entry:

> A chronological listing of the U.S. Exclusion Acts illustrates the intersection of morality and race, class, gender, and sexuality in the construction of Asian peoples as the "yellow peril." It was the 1870 hearings on Chinese prostitution that led to "An Act to Prevent the Kidnapping and Importation of Mongolian, Chinese, and Japanese Females for Criminal and Demoralizing Purposes." This act granted immigration officers the right to determine if women who chose to emigrate were "persons of correct habits and good character." (Mohanty 1991, 25)

Emphasis on gender and sexuality as criteria for entry into the United States does not minimize the significance of Asian immigrant women as wage laborers given the largely economic rationale underlying the exclusion laws. Nevertheless, their immigration was clearly determined relationally—by what effect it would have on male labor. In commenting on the consequences of this relational dependency for women's citizenship, Nira Yuval-Davis writes, "Women have tended to be differentially regulated to men in nationality, immigration and refugee legislation, often being constructed as dependent on their family men and expected to follow them and live where they do" (Yuval-Davis 1997, 24). The fact that a woman's relationship to the state is read through a man's potentially compromises her civic participation and access to the full rights of citizenship.

To be embodied before the state fundamentally contradicts the notion of the abstract citizen-subject underlying democratic universalism or what Lauren Berlant calls the "fantasy of a national democracy . . . based on principles of abstract personhood" (Berlant 1997, 18). The democratic ideal supposes a connection between citizenship and impartiality, an impartiality that, as Iris Marion Young writes, "requires constricting the idea of a self abstracted from the context of any real persons" (Young 1987, 60). Advancing collective interests presumes a citizen who "is not committed to any particular ends, has no particular history, is a member of no communities, has no body" (60). Citizenship thus depends on the disavowal of difference and the projection of equivalence or uniformity. The necessity of projecting homogeneous national citizens erases embodied difference as a predicate of uninterested civic participation and the promotion of the common good. Under such a dictate, the Asian female subject of Mirikitani's poem inhabits the space of irreducible sexuality that marks her as alien to the national democratic project.

Projected as a neutral body, the body politic is yet implicitly masculine; the necessary fiction of homogeneity masks the fact that the "universal" citizen-subject is white and male.[2] In exposing this false universalism, feminist political theorists have argued that women's embodiment and exclusion from the body politic not only compromises women's equal participation in civic life, but *produces* the very notion of a rational, disinterested citizenship among equals: as Robyn Wiegman has suggested, "the reduction of woman to her anatomy provides the difference against which masculine disembodiment can be achieved" (Wiegman 1995, 88). Women's specificity is not merely excluded in the projection of abstract, disembodied citizenship but is fundamental to its construction.[3] Yet to be embodied before the state signifies that one is incapable of acting rationally and beyond particularist interest, in other words, incapable of acting in accord with the democratic, consensual process. Thus, the association of individuals and groups with partiality and affect is a sign of the very contingent and partial nature of their national incorporation.

One consequence of women's embodiment is limited political agency: women's political allegiance is positioned not as a reflection of their own views but is inferred through heterosexual alliance. Marking women's relationship to the state as one of compulsory heterosexuality, Carole Pateman's *The Sexual Contract* reveals the social contract and the sexual contract to be one in the same. What I want to examine here, however, are the broader implications of this connection: the fact that women's political agency is both contingent on and compromised by embodiment. The exchange of women underlying gender differentiation is aptly portrayed in Ruthanne Lum McCunn's *Thousand Pieces of Gold* (1981), which novelizes the life of Lalu Nathoy, later known as Polly Bemis. McCunn's depiction of Lalu's slavery and eventual "freedom" through her marriage to an American suggests that sexuality is the price of both her cultural belonging and legal status. Upon being told that the "only way a Chinaman can become an American is to be born here,"

Lalu draws a connection between feminine sexuality and the rights of citizenship:

> Here or in China, slave or free, it was the same. She needed a protector. She rubbed her hands across Charlie's back, unknotting the tight muscles. He turned. Mechanically she began unbuttoning his shirt. (Lum McCunn 1981, 164)

As the autonomy Lalu hopes for proves to be illusory given racist naturalization policies, she bitterly concludes that her body is the only bargaining chip she possesses that can be traded for the security and legal authority that her future husband's citizenship represents.[4] At first glance, her freedom depends on the "choice" among three men—the Chinese slave owner who initially buys her, the Chinese American man who hopes to marry her, and the American who "wins" her in a poker game in order to set her free. The novel suggests the limits of Lalu's freedom by blurring the distinction between bondage and marriage; at the moment Charlie tells her she is free, she notices the bruises left from his hold. The biographical novel foregrounds the element of domination involved in women's "free" choice of marriage, a condition that Pateman views as intrinsic to the contractual agreements that underlie civil society. Pateman argues that as a contract that "generates political right in the form of relations of domination and subordination" (Pateman 1988, 8), marriage "is not an exchange but produces social relations of subordination" (148). The novel renders the voluntary nature of marriage suspect by unveiling the underlying asymmetry between the individuals involved in the contractual agreement: "When social inequality prevails," Pateman notes, "questions arise about what counts as voluntary entry into a contract" (62). The marriage contract bears striking resemblance to the "contract" of citizenship: both specify the exchange of obedience for protection. The novel's parallel between the status of slave and wife hinges on Lalu's recognition of her corporealization; this parallel suggests that national inclusion is contingent on sexual exchange. While the novel eventually contains its radical premise by displacing Lalu's contractual agreement with the aura of romance, it nonetheless suggests that conjugal servitude, her consent to the use of her body, is a condition of the rights of citizenship. For Lalu, cultural participation and entitlement demand that an identification with patriarchal nationalism be expressed through sexual-as-national fidelity.

Narratives such as *Thousand Pieces of Gold* attest to the embodied contingency of women's national incorporation irrespective of their formal citizenship status even as the demand for democratic homogeneity would disavow difference. If women's political agency is read as an expression of their sexuality, women's civic participation and public representation become compromised; as theorist Moira Gatens writes, "[T]here is a lot more to be said about methods of exclusion than formalized principles of equity can address. If woman speaks from this body, she is limited in what she can say" (Gatens 1997, 85). Her statement also applies to those who embody other visible markers of difference, in Berlant's words, those "women, African Americans, Native Americans, immigrants, [and] homosexuals" who are deemed "not American enough to be sustained by the fullest resources of democratic national privilege" (Berlant 1997, 19). While equality among citizens has been enforced by the removal of some overtly discriminatory barriers, nevertheless, formal membership in the nation-state has not produced equal representation or equal access to state institutions. Those exclusions produce, in Berlant's terms, only partial citizenship. For women of color, there is no position to speak from but a position of embodiment. For Asian American women constrained by their association with hyperfemininity, sexualized representation significantly impacts notions of equal citizenship.

In discussing the ways that representations of women regulate society, Elisabeth Bronfen has noted that women must be eliminated in the public sphere through death: "Over her dead body, cultural norms are reconfirmed or secured, whether because the sacrifice of the virtuous, innocent woman serves as a social critique and transformation or because a sacrifice of the dangerous woman reestablishes an order that was momentarily suspended due to her presence" (Bronfen 1992, 181). Her point highlights women's symbolic role in boundary maintenance and the ways that their impact on civic life is contingent on their absence. Similarly, I want to suggest that Woman's emergence in the public sphere depends on her appearing as a woman, that gender role conformity is the very condition of her civic participation. For women, citizenship is inseparable from the performance of femininity and, in turn, femininity mediates women's identification with the nation. The demonstration of national fidelity, then, lies in both ritualized gender performance and in witnessing that performance.

If national incorporation for Asian American women as for other women of color is inseparable from questions of sexual availability, then the public display of the body becomes one of the few avenues through which women can attest to communal fealty. Visibility has become a primary trope of Asian American claims to political rights, but as a determiner of political representation, visibility has specific consequences for women. Jeanne Wakatsuki Houston's and James D. Houston's 1973 *Farewell to Manzanar*, a personal narrative on Japanese American internment, provokes questions about the relationship between hyperfemininity and the construction of a loyal citizenry. Jeannie's innocent postwar speculation—"I wondered why my citizenship had to be so loudly affirmed" (116)—may appear as somewhat disingenuous in light of Houston's depiction of internment and her deliberate attempts to modify the wartime meanings ascribed to her race—disloyal, traitor, saboteur, enemy. Her efforts at integration point to a contradiction between the public actions that mark her as a "strictly female female" and the necessity of undergoing deracination as a predicate of equal democratic representation in the abstract. She tries "desperately to be as American as Doris Day" in an attempt to counter the racial hatred that Japanese Americans faced upon release from the internment camp at Manzanar:

> By that time I was desperate to be "accepted," and baton twirling was one trick I could perform that was thoroughly, unmistakably American—putting on the boots and a dress crisscrossed with braid, spinning the silver stick and tossing it high to the tune of a John Philip Sousa march. Even at ten, before I really knew what waited outside, the Japanese in me could not compete with that. (79)

As a resolution to the crisis of citizenship that internment represents, Jeannie's role-playing appears to reconcile her Japaneseness to Americanization through ritualized gender conformity; offering herself as the gazed upon object is a concession to masculinized state power. On the surface, this means of achieving acceptability, like the other costumes that Jeannie tries on—carnival queen and orphaned confirmation "bride"—seems to capitulate to the gender dictates of the times in order to mitigate the visible signs of race, or in Wiegman's terms, the "epidermal iconography of difference" (Wiegman 1995, 117). The underlying question is whether the spectacle of the Asian body performing the public rituals of citizenship creates cultural dissonance in the form of disruptive mimicry, or whether it merely works to normalizing effect.

It could be said that the only D-Day Jeannie's actions invoke is Doris; the challenge of her self-acknowledged goal lies in transforming her public representation from a reminder of war into a symbol of wholesome femininity. A big, relentlessly perky, and optimistic blond of the 1950s, Doris Day was an icon of flush times; it is not surprising that she symbolized America as her image was exported to the Third World. Such is the connection that Bharati Mukherjee draws in her 1993 essay, "Love Me or Leave Me," a meditation on her identification with Doris Day, which prefigured her immigration from India. In exploring her initial response to America through a Hollywood musical, she locates herself not as a participant in a spectacle of femininity with national overtones, but as its witness. Both Houston's and Mukherjee's narratives reveal that national affiliation has gendered terms of admission; sexuality is at once the pathway to inclusion and either a resolution or catalyst to an implied betrayal. In drawing these connections, this chapter asks whether feminine role-playing suppresses racial markers to mitigate a threatening differ-ence that cannot be incorporated by the body politic. What I am inter-ested in, then, is an understanding of citizenship, in the words of Yuval-Davis, "not just in the narrow formalistic meaning of having the right to carry a specific passport, but citizenship as an overall concept which sums up the relationship between the individual and the state" (Yuval-Davis 1991, 58). Understood in part as an identification with patriarchal na-tionalism, citizenship exceeds its legal definition to encompass the public enactments of "private" identity that attest to national belonging.

Masquerade and the Dictates of Citizenship: *Farewell to Manzanar*

If there is a "representative" fact about *Farewell to Manzanar*'s depiction of the internment it is that Jeanne Wakatsuki Houston's story, initially told from the point of view of a seven-year-old, reflects the experiences of the "army of tots and teenagers" who comprised the bulk of the interned nisei (Weglyn 1976, 134). The youthfulness of the majority of internees in part accounts for the Japanese American community's lack of political leverage in the years leading up to Executive Order 9066, the call for mass evacuation in 1942. The overt reason behind the imprisonment of 110,000 people of Japanese ancestry, aliens and citizens alike, was "mili-tary necessity," the fear of disloyalty and acts of sabotage against the war effort. The underlying facts proved this fear to be unfounded—a report submitted to President Roosevelt prior to evacuation revealed no reason to suspect the loyalty of issei, nisei, or kibbei. The adminstration's covert reasons were as equally compelling influences as the stated one: fear of "the Japs" must be at once incited and assuaged in deference to public opinion; the economic interests of the California growers lobby could be appeased (Takaki 1989); the United States would have a potential hos-tage pool to safeguard the interests of American prisoners of war overseas (Weglyn 1976). These motives not only countered the fear of subversive activity as the stated reason for internment, but were deemed significant enough wartime necessities to abrogate the Constitution.

Japanese American internment is not merely an aberrant blot on the American historical record but remains significant as an instance in which the contractual agreement that citizenship represents was rendered inva-lid by the state. The evacuation order mandated a loss of rights in spite of the formal rights of citizenship both in the detention of individuals for an unspecified duration without the filing of criminal charges, and in the forced liquidation of personal property. It was clearly a case in which visual markers of racial difference trumped other facts: that citizenship protected against such measures, that there was no evidence of disloyalty, that children and infants could not possibly enact sabotage, and so on. Ironically, one right would be restored prior to the release from camp: the right to volunteer for military service in the defense of the state that had imprisoned them. In a reversal of the very logic that made him sign Executive Order 9066 authorizing mass internment, President Roosevelt decreed, "No loyal citizen of the United States should be denied the democratic right to exercise the responsibilities of his citizenship, regardless of his ancestry" (Takaki 1989, 397). To this end, all internees over the age of seventeen were required to fill out the infamous "Application for Leave Clearance" that was, in reality, a loyalty oath.

Elaine Kim has noted that what is "crucial about *Farewell to Manzanar* as a work of Asian American literature is not the story of the internment so much as the story of a *nisei* woman's response to racism" (E. Kim 1984, 84). Kim's comment suggests that the autobiography's novelistic structure counters its contribution as historical testimony. Her assessment depends on an evaluation of the autobiography not as an inaccurate but as a partial and particularist account of the camps from the point of view of a child. Houston's text represents Manzanar as a psychological effect; the narrative tension and resolution must therefore come about as the adult narrator's individual catharsis:[5]

> Until this trip I had not been able to admit that my own life really began there. The times I thought I had dreamed it were one way of getting rid of it, part of wanting to lose it, part of what you might call a whole Manzanar mentality I had lived with for twenty-five years. Much more than a remembered place, it had become a state of mind. Now, having seen it, I no longer wanted to lose it or have those years erased. Having found it, I could say what you can only say when you've truly come to know a place: Farewell. (140)

The narrative's trajectory follows that of successful therapy: once made conscious as the source and manifestation of the narrator's "shame and the guilt and the sense of unworthiness," Manzanar can be let go. Consciousness initiates recuperation. As the foreword notes, the Houstons' idea was to avoid framing the experience around political issues in deference to a white audience that was "issued out" presumably by the Vietnam War and the civil rights movement. Thus the autobiography's point of view represents history not as an overtly political terrain of struggle but as psychic conflict, a move that potentially reduces the collective history of the internment to a matter of individual trauma with a very individualized pathway to resolution and redress.

What lies within Jeannie's control, the narrative implies, is not racism but internalized racism. The idea of internment as psychological syndrome also underlies the structure of John Okada's *No No Boy* (1977), albeit there, Ichiro's malaise stems specifically from the fallout of his refusal to be drafted as a sign of political allegiance. The novel rehearses the shortcomings and contradictions of each position on the draft through interior reflection; Ichiro must overcome the postwar "no no" stigma to be reintegrated into community. Yet like Okada's novel, *Farewell to Manzanar* does not push the internment out of the realm of politics through its emphasis on interiority. The abrogation of individual rights and the violation of the civil rights of a group specifically targeted by the state remain salient: the text implies the absolute innocence of the stigmatized group by grafting such innocence onto a child. The historical parallels to the individual's process of healing also become clear: bringing to light a painful and repressed history is therapeutic for an American collective conscious haunted by the memory of the very undemocratic measures that it took to secure democracy. (Drawing a chilling correspondence between the bureaucracy of Japanese American internment and that of the Holocaust, historian Michi Weglyn quotes Hitler's prophecy: "Those who now most oppose our methods will ultimately adopt them" [cited in Weglyn 1976, 75].) One of the text's contributions lies in its treatment of the very terms of communal belonging that mass evacuation brought to a crisis—not the privileges or rights accorded within legal definitions of citizenship but what exists in excess of those definitions. The history of internment reveals the tenuousness of citizenship as the primary sign of national belonging; as the narrative reveals, citizenship can be rendered moot according to the whims of the state. But the text also chronicles the public enactments of "private" identity that attest to national loyalty; the text specifies the identifications necessary to authorize at least the appearance of communal belonging and reveal woman's relationship to the nation to be a function of her sexual corporealization. Ultimately, Jeannie's racially valenced "disloyalty" must be redeemed by her femininity.

Farewell to Manzanar reads as an oedipal drama between the issei and nisei with the state cast as the ultimate phallic father. The Freudian language the authors invoke cannot help but situate acculturation as an oedipal process whose successful end is an identification with patriarchal nationalism. This explains, in part, why the narrative centers on the father/ daughter relationship: "Papa's life [ended at] Manzanar. He didn't die there, but things finished for him there, whereas for me it was like a birthplace. The camp was where our life lines intersected" (34). The neutral portrayal here of the coincidental intersection of two journeys, the father's fall and the daughter's rise, belies the fact that the daughter's social integration is precipitated and enabled by her father's social death in camp. An alien ineligible for citizenship because of his race, her father is rendered effectively stateless in answering affirmatively to the question, "Will you swear unqualified allegiance to the United States of America and faithfully defend the United States from any or all attack by foreign or domestic forces, and forswear any form of allegiance or obedience to the Japanese emperor, or any other foreign government, power, or organization?"[6] The loss of his domestic authority is portrayed as a classic oedipal melodrama in which the nisei son challenges his father over the abuse of his passive and resigned mother ("Kill me then. I don't care. I just don't care" [49]). Kim points out that as narrator, Houston hides behind the "dashing" figure of her father out of an uncertainty about the representativeness of her own experience; the overall effect, however, is not of a daughter who merely witnesses the destruction of patriarchal authority but of one who wills it.

The narrative depicts issei male disenfranchisement as castration: "He had no rights, no home, no control over his own life. This kind of emasculation was suffered by all the men interned at Manzanar" (48). Her father's cane, the "sad, homemade version of the samurai sword," contrasts with the daughter's own instrument of entry, the majorette's baton, as the symbol of her limited phallic power and need to identify with its true owner. In a fort/da game of its own, the state has the power to effect the father's disappearance and to restore him. Prefiguring Jeannie's understanding of the two social options open to her upon release from camp—invisibility or acceptability—her father's detention at Fort Lincoln first renders him invisible and then replaces him with a pacified, disempowered, "acceptable" version of his former self. The daughter's rage at the loss of her mother upon her father's return from the FBI's interrogation center in North Dakota ("I slept with her every night . . . until Papa came back" [16]) precipitates her apprehension of where the phallus really resides: outside the camp. Jeannie identifies with masculine authority beyond the fence; a child tagged with an identification number during evacuation, she attempts to ingratiate herself to the instrument of state power by smiling at the bus driver who ignores her. She blames her father not merely for his failure to protect the family from internment but for his unrepentant ethnic visibility, as she correctly apprehends, the sole basis on which ethnic Japanese were interned: "I was ashamed of him . . . and, in a deeper way, for being what had led to our imprisonment, that is, for being so unalterably Japanese" (119). Houston's repeated emphasis on race as a visible marker of difference enforces a division between the domestic and public spheres that the camp experience has eroded: she tolerates and submits to the "private" enactments of her father's Japaneseness in the form of his claims to masculine entitlement but recoils at the public expressions of his ethnicity that force others to see him as alien, Old World, and "unforgivably a foreigner."

Against the text's implications, it is not only the state that has castrated him but Jeannie herself; beginning with her fantasies about a camp

orphan, her attempt to integrate into the social fabric is ultimately parricidal. The child-narrator envies the orphan's confirmation ceremony: on
a conscious level it appeals to her sense of performance and ritual—and
unconsciously, masquerade. Being the center of attention is part of the
appeal, but her desire speaks to the fantasy of being orphaned, of killing
both her father and mother as the impediments to her social mobility. The
orphan's confirmation is also the posture of perfect innocence, an innocence that veils the murderous desires she holds toward her parent-
objects and the challenge they represent to her identification with a higher
authority—here, God, and later, the nation. The orphan's representation
as "bride" in a symbolic union with God is a displaced desire for an
alliance with the "outside," with the unseen authority existing outside the
camp gates. This association is made textually overt in Jeannie's test of
religious belief in which she prays for dried apricots; while God does not
answer her prayers, she loses what little faith she had without ever relinquishing "faith in the outside where all such good things could be found"
(94).

One of the other appeals of the church lies in the stories of female saints
like Saint Agatha, "whose breasts were cut off when she refused to renounce her faith" (31). Jeannie becomes "fascinated with the miseries of
women who had suffered and borne such afflictions" and pictures herself
among them, "up there on the screen of history, in a white lace catechism
dress, sweating and grimy, yet selflessly carrying my load" (31). Her desire may suggest a masculine identification in the image of displaced female castration ("breasts cut off"), a renunciation of the female body
through an association with the abstract spiritual realm. However, the
dream of martyrdom more specifically resonates with the very historical
process in which the child is an actor: the Japanese internees are martyrs
to the need to satisfy American public perception; she is thus already on
the "screen of history" in a particularly racial sacrifice. More important,
the stories evoke the public spectacle of suffering and mutilation enacted
on the female body that prefigures Jeannie's bodily offering to America of
the 1950s.

Once released from camp, Jeannie responds to the experience of segregation by overcompensation; reflecting a masculine bias in language as
in ambition, she notes, "I wanted to declare myself in some different way
. . . I wanted *in*" (115). Seemingly a protest of the racist interests that
brought about internment, integration is presented as a matter of master-
ing and publicly performing certain roles, roles that could be said to mitigate her racial difference. In regard to Jeannie's majorette costume, Kim
writes, "Wearing a braided costume with boots draws attention away
from her Japanese American identity. Fastening on clothes and roles—as

majorette, as carnival queen, as nun, as confirmation 'princess'—is part of the desire to be invisible and acceptable at the same time, just as U.S. Army uniforms have made men from minority groups feel more 'American' and less Asian, Black, or Chicano" (E. Kim 1984, 87). The willingness of nisei volunteers to serve is a tangible, if ironic, indicator of allegiance; for them, as for other men of color, the military uniform functions as an indicator of the "uniformity" necessary to the idea of disembodied and homogeneous citizens. If military service is one sign of loyalty recognized by the state, what options are open to women to display a comparable fidelity?

Farewell to Manzanar's portrayal of Jeannie's postwar years suggests that the display of feminine sexuality is one of the few means of publicly signifying women's identification with the state. Jeannie's speaking of her experience as a majorette for the Boy Scout corps after being excluded from the Girl Scouts because of her race, Houston writes,

> The boys in the band loved having us out there in front of them all the time, bending back and stepping high, in our snug satin outfits and short skirts. Their dads, mostly navy men, loved it too. At that age I was too young to consciously use my sexuality or to understand how an Oriental female can fascinate Caucasian men, and of course far too young to see that even this is usually just another form of invisibility. It simply happened that the attention I first gained as a majorette went hand in hand with a warm reception from the Boy Scouts and their fathers, and from that point on I knew intuitively that one resource I had to overcome the war-distorted limitations of my race would be my femininity. (117)

Jeannie's participation announces her sexual availability to (white) men in what feminists recognize as the "traffic in women" that underlies gender differentiation. On the surface, her desire to be the eroticized front of a pseudo-military parade suggests Luce Irigaray's concept of the capitulative feminine masquerade in which women "submit to the dominant economy of (masculine) desire" in order to "recuperate some element of desire but at the price of renouncing their own" (Irigaray 1985, 133). But the child/woman's intuition about how to be pleasing to authority has implications beyond Marxist feminist understanding of woman as commodity or woman as the object of the masculine gaze in feminist film theory. Here, heterosexual gender conformity is a means of signifying loyalty, of performing citizenship on the "screen of history" as a concession to the phallic power of the state. Jeannie's public performances challenge the war-distorted perception of a separatist, clannish Japanese American community by demonstrating Japanese men's willingness to place "their" women in circulation to share with others; as Houston notes in an essay, the connection she makes between sexuality and social integration has the support of her brothers, who would buy her the "sexy" sweaters that her Caucasian friends wore, but that her mother refused her (Houston 1980, 21).

Jeannie's hyperfeminine display as the means of signifying her identification with patriarchal nationalism seems to reflect the specific association of gender with assimilability operative within Asian American letters. Here, however, the belief in Asian women's acceptability to the dominant culture is supported not by conspiracy theories about a powerful, white feminist publishing cabal as I discuss in chapter 3, but through a complex dynamic in which femininity replaces the irreducible difference of race with the familiarity of gender difference. To paraphrase Bharati Mukherjee, Jeannie's costume transforms "real foreignness" into the benignly exotic. Certainly, her use of sexuality as a means of getting "in" seems to enact the very idea of racial acceptability that Frank Chin and Jeffrey Paul Chan decry as "racist love," white preference for pacified, servile, and ultimately "womanly" minorities (Chin and Chan 1972). According to this logic, Jeannie's posturing enforces the perception that heterosexual women of color betray ethnic community through sexual capitulation. But contrary to the suggestion that the nation can incorporate women of color not as nonwhites but as women, feminine corporeality delimits women's ability to represent the universal citizen subject. What are the consequences, then, of Jeannie's efforts to claim a space in the public sphere through ritualized hyperfemininity, to claim, in effect, a partial citizenship?

Farewell to Manzanar represents femininity as a pathway to Jeannie's acculturation in the same way that Michael Rogin suggests racial cross-dressing did for Jews. In his reading of Al Jolson's *The Jazz Singer*, in which Jack Robin née Jakie Rabinowitz "adopts a black mask that kills his father" (Rogin 1996, 79), Rogin argues that "motion picture blackface . . . turned Europeans into Americans" (Rogin 1992, 12). The racial masquerade—Jakie's appropriation of "the surplus symbolic value of blacks"—facilitates his entry into America via popular culture. The link between racial masquerade and parricide bears relevance to Jeannie's own desire for integration: her public identity is contingent on the social death of the father and her willingness to play with racial meanings through masquerade. Like Rogin's blackface performers, racial cross-dressing is a means to Jeannie's bid for acceptance as carnival queen.[7] In discussing her winning strategy, she notes,

> I knew that I couldn't beat the other contestants at their own game, that is, look like a bobbysoxer. Yet neither could I look too Japanese-y. I decided to go exotic, with a flower-print sarong, black hair loose and a hibiscus flower be-

hind my ear. When I walked barefooted out onto the varnished gymnasium floor, between the filled bleachers, the howls and whistles from the boys were double what had greeted any of the other girls. (124)

While presumably girls in the school have a vote, the passage implies that it is only the response of the boys that matters, an implication in keeping with Mary Ann Doane's point on female spectatorship that "the woman as subject of the gaze is clearly an impossible sign"; the implied spectator is always white and male, and more explicitly as in the case of the Boy Scout parade, a former Navy man (Doane 1982, 84).

Like blackface, Jeannie's racial cross-dressing as "native" is not intended to mask her own difference as much as it is to take on the racial attributes ascribed to another group and use them to transform her own. To this end, playing to fascination with Hawiiana in the postwar era, she puts on not the "ghastly white" face of the Japanese geisha, but the overtly sexualized garb of the receptive native woman. In evoking the Pacific Islands, the costume brings to mind a site that witnessed intensive American involvement during the war, a site now successfully pacified, secured, and, hence, available. (Ironically, ethnic Japanese living in Hawaii were *not* interned.) Houston's strategic racial cross-dressing recalls an instance embedded within her description of internees' attempts at American "normality" inside the camps. Details of yearbooks, school plays, and hillbilly bands are supplemented by her memory of an Indian "billing himself as a Sioux chief, wearing bear claws and head feathers" who sings and dances while hundreds of internees watch (73). It is as if witnessing the performance of putative Native ethnicity creates putative Americans: the internees participate in American culture by joining the subjugation of another group elevated to the art of public spectacle. In the mastery implied by the act of watching, they are transformed from prisoners of war into tourists. In both instances, going native is a means of becoming American.[8]

The internment demonstrated the dangers of American fascination with ethnic visibility; what was punishable was not actual acts of sabotage but appearance, the fact that Japanese in the United States looked "exactly like the enemy" (6). As internee Mary Oyama laments in an essay ironically appearing in *Liberty* magazine, "My only crime is my face" (Mary Oyama, "My Only Crime is my Face," *Liberty Magazine*, 1943). Scholars such as Elena Tajima Creef and Wendy Kozol have analyzed government attempts to refashion this image through highly selective, state-sanctioned photographs that depict camp experience and resettlement as having the willing cooperation of loyal citizens. In looking at the WRA photographs of internment taken by official photographers such as Dorothea Lange and Ansel Adams, among others, both Creef and

Kozol demonstrate the ambivalence of these photographs' staging of citizenship against the government's propagandist intent. Both suggest a similar connection among gender, visibility, and Americanization that Houston's text so self-consciously portrays. Creef's analysis of a postwar *Saturday Evening Post* spread on Japanese war brides—"hamburgers, Hollywood, and home on the range"—highlights the ways that domesticity is a vehicle for Americanization. Her investigation of these photographs, which depict a group of newlywed Japanese women taking classes in American culture to prepare for immigration, suggests that nationality is "learned" through gender conformity. Hers is a particularly fraught academic exercise, given that one of the students in the photograph is her mother.

Kozol also emphasizes gender's role in regulating race in her reading of a WRA photograph of Japanese American women's resettlement in Chicago. Portrayed as bathing beauties in ways that mirror the pin-up poses in popular magazines such as *Life* and *Look*, these women are presumed to be incorporated into American society through consumerism; the caption reads, "Another freedom of considerable importance to the young feminine mind in America is the freedom to shop for and wear pretty clothes" (Kozol, 236). Nevertheless, Kozol also argues that other idealized images of domesticity intended to normalize the traumatic experience of internment are destablized by the photographs' composition. In marking the dual and potentially contradictary resonances of these WRA photographs, she suggests that while the photographs of internees documented Japanese Americans' cheerful compliance with the policy of evacuation, they nonetheless also "argue for the citizenship status of the internees through recognizable domestic arrangements and material objects that help to secure their identity as Americans" (Kozol, 231). Kozol suggests that in operating out of a colorblind aesthetic, the photographs enable the viewer to visualize the humanity of subjects who refuse victimization. Nevertheless they also serve the purposes of the state by imbuing an unconstitutional violation with national ideals.

Both these documentary photographs of the camp experience and Jeannie's effort to subvert the "epidermal iconography of difference" through costumes and uniforms suggest a cooperative relationship between hyperpatriotism and gender as a familiarizing discourse. They also indicate the potential uses and limits of mimicry to enact or challenge the status quo. Theories of mimicry, masquerade, drag, passing, blackface (or yellowface), and gender performativity contest the idea of the body as the origin of identity and emphasize the transgressive possibilities of play. Not all are applicable to Jeannie's methods of claiming visibility in the public sphere; her actions cannot be properly described as masquerading as American—she is already American, a point ignored by the state. Nor does she pass as white; given the public nature of her activities, she makes no attempt to mask the visible signs of racial difference.[9] Her attempt to assign to Japaneseness another valence through femininity could be understood as the desire for likeness, as a mimicry of white womanhood. While her narrative relegates white women to secondary positions in two instances—as second majorette and attendants to the queen—Jeannie's threat to white women is limited. She is not only excluded from socializing with her white classmates on the basis of race, but her retrospective analysis recognizes that her crown is, in fact, only cardboard, the mimicry imperfect. Twice, committees representing the institutional state apparatus—the school system and the Boy Scouts of America—confer and contest the desirability of her representing their public face out of fear of being accused of supporting racial integration. A successful mimicry of white women would only situate her in the space they occupy vis-à-vis the nation—as Wiegman notes, excised "from the public domain of enlightened citizenship" (Wiegman 1995, 45). The success or failure of her attempts at integration via femininity only exposes the degree to which, to paraphrase Cherríe Moraga, she can never become the white man, only the white man's woman.

Yet Jeannie's role-playing as a means of demonstrating civic loyalty can be understood as more than an effort at mimicry if femininity itself is seen as a masquerade that disguises an underlying phallicism. In "Womanliness as a Masquerade," Joan Riviere suggests that excessively feminine behavior unconsciously disguises women's phallic desires. Speaking in regard to an intellectual woman whose need to solicit reassurance from men after her public lectures takes the form of "flirting and coquetting" as a means of soliciting "sexual advances" from father-figures, Riviere theorizes that such behavior originates from a woman's desire to placate masculine authority for the affront of her own intellectual display (Riviere 1986, 36). "Womanliness," she writes, "could be assumed and worn as a mask, both to hide the possession of masculinity and to avert the reprisals expected if she was found to possess it" (38).[10]

Jeannie's public demonstrations of "girlness" might thus enact a masquerade that disguises the presumptive desire for social equality on the part of a Japanese American woman. Her appearance as uniformed military nymphet and later as carnival queen obscures the essentially phallic nature of her desire to participate in civic life—and potentially not only as an equal, but as a leader. Like Riviere's masquerading analysand, whose hyperfeminine behavior compensates for her castrating intellectual performance, Jeannie's willingness to please masks the affront represented by the exercise of her freedom to participate in the civic life of her community as befitting her status as citizen. Her attempts at public visibility appear as the resolution to the narrative's oedipal drama with her own father, but it is the punishing state, not the father, who must ultimately be placated. While her actions suggest a willingness to situate herself as racialized and feminine object before the national gaze, they can also be read as compensations for the transgression of claiming a public presence.

The daughter lacks the means to prove her loyalty in ways open to the son and is thus without a formal means of demonstrating the success of an oedipal process whose end is an identification with nation. Her brother's military service presumably affirms his likeness to white men (albeit from the safe distance of a segregated unit), and, as the text notes, restores the family honor if only by demonstrating that the rebellious line of the Wakatsuki family is alive and well and in bed with the occupying forces. In contrast, the phallic daughter must redress the affront of Manzanar through her own circulation as a woman, revealing the social contract to be indistinguishable from the sexual contract.[11] According to the logic of internalized racism operative in the narrative, interracial marriage as "the ultimate assimilation" is the most obvious sign of acceptance, the successful end to Jeannie's hope for integration. In the context of the internment, the importance of cross-racial alliance does not remain in the realm of the unconscious but specifies degrees of democratic freedom; movement is measured through the proximity of Caucasians: "you could measure your liberty by how far they'd let you go—to Camp Three with a Caucasian, to Camp Three alone, to Camp Four with a Caucasian, to Camp Four alone" (77). These degrees of freedom become associated in the child's mind with illicit, cross-racial alliance: her one night outside the camp on a field trip is specifically arranged to enable the courtship of a nisei and a Quaker volunteer. Thus, "flirting and coquetting" are not only methods of appeasing castrating authority but are intrinsically connected to the basic freedom of mobility.

Does the question of integration for male internees also hinge on the corporeal? Okada's *No No Boy* engages a potent image of the body politic and internment in the character of Kenji, a "yes yes" veteran whose war injuries result in a gangrenous leg and his eventual death. His condition is at once symbolic of the desire to excise Japanese Americans from the national body for fear of the contagion of disloyalty, and the internal, putrid side of democracy—the better-left-forgotten history of the very undemocratic measures that it took to secure democracy. But unlike Houston's text, *No No Boy*'s resolution does not rest on the sexual; sexuality, it implies, is something women, not men, possess, and it is a gift they bestow as a sign of men's ethnic communal integration. A more apt parallel is David Mura's 1993 essay connecting sex addiction and the legacy of the camps, "No-No Boys: Re-X-Amining Japanese Americans."[12] Although a sansei and a son of internees, Mura self-consciously links his feelings of sexual inadequacy to the racial shame inherited from internment:

> To move from the Japanese-American internment camps to the sexuality of one Japanese-American boy in a suburb of Chicago—even I can look at this as a movement from tragedy to farce. A large scale, community-wide anguish and humiliation is replaced by an adolescent's discomfort and awkwardness, not very different from any other American boy's coming to terms with sexuality, whatever his color. (Mura 1993, 146)

Mura's retreat into the privatized world of pornography, promiscuity, and drugs acts out his internalized self-contempt derivative of the inheritance—not the experience—of the camps. The physical exclusion represented by his parents' internment mirrors his seeming exclusion from the economy of desire:

> I felt I recognized in this image [of porn miscegenation] the grid against which I was to look at my sexuality. Beauty and intelligence was [sic] there with the whites, sexuality and the body was what characterized blacks. And I as a Japanese American? I was the one who watched, who did not participate, who was outside of that history. I was the neutered Hop-Sing or the houseboy of *Bachelor Father*. (Mura 1993, 150)

His self-designation as castrated bystander before "multicultural" porn masks the essentially phallic nature of his private enjoyment: he recovers the mastery denied his race in the camp experience through masculine spectatorship, as a witness-participant in the domination of white (and nonwhite) women. Although he comes to pinpoint the internment legacy as one source of his sexual addiction, his resolution is not activism in the form of the redress movement, but therapy in the form of a twelve-step program. The therapeutic process initiates political consciousness and his growing identification with people of color and with the "No No boys" who protested the placating stance of the Japanese American Citizen's League.

Like Houston, Mura's response to social exclusion is symbolic parricide. He blames his father for not resisting, for passing on to him an accommodationist, "yes yes" mentality. Ironically, he sees this legacy as a result of, for one, his parents' placement in Jerome, Arkansas, where the symbolic castration of Houston's text becomes a literal fear of lynching in the Deep South. In speaking of "No No boy" Gordon Hirabayashi, who brought suit against the U.S. government over the internment, Mura writes, "if this man had been my father . . . I would not only know more about the camps or history, I would not only have grown up with different political beliefs. I would have felt differently about my sexuality, about my body, I would not have seen them as a source of wounding and shame" (Mura 1993, 152). Unlike Jeannie's parricidal impulses, his desire to kill his father and replace him with a more heroic model arises from what he sees as his father's responsibility for Mura's own psychosexual pathology. Rather than suggesting an ideological difference between Japanese American male and female narratives depicting the relationship between sexuality and citizenship, between a man's identification with a No No boy's protest and a woman's desire for national incorporation, "No-No Boys: Re-X-Amining Japanese Americans" and *Farewell to Manzanar* reach similar conclusions. Not only does their characterization of internment as psychological syndrome enable specific political resolutions, but Mura's "recovery" implies a return to the monogamous, heterosexual fold from a space of perversity and "sickness" that mark him as an outsider to national community. His desire for therapy and historical accounting, then, can be read as a similar desire for communal integration albeit through an identification with masculine, antinationalist figures.

A major consequence of racism, Mura' confession suggests, is sexual repression and shame: "The questions about how our desires are formed or where they came from are somehow too troubling [to inquire into very deeply]" (Mura 1993, 147). Mura's conclusion that the high outmarriage rate in the Japanese American community is due to ethnic self-contempt is a problematic consequence of applying his individual circumstances to a collective, historical phenomenon, a "farcical" leap that he readily acknowledges but nonetheless relies on. His causal connection between outmarriage rates and negative self-perception fails to account for the material conditions that truncated the development of ethnic community, namely, the 1917 Gentleman's Agreement between the United States and Japan to curtail immigration from Japan, and President Roosevelt's deliberate policy of dispersing Japanese American families upon resettlement. Nisei hoping to relocate to the Midwest and East were told by authorities "not to congregate in public, not to walk on the street in groups of more than three, or sit in a restaurant in groups of more than five" (cited in Nagata and Takeshita 1998, 592–93). This resettlement policy was not intended to facilitate integration, but was implemented out of concern that white communities would be offended by Japanese American presence. Rather than reflecting a condition of psychosexual and racial pathology as Mura's comments imply, the outmarriage rate is a consequence of prohibitions to reproducing community deliberately imposed by the state. His conclusions exemplify the problem inherent in grafting the collective experience onto an individual, interior reflection. Moreover, his text reveals that reading through the lens of oedipal drama is necessarily limited if such an analysis merely derives sociological truisms from individual experience or privatizes national history as family romance.

In contrast to Mura's anticommunal sexual predilections, Houston's text depicts feminine sexuality as intrinsic to the performance of citizenship. Her attempts at integration as a means of redressing the implicit charge of disloyalty highlight the public nature of women's circulation and testify to the degree to which there could be no female equivalent to the "No No boy." Were there a means for women to mark national allegiance in defiance of their corporealization, to echo internee Mitsuye Yamada, it would not have made a difference to anyone (Yamada 1981). Nevertheless, Jeannie's desire for inclusion supports the project of nationalism by confirming the nation's desirability—and exclusivity. The autobiography's "yes yes" logic might mark it as a form of what writer Frank Chin calls "ventriloquism," the capitulative writing that speaks through the disciplining forces of white power. No doubt, some may attribute such co-optation to James D. Houston's coauthorship in ways that provide a corrective to the daughter's oedipal struggle; it is the authorial manipulation of the disembodied white male citizen who castrates the Japanese father after all. But in keeping with the dynamic I highlight in the chapter's introduction and later in chapter 4, such a reading implies that Houston has no political agency of her own and no control over the ideological import of her story.

Farewell to Manzanar does exhibit a 1970s retrospective awareness of the terms of inclusion as Jeannie rethinks the authenticity of her bid for acceptance. Her self-consciousness bears queer resonance to Houston's 1993 depiction of a preinternment childhood encounter with a pinhead in a freak show and the violence of public display:

> I see a sharp picture of the pin-head dressed in a Japanese kimono, nervously twisting a sequined purse with thin blue-veined hands. He especially intrigued me because he was small, not much taller than me, and wore heavy make-up, bright lipstick and face powder which failed to cover the purple five o'clock shadow of his lower face. His hair was swept up into a small bun from which dangled Japanese ornaments.
>
> One day, as I gazed at him—more awed than curious—he looked me straight in the eyes. I remember being shocked, feeling a pang of pity, feeling badly and not understanding why. I know now those beady black eyes had drawn from my childish heart its first feeling of compassion. I never went back. (Houston 1993, 60)

What fascinates the child is perhaps not the monstrosity of the pinhead's difference but his likeness to her, here, in recognition of his stature but no doubt also in regard to his attempts at Japaneseness or what Renee

Tajima calls DRAG—downright retrograde asian getup (Tajima 1989). Her feeling of compassion is an unconscious recognition of the dehumanizing nature of specular violence. As Rey Chow notes, "The activity of watching is linked by projection to physical nakedness. Watching is theoretically defined as the primary agency of violence, an act that pierces the other, who inhabits the place of passive victim on display" (Chow 1993, 29). It is thus that the freak show is both pornographic and objectifying; in gazing upon his "defiled, degraded image" (Chow 1993, 30), Jeannie is nevertheless forced to recognize his subjectivity as he, the failed replica, returns her gaze. What is shocking, however, and perhaps what commits this image to her memory, is seeing her own femininity and Japaneseness as supplements to freakishness and potentially the very signs and condition of the pinhead's "captivity" and display. Yet the moment does not move her to comment on her own self-representation as Japanese American. Her resistance is a refusal to look; her complicity, her use of him to feel emotion.

The child's horror in looking cannot anticipate the ways in which she herself will be held captive on the basis of her difference and subsequently displayed as the price of conditional national inclusion. The adult retrospective may acknowledge the inauthenticity of her feminine performance in terms of seeking a hybrid ethnic identity, but it does not admit its violence because the text ultimately marks integration as empowering. Rather than standing as evidence of a capitulative fantasy, however, Houston's text exposes the very dictates of national inclusion for women and the extent to which their public circulation may service national agendas. If Riviere's "phallic woman" has significance for the idea of citizenship, it lies in the fact that feminine posturing may veil a greater affront than that of women's intellectualism—namely, the desire for (racial) social equality. Hyperfemininity masks an aggressive—although not ultimately empowering—move to establish a visible public presence as a challenge to the physical segregation Manzanar represented. Here, the feminine does not itself represent lack but is a compensation for a perceived lack—that of political fealty. *Farewell to Manzanar* may well expose the contingent nature of citizenship and national inclusion through its depiction of both a discriminatory history and the pleasures of girlness.

Feminine Identification as Sexual Ruthlessness: Mukherjee's "Love Me or Leave Me"

When the hyperfeminine woman appears on the screen of history, her function, as Diane Taylor notes, is to keep "homosocial society from becoming a homosexual one," to assure that the masculine drive for possession and control has its proper object (Taylor 1997, 68). The appearance of the symbolic Woman functions differently for the female spectator, particularly one who by race or origin of birth is perceived to be an outsider to national community. Houston's text, which testifies to the performative nature of imagining citizenship through the embodiment of this symbolic Woman also speaks to a reciprocal dynamic, that of identifying with hyperfemininity. While *Farewell to Manzanar* does not pedestal an actual figure of Jeannie's identification with the phallic woman, other texts portray the process of witnessing such role models as a prelude, I would suggest, to imagining national incorporation. One could say that Mukherjee's autobiographical essay, "Love Me or Leave Me" (1993), recounts the origins of the political views embedded in her fiction; it depicts a single, decisive moment in her sheltered and privileged Calcutta adolescence that initiates her decision to immigrate. She watches a Doris Day musical at the local cinema and walks out transformed: "What *could* I have discovered in a story about an obscure chorine in Chicago who meets a crooked nightclub owner and allows him to help her become a singing star even though it means denying or delaying true love?" she rhetorically asks (Mukherjee 1993, 190). "I" in this case is a fifteen-year-old convent-educated Bengali Brahmin awaiting, as she implies, the somewhat fated life of an Indian elite, a traditional woman's life if one slightly modified in the wake of postindependence progressiveness. The essay depicts the transformation of consciousness that precedes physical immigration and the exchange of formal citizenship to be the result of feminine identification.

Psychoanalysis has theorized identification as a means of restoring a lost love-object and, as such, Diana Fuss notes, it is a process intrinsically tied to the formation of identity, "the detour through the other that defines a self" (Fuss 1995, 2).[13] Identification, she writes, is "the play of difference and similitude in self-other relations" that brings identity into being, the point "where I become other" (2). What Fuss emphasizes and what I want to highlight here is that identification is an intrinsically political and historical process as it comes to structure the affiliations that underlie identity. Identification is, in her words, "a question of *relation*, of self to other, subject to object, inside to outside" (3).

Thus, in "being a girl" there resides not only pleasure but a specific social function as well: witnessing and identifying with spectacles of girlness is a means of becoming something other, in this case, I would argue, an American. Nowhere is the relationship between feminine sexuality and American acculturation so forcefully drawn than in Mukherjee's work. Almost all the stories in Mukherjee's *The Middleman and Other Stories* (1988), for example, end with a sexual act. Whether violent and coerced or ambiguously consensual, sex becomes a shorthand for depicting her immigrant characters' conquest of America; in effect, an evolving sexual freedom maps immigrant women's transformations and serves as a gauge of their progressive integration. Mukherjee's positive connotation for assimilation—one that encompasses a reciprocal influence on the immigrant who voluntarily sheds ethnic culture and on the American landscape—marks the controversial nature of her fiction among critics. Deemphasizing racial difference in its privileging European immigrant models of adaptation and integration, her writing ignores the state to address the nation. Nevertheless, her work raises questions about the nature of feminine identification and sexuality's role in staging citizenship for Asian women. In her fiction, cultivating public femininity is represented as a condition of immigrant women's cultural adaptation. In its portrayal of an immigrant's embrace of America, for example, "A Wife's Story" depicts a transplanted Indian woman's response to a New York tour guide's falsely enthusiastic effort to work the crowd:

> "Right your highness? Look, we gotta maharani with us! Couldn't I have been a star?"
> "Right! I say, my voice coming out a squeal. I've been trained to adapt; what else can I say?" (Mukherjee 1988, 36)

The guide's racist attempts at humor elicit Panna's self-conscious approval as the sign that she is in on the joke; the moment suggests that learning to deal with racism is a necessary adaptation; it is controversial because it portrays this adaptation as resigned acquiescence ("what else can I say?"). Panna's accommodation forces a connection between feminine posturing and public identity. Her familiarity with New York pushes her into an alien role reversal in regard to her tourist husband who, once out of the sphere of his control, appears to her as quaintly Old World, almost childlike in his need of direction. But vis-à-vis American men in public exchanges such as this one, which is to say, within a national gaze, adaptation to America means taking on a persona that is goodnaturedly insincere and femininely puppyish: she becomes a cheerleader, an insider, to a grotesque patter literally intended to acclimatize the outsider to the metropolis. Panna's awareness of the indignity of this posture is both redeeming of her character (she is not merely a fool) and condemning of it (she accepts this accommodation in exchange for the payoff, the opportunity for self-transformation through exposure to America).

In analyzing her youthful response to Charles Vidor's film about the rise of singer Ruth Etting, *Love Me or Leave Me* (1955) starring Doris Day, Mukherjee unintentionally validates a Marxist cliché about the effect of American pop culture on the Third World, that ideological (here deemed "subliminal") messages about capitalist individualism come through loud and clear. Her essay nevertheless also reveals the complexity of imagining national belonging by suggesting that to identify with a phallic woman is to enter into the promise of American democracy. Like Houston's narrative, in which Jeannie performs the rituals of citizenship through gender role conformity, Mukherjee's essay suggests that developing national loyalty lies in identifying with spectacles of (white) women's availability. In complement and contrast to Houston who not incoincidentally also found in Doris Day a model for acculturation (Houston 1980, 17), "Love Me or Leave Me" reveals that one can enjoy witnessing as well as performing femininity.

Echoing Jessica Hagedorn's portrayal of Third World fascination for American movies in *Dogeaters* but without her incisive indictment of the neocolonial relationship such fascination enforces, Mukherjee writes of 1950s Calcutta, "In that transitional decade, when preparations to flee the city seemed cowardly and prayer little more than escapism, Doris Day was an abstraction for democracy. A person with gumption—any person, even a ten-cents-a-dance taxi dancer like Ruth Etting—could turn her life around. The handicaps of caste, class, and gender could be overcome" (189). Mukherjee's thoughts of democracy do not remain at home even at the moment that India's postindependence democracy seemed, locally at least, to be poised at a crisis. Democracy is elsewhere, namely, at the cinema in the highly sexual figure of Doris Day as Ruth Etting; it is, in this and in other work by Mukherjee, not a political system as much as a symbol of opportunity, particularly the opportunity for self-transformation. In this case, the only "handicap" that allows her a point of alliance is gender; while the controversial nature of Mukherjee's proassimilation politics is more obvious in her fiction, what I am interested in is how witnessing the feminine appears as a means to the spectator's imagining herself "in," the suggestion that women's symbolic access to nation occurs through the projection of a phallic femininity.

Celebrating Ruth Etting's careerist ambition, Mukherjee writes, "I identified with her totally. I, too, intended to go places, be somebody" (190). Ruth's passion for performance is easily transposed onto her own desire to write; the fact that sexuality can be traded for a shot at establishing a public persona is an easy parallel. Both are illicit; neither sexual manipulation nor writing is something good girls do. Here, the allure of America lies not in class mobility but women's artistic freedom. In the film, the promise of both women's creativity and career success appears to be inseparable from performing sexual availability ("Come on, big boy, ten cents a dance"), and using sexuality more literally as a unit of barter in exchange for "a break." What specifically incites Mukherjee's imagination is Ruth's ambiguous moral code that later figures as an American character trait in her fiction: "She guaranteed us women who fancied ourselves talented extraordinary absolution" (191). For Mukherjee, absolution is required not merely for her eventual career and outmarriage, but for the symbolic castration of the patriarch that accompanies them. In the essay, ambition for a public voice prefigures the choice of America; as in Houston's narrative, this implied betrayal of fatherland has explicitly oedipal overtones.

Mukherjee's fascination with *Love Me or Leave Me* is born of her father's obsession with Doris Day, albeit not exactly the image of wholesome yet teasing virginity that he fixates on; the film casts Day somewhat against type as an opportunist who straddles the border between virgin and whore, a feat that Day manages without compromising her status as, in Mukherjee's terms, "an icon of spunk." Her own future, Mukherjee suspects, has been partially written by her father's investment in Day as a figure of postindependence optimism: "He sent us to America, a country he himself had not seen, instead of to Europe, where he had been a happy graduate student, because he was in love with the world of Doris Day and all MGM musicals" (187). The exchange of India for America is enabled by her own homoerotic identification, part symbolic possession and part mimicry. She portrays in detail the moments leading up to this transformative identification:

> I try not to think now how we must have appeared to the street people and beggars outside the Metro Cinema or how we might have appeared to Charles Vidor, the director, if he had seen us being chaperoned by servants from cars to the movie theater. We were ten adventurous but shockable young ladies dressed in our mothers' evening saris, with hair pinned up in elaborate chignons and smelling of sandalwood soap and jasmine. I remember I wore a peach-colored French chiffon sparkling with sequins. (190)

This passage turns her into a spectacle as an ironic prelude to witnessing the spectacle of femininity that is Doris Day. In turning the gaze back on herself, she portrays a self-consciousness awareness of (as well as an attempt to repress) the ludicrousness of upper-class leisure to those in want, of Indianness marking her as an alien, unintended audience to the film, and most significantly, of woman as a visually constructed object. Rather than signifying simple vanity, her minute recall of what she is wearing foreshadows the moment the film will model new but yet ill-fitting roles, the first and most immediate, that of woman not child, and the second, future immigrant. The fact that she is literally dressed in her mother's clothes prepares her to take her mother's place through a symbolic identification with a figure of putatively empowered sexuality. The question the essay raises is, what must be repressed to allow this identification with the phallic woman as the symbol of American potency to emerge? It is not, as I suggest in chapter 3, the disempowered mother but another version of the castrated ethnic outsider.

The essay's validation of a New World laced with possibility is dependent on Mukherjee's repressing an identification with the film's "villain," the mobster and Ruth's self-appointed promoter, Marty "The Gimp" Synder, played by James Cagney. She acknowledges that screenwriter Daniel Fuchs's interest might lie more in Marty than in Ruth—she mentions that Fuchs is known for his proletariat novels about Brooklyn Jews. Unschooled in the history of American ethnic relations, her adolescent screening misses the implications of Marty's "lusting after a spirited blond goddess" as a working class, disabled Jew. The admission is an interesting one in the context of Mukherjee's efforts to locate in the film the origins of her national desire. While Etting's story may demonstrate that any individual with talent, gumption, and frontier ethics can make it, the essay's validation of American democratic possibility can only be effected by keeping Marty on the periphery of the narrative. While Mukherjee sees in Marty an American archetype in "his splendor, his power, his pathetic hollowness," the essay denies him as an alternative means of accessing the national imaginary and recasts him, instead, as an Indian patriarch.

As part of the criminal underworld, Marty's cultural influence is based on money and muscle. His America does not acknowledge an ideology of meritocracy, a point the film drives home in a scene where Marty explores his options for "putting the squeeze" on radio stations to get Ruth on the air; the fact that producers might want to do so because she has talent does not initially occur to him. An outsider to American culture like Mukherjee herself, he can only imagine social legitimation through sexual possession once his financial and emotional independence become compromised by his obsession with Ruth. The twinning between Marty as foreigner and Mukherjee as postcolonial spectator who also "lusts after the spirited blond goddess" must remain veiled to allow for the essay's celebration of the American promise embodied in Day/Etting. Distancing herself from Marty, Mukherjee casts him in the role of Indian father by transposing his "monstrously possessive, Othello-like love that turned the beloved into chattel" to Calcutta's rigidly hierarchical culture: "In Marty's 'Didn't I do wonders for her?' guilt made me imagine I was hearing a patriarch's lament" (193). What Chicago of the 1920s and Calcutta of the 1950s have in common is the repression of gifted women. Seeing in Marty a father's effort to control through obligation, Mukherjee not only enforces her identification with Ruth but in part justifies her "betrayal" of India and her father's intention that her overseas education serve merely as a dowry substitute and as the sign of his own postindependence progressiveness. Mirroring the film's melodramatic title, "Love Me or Leave Me," the essay seems to apply the ultimatum to territory as well as to romance; Mukherjee's title might as well be, "India: Love It or Leave It."

In this sense, Mukherjee's desire for Doris Day might be read merely as an identification with whiteness unadulterated by ethnicity, as a seduction to identify with relations of power as in Fanon's concept of the pyschic processes of colonial subjugation. However, the fact that Mukherjee's overt point of identification with Ruth lies in her own desire to write adds a complexity to the oedipal conflict the essay unintentionally inscribes. Suggesting a link between Riviere's analysis and autobiography, Butler notes, "[T]he rivalry with the father is not over the desire of the mother, as one might expect, but over the place of the father in public discourse as speaker, lecturer, writer—that is, as a user of signs rather than a sign-object, an item of exchange" (Butler 1990, 51). The struggle is not merely to wrest Doris Day away from Mukherjee's father by assigning her feminist meaning but to seek a potentially nonthreatening model for "Woman as Artist." Like Jeannie's method of defying the invisibility forced by internment, Day/Etting's overt sensuality, like that of Riviere's flirtatious analysand, masks the affront of her attempt to claim a public voice. Identifying with the film's female protagonist—not its ethnic one in Marty—encourages Mukherjee's ambition to be a producer of signs, an intellectual, at the same time that it places that desire in the socially acceptable form of a hyperfeminine (although potent) white woman. In desiring the same image, Mukherjee is more like Marty and her father than not. Unlike them, she is Doris Day's successful suitor: imbuing Day as Etting with national resonance allows Mukherjee to imagine both becoming and possessing the phallic woman, a possession that symbolizes her American incorporation. As in the case of Houston, her feminine identification hints at a desire to identify with the masculine subject position. The essay suggests that homoerotic identification with white women over the body of the disempowered ethnic man is one means of accessing the national imaginary; in this case, however, the eroticism is reserved for the abstract promise of American democracy rather than the body of a woman. Homoerotic desire is in the end subsumed by the heterosexual imperative and the enjoyment of being (like) a girl.

If the essay inscribes a desire for American national incorporation through the erotics of feminine possession, its resolution—that "[t]hings would work out for me as a writer as long as I rejected both the Johnnys and the Martys," in other words, both the risk-takers and the conformists—veils the brief reference as to why choosing America is a legal possibility in the first place: she marries an American man. The state impediments to formal citizenship are removed by heterosexual alliance. Yet this marriage never figures as the logical culmination of the adolescent lessons Mukherjee takes from the film. In contrast to Ruth's choice to sexually manipulate men in the pursuit of her career, Mukherjee's own marriage is deliberately cast as a love match that renders national affiliations inconsequential ("I might just as easily have fallen in love with a Frenchman or a Briton"). This portrayal is entirely incongruous with the essay's emphasis on the film's impact on Mukherjee's adolescent imagination, a lesson on how the end justifies the means of a female opportunism marked as ruthlessly (and therefore positively) American. We are led to believe that taking Ruth as a role model never materializes as a form of mimicry for Mukherjee; however, this is not the case for her characters. In light of the disjunction between the lesson she imbibes from the film and its biographical eventuality, the essay should be read not only as one immigrant's career primer but as a meditation on how Charles Vidor Americanized her fiction. A sexually manipulative "icon of spunk," Doris Day as Ruth Etting is reborn many times over in Mukherjee's Asian immigrant women. Fuss's articulation of identification as a "detour through the Other that provides access to a fictive sense of self" (Fuss 1995, 143) is quite literally evidenced in multiple fictional selves. Ironically, such characters owe their inspiration to Doris Day and the complex processes whereby national desire is channeled through the body of a white woman and abetted by the promise of feminine likeness.

Hyperfemininity and Social Being

In portraying the transformation of resident aliens to immigrants, Mukherjee's work depends on the construction of a genderist India wherein women lead an existence both secluded and frozen in time. This concept of India must repress the very adaptations that Indian women have undergone under colonization in order to represent Indian women as largely undefiled by Westernization. Mukherjee's portrayal of gender as performance in an American context, of modeling American standards of female behavior as a dictate of acculturation, necessitates naturalizing gender in India to portray women's lives as fated, calcified, and timeless. Mukherjee's India cannot acknowledge the possibility that women may themselves perform what Homi Bhabha calls colonial mimicry, a challenge to colonial domination through the repetition of Western norms "with a difference." Colonial hybridity, he writes, "unsettles the mimetic or narcissistic demands of colonial power but reimplicates its identifications in strategies of subversion that turn the gaze of the discriminated back upon the eye of power" (Bhabha 1994, 112). Nor can this concept of a resistant colonial mimicry be transplanted to the American context of Mukherjee's writing; mimicry does not serve to reveal the ragged edges of inadequate resemblance, the "not quite/not white" (92) of Bhabha's conception. While Mukherjee's work reveals feminine mimicry to be a requirement of national belonging, it does so in order to validate immigrant women's willingness to accede to it. To some extent, her characters' hyperfeminine masquerade or use of sexuality for self-promotion are represented as "above" culture in the sense that both appear as, in the words of her title character, Jasmine, "genetic" character traits rather than gender effects. For Mukherjee, being an American has more to do with individual daring and the capacity for optimism than cultural context; it appears as a not so latent personality trait rather than a condition of formal rights.

Mimicry in both *Farewell to Manzanar* and visual representations of internment works more ambivalently than in Mukherjee's work; as Wendy Kozol aptly points out, documentary photographs of camp life serve national agendas at the same time that specific images may question such agendas. Houston's text at times reflects a self-consciousness of this ironic distancing that signals the inadequacy of repetition, the dissonance caused when Asian bodies people scenes of American domesticity. Manzanar's high school yearbook, for example, describes the school play, *Growing Pains*, as "the story of a typical American home, in this case that of the McIntyres . . . with Shoji Katayama as George McIntyre, Takudo Ando as Terry McIntyre, and Mrs. McIntyre played by Kazuko Nagai" (74). The text's juxtaposition of the Japanese surnames and the "typical American" domestic drama signals the dissonance of inexact repetition at the same time that it provides evidence of "normality" inside the camps. This ambivalence introduced by repetition is highlighted in Lisa Lowe's discussion of translation, which is not in her view predicated on fidelity to an original but underscores instead "the ambivalence or double valence of the translation enterprise—translation is both an apparatus of cultural domination . . . and . . . the means by which the dictation is adulterated, resisted" (Lowe 1994, 42).

It would be difficult to claim either Mukherjee's role-modeling or Jeannie's feminine role-playing as a form of ambivalent translation in Lowe's view, as resistant colonial hybridity in Bhabha's, or as a form of mimicry in the empowered sense of Irigaray's description whereby women "convert a form of subordination into an affirmation" by making gender visible through "an effect of playful repetition" (Irigaray 1985, 76).[14] It seems enough to say that a woman's acting "like a woman" does not constitute role transgression. Could Asian women's representation as hyperfeminine be said to function as a kind of feminine parody akin to Judith Butler's discussion of drag as disruptive gender performance? In dramatizing "the signifying gestures through which gender itself is established," drag destabilizes distinctions between the natural and artificial. Butler argues that the "parodic repetition of 'the original' . . . reveals the original to be nothing other than a parody of the idea of the natural and the original." If the "original" in this case is white womanhood, the Asian woman as the "strictly female female" represents gender inscription taken to excess. But unlike Butler's view that drag displaces gender constructs through "hyperbole, dissonance, internal confusion" (Butler 1990, 31), the potential for this sort of gender hyperbole as a form of camp may be undermined by its racial conjoining; the hyperfemininity that Houston and other Asian women embody may not testify to gender's social construction but, in fact, to its naturalization. Houston's camp experience argues for a reevaluation of feminine camp and the consequences of nonparodic repetition for national incorporation.

If the excess of Asian femininity typified by Nancy Kwan's mirror dance fails to subvert imposed identity it is because the representation of the Asian woman as *Überwoman* is often taken not as evidence of disparaging racial objectification, but as a compliment. As one Asian American woman interviewed for a *New York Times* series on race in America reasoned, "There are definitely people who think Asian girls are hot. It's flattering. Why is it offensive? They're not saying we're ugly" (cited in *New York Times Magazine*, 16 July 2000, 59). Bhabha's point on the dual nature of stereotype, which is "mixed and split, polymorphous and perverse, an articulation of multiple belief," explains in part why hyperfemininity and its twin, hypersexuality, do not appear as contradictions.[15] The film, *Priscilla, Queen of the Desert*, in which drag queens in the Australian outback are upstaged by a Thai mail order bride shooting ping pong balls from her vagina dramatizes the difference between drag and hyperbole. In contrast to the cross-dresser's exuberant playfulness, the "real" woman's manic, jealous performance is dependent on her embodied difference. The comparison is meant to suggest that being a lady is not a matter of nature but of "civilized" behavior; it is precisely the monstrousness of the Asian female body that renders such behavior impossible. The white male drag queens become the other-worldly Ariels— an image enforced by filming their sequined and feathered costumes against the stark landscape of the outback—in juxtaposition to a feminized Caliban who is wholly body. In the end, the film suggests that it takes a white man to show an Asian woman how to be a lady.

As a resolution to the crisis of citizenship, Houston's and Mukherjee's narrators develop (or become inspired to develop) a hyperfeminine public persona as a means of forging a new relationship with political community. The texts suggest that an identification with the nation may be expressed through the very processes of gender role conformity. As a requisite of civic participation, likeness, or uniformity, might well be enabled by the performance of a seemingly transhistorical femininity. Feminine role-playing here functions as a "uniform" that suppresses racial markers to mitigate a potentially threatening difference that cannot be incorporated by the body politic. As Mukherjee's narrative attests, a gendered identification (here, indistinguishable from an identification with sexual opportunism) allows access to American national promise. Houston's example is a reminder that what constitutes full access to rights and effective involvement in the public sphere is often independent of the formal status of citizenship. While the state attempted to coerce an identification with patriarchal nationalism in the form of a loyalty oath aimed at nisei men, Houston's text reveals that for women, the demand for national identification must be enacted on the level of the specular. For both, highly sexualized public images of women serve as a means through which women must imagine civic presence.

What are the consequences of hyperfeminine representation for civic participation? In suppressing racial difference through feminine role-playing, Jeannie's actions attempt to homogenize difference as a requirement of public participation, a requirement that Young suggests is the result of associating the democratic public realm with universality and privacy with particularity and self-interest (Young 1987). Race and gender difference must be subordinated per the dictates of a political representation contingent on the citizen's universalist abstraction; as Lowe notes, "the discourse of equal citizenship under democracy is . . . inherently contradictory, since it holds out the state as an inclusive unity, but asks for the suppression of particular and local differences as a requirement for representation by that state" (Lowe 1994, 53). While Jeannie's public performance intends to reassign racial signifiers that prohibit access to the nation in deference to the need to suppress her embodied particularity, it also ironically reifies her feminine corporeality. For Mukherjee, this feminine embodiment signifies the nation and capitalizing on that body is projected as a vehicle of integration. In both cases, one would have to work to make a convincing case for the emergence of a sexuality through mimicry or repetition that is not, in Butler's words, "a simple replication or copy of the law itself, a uniform repetition of a masculinist economy of identity," or for a view of gender that is more than a conciliating gesture (Butler 1990, 29). Likewise, one would have to work to convince that these textual personas do not simply betray ethnic solidarity in their longing for national inclusion. Nevertheless, I would argue that both texts nuance the relationship between state and nation, casting one as the punishing father and the other as the improper love-object. Moreover, both texts expose women's role in solidifying collective affiliations and securing group cohesion. The textual personas that both narratives inscribe hope to embody that symbolic Woman, who, as Taylor notes, prevents the homosocial society from appearing as a homosexual one. The question left open is whether or not such inscriptions betray the homosocial nature of nationalism if on an overt level both ascribe to its terms.

It is the public nature of women's circulation, of making allegiance visible, that appears as a condition of women's civic participation even as that condition specifies the very partialness of their democratic enfranchisement. My analysis is not meant to suggest that citizenship, to invoke Bryan Turner's terminology, is wholly passive and that rights are merely handed down from above (Turner 1990). Certainly, women exhibit political presence through activism or more traditional electoral channels, a presence that is not wholly contingent on feminine embodiment; Japanese American women's involvement in the internment redress movement is a case in point.[16] Nor do I mean to imply that these public demonstrations of "girlness" forestall collective activism. Nevertheless, women's civic participation and public representation become compromised if their social being is read through their sexuality as the singular means of perceiving allegiance. Visibility as a primary sign of political representation thus has its limitations, especially for women of color.

The unfortunate consequence of being assigned a position, to echo Kim, of having nothing else but sexuality is that corporealization spells only a partial citizenship. Claiming embodiment as a strategic political move akin to Donna Haraway's recognition of situated, embodied knowledges may not be an option if, as Gatens suggests, "our political vocabulary is so limited that it is not possible, within its parameters, to raise the kinds of questions that would allow the articulation of bodily difference: it will not tolerate an embodied speech" (Gatens 1997, 86). If the abstract principles of democratic equality have always been a political fiction, women of color in particular must remain wary of the ways in which feminine uniformity merely tokens national inclusion. The two texts reveal that nations have informal terms of admission, and that claiming a space in political community is neither natural nor, at times, uncoerced.

Three

The Triumph of the Prefeminist Chinese Woman?

INCORPORATING RACIAL DIFFERENCE THROUGH
FEMINIST NARRATIVE

> "Have you read this new novel *Lucknow
> Nights Without Joy in Chinatown*?"
>   Raymond had tried but could not get past the
> first chapter. Red continued without waiting
> for an answer. "Man, what a tearjerker when
> Mei-mei and her mother triumph over the vicious
> cycle of Chinese misogyny and despair."
>   (*Shawn Wong*, American Knees)

SHAWN WONG'S BRIEF PORTRAYAL parodies *The Joy Luck Club*'s feminist plot structure and the triumphalism and sentimentality that drive it. While his male protagonist would reject such a narrative as exalting Chinese American women at the expense of Chinese culture, ironically, Wong's own story of the originary moments of Asian American literature is both sentimental and ultimately triumphant. A young college student desirous of being a writer in the late 1960s, he could find no ethnic role models and sets out to recover Asian American male writers forced into obscurity by the vicious cycle of American racism and indifference: "I asked myself at the age of 19, 'Why am I the only Chinese American writer I know?'" Trying to find an answer to the question connects him with a number of his contemporaries, and together they begin a quest to recover, in flesh and in print, a previous generation of Asian American writers and writing. As Wong explains in hip staccato, the search for these writers was at times embarrassingly easy: "They were not hiding. They were not gone. Some were not even out of print. They had not stopped writing" (Shawn Wong 1993, 125). The quest required few feats of heroism; as he tells it, bringing a generation of writers to light at one point simply meant looking up Toshio Mori's name in the phone book.

There is, perhaps, an unintended irony to this story of literary excavation: it bears striking resemblance to what feminist critics were doing at the same time revealing, perhaps, that cultural nationalism has its sentimental side. It is the truncated, Asian, male version of Alice Walker's

1975 "Looking for Zora." In re-creating the search for Hurston, a forgotten literary foremother, Walker's personal narrative thematizes what Jane Marcus has noted as the recuperative model of feminist criticism, a critical process focused on recovering and recontextualizing "lost" women writers (Marcus 1988). In both cases, the political significance of such a model lies in the belief that to restore the gendered or racial subject's voice is to restore his or her worth, that canon inclusion produces a more accurate and well-rounded account of American letters. These concurrent efforts at recuperation locate in ethnic and feminist literary activism similar goals. But while such contributions have been acknowledged, they are also viewed as politically and theoretically limited, expressive of a reductive pluralism unable to address fully the mechanisms through which social differences are produced and maintained. And as Raymond Ding's nonplused response to a Chinese American feminist "tearjerker" implies, race and gender do not always signify analogously; in this case, triumphant feminism does not maintain the veneer of oppositionality, but rather, of capitulation to the most easily commodified common denominator of cultural norms.

In parodic shorthand, Wong names an identifiable plot structure that appears in women's texts across Asian American ethnicities, a structure perhaps even unwittingly underlying his own story of ethnic literary excavation. The depiction of the subject's movement from silence to voice with a future-oriented, salutary effect on a succeeding generation not only structures Wong's own story, but functions as an organizing movement in women's writing. In *The Joy Luck Club*'s perhaps paradigmatic narrative structure, storytelling is a medium for understanding gender oppression in ways that can lead to self-affirmation; the work locates the mother/daughter relationship as the site for a reenvisioning of self both based on and potentially transcending a maternal legacy. What the title of Julie Shigekuni's novel, *A Bridge Between Us*, or Moraga and Anzaldúa's ground-breaking anthology, *This Bridge Called My Back*, make explicit is that connections between women are forged through the recognition of mutual oppression; in this feminist narrative, a previous generation of women's experiences serve as a foundation, albeit a traumatic one, authorizing a better future. The effect of coming to this consciousness is both didactic (e.g., I learn from my mother's oppression) and salutary (e.g., I can be healed by challenging the restrictions she once faced), producing the idea of a transnational, transhistorical women's community that exposes patriarchy as one arena of domination. Culminating in a more "liberated" subject, the trajectory of such narratives is ultimately progressive, at times explicitly affirming the hope expressed in *This Bridge* that by "the third generation the daughters are free" (Levins Morales 1981, 56).

The problem with the underlying progressivism of such narratives is that they require women's oppression to assume an air of pastness. The association of women's oppression with feudal tradition has long appeared as a tactic of postcolonial nationalism, which has harnessed incipient women's movements to mandates for modernization in the reorganization of traditional solidarities and identities. In an American context, progressive narratives of women's liberation have specific relevance for texts dealing with first-generation immigrants and their American-raised children; gender dynamics are necessarily inscribed with messages about citizenship and racial progress. By linking the hope of genealogical transmission ("You will inherit a better life because of my suffering") or, more generally, an increasing liberalism regarding gender rights ("Don't the Chinese admit that women have minds?") to acculturation, these Asian American works map a developmental narrative about the First and Third Worlds onto narratives of women's bonding or struggle for autonomy. Shawn Wong's *Lucknow Nights Without Joy in Chinatown* is a response to the politically charged yet narratival necessity of representing, in this case, China as excessively genderist so that misogyny appears expressly as a backward, Old World holdover. While such equivalences are obviously overly simplistic, nonetheless, if I, like the stereotypical feminist, fail to see the humor in the parody I take as my epigraph, how can I begin to interrogate it without acknowledging why it also works?

Reflecting Hisaye Yamamoto's "Seventeen Syllables" and "Yoneko's Earthquake," contemporary women's narratives often place the female protagonist in a position of witnessing women's oppression, either that of the previous generation or of contemporaries associated with an ethnically distinct home-space. This plotline appears with differing degrees of significance in Kingston's *The Woman Warrior*, Lee's *Still Life with Rice*, Hagedorn's *Dogeaters*, Meer's *Bombay Talkie*, Lee's *Disappearing Moon Cafe*, Kadohata's *The Floating World*, Tan's *The Joy Luck Club* and *The Kitchen God's Wife*, Keller's *Comfort Woman*, Lan Cao's *Monkey Bridge*, and so on. Certainly, not all Asian American women's literature suggestive of this structure signifies in identical ways.[1] But one of the underlying features of work portraying genealogical transmission between women is the belief in the individual's capacity to choose—and, more specifically, to choose a better life.

Texts in which immigration to the United States figures as the resolution to narrative conflict raise similar questions about the national resonances grafted on to feminist plots. For example, in as cogent a neocolonial critique as Hagedorn's *Dogeaters*, what are we to make of its immigration ending in which Rio's rejection of models of feminine behavior she witnesses in the Philippines is a movement toward women's self-sufficiency and the possibilities of artistic self-fulfillment in the United

States? Is there a space of women's "freedom" for Rio that is not coded as Western even as the novel's content works to expose the abuses of an elite intent on mimicking the West?[2] Likewise, in Anchee Min's *Red Azalea*, the desire to immigrate is a response to political-as-libidinal disillusionment, the recognition of the state's investment in sexual repression. "America" appears in such texts—although not unequivocally—as a symbol of futurity linked to increasing the possibilities of women's self-determination (and, in the case of *Red Azalea*, as determining one's relation to the erotic). Like portrayals of generational clashes over issues of liberal feminism, these immigrant endings locate gender as one site where the division among tradition and modernization, collective identity and competitive individualism, is enacted. This association among rights, self-determination, and the West underlies my discussion of the universalism of human rights as women's rights in chapter 5.

To some extent, narratives of gender progress that portray Asian women as prefeminist-but-becoming-enlightened seem to promise a teleological movement toward modernization expressed through the hope of increasingly *democratic* gender relationships. Reflecting although not identical to the trope of the coerced marriage, the "bad marriage" in *The Kitchen God's Wife* and *The Joy Luck Club*, for example, models this by imbuing future, egalitarian marriages with American national resonance, paralleling freedom and Americanization, Westernization and self-fulfillment. These "democratic" hopes are not exclusively placed on the West in other texts but appear as endemic to the project of postcolonial modernization. For example, in Fiona Cheong's *The Scent of the Gods*, the possibility of gender (and ethnic) equality are debated as evidence of an advanced, Brave New society promised by Singaporean nationalism:

> "Yes," said Auntie Daisy. "But you know, even in Singapore, men get better treatment than woman."
> "Like Malays and Chinese?" Li Yuen asked.
> "Yes," said Auntie Daisy.
> "It'll change," Li Shin said. "The Prime Minister has promised, everyone a first-class citizen." (Cheong 1991, 54)

This promise of equality under national citizenship suggests a rhetorical interaction between discourses of gender and nationalism that is not limited to, but resonates particularly within an American context informed by liberal multiculturalism.

The vision of individual agency cast within a narrative of progressive history—what Hayden White (White 1973) would deem the Romantic mode of historical emplotment—coincides with the notion of racial progress articulated as the hope of class advancement. Clearly, American exceptionalism depends on an idea of history invested with the implicit promise of futurity; this Romantic plot grants "America" symbolic potency. Scripting this notion of history may inevitably serve as the mark of a text's national investment. What is notable about feminist plot structures across Asian American women's texts is their use of gender freedom as a gauge of progress. What are the attendant implications of this specific intersection of racial, national, and gender discourses?

Inevitably, a specific construction of Asia is necessary to the working of these narrative structures, one that presents Asian cultural traditions as excessively genderist. Feminist theorists have recognized the dangers of characterizing women's freedom from patriarchal restraint as singularly possible within the West or representing traditional family structures and gender roles as antithetical to women's self-actualization. Such characterizations enforce the unfortunate Western bias in global feminist discourse that selectively defines specific women's issues—coerced marriage, female infanticide, limited access to birth control and family planning, or domestic abuse, for example—as problems of the Third World. This is precisely the kind of bias that Aiwah Ong warns against in her analysis of Western feminist scholarship on women in non-Western societies or "women in development studies." These studies, she writes, situate the question of gender inequality simply as the failure to achieve modernity, differing only over whether "modernization of the capitalist or socialist kind will emancipate or reinforce systems of gender inequality found in the Third World" (Ong 1988, 83). As Nalila Kabeer suggests, bias is endemic to modernization theory, which portrays development as evolutionary and unilinear (Kabeer 1994).

The representation of Asian women as prefeminist certainly surfaces in Western feminist scholarship; for example, Cleo Odzer's *Patpong Sisters: An American Woman's View of the Bangkok Sex World* (1994) argues that prostitution is liberating for Thai women because it offers them economic autonomy, freedom from rigid sex roles, and greater control over their lives, all positively coded changes apparently not possible within Thai patriarchy. These advances for women are characterized as somehow also redeeming of the risk of contracting AIDS—an unintended corollary to this logic. In contrast, postcolonial discourse has shown through British outlawing of sati, for example, how gender "liberation" colluded with imperialist endeavors, a phenomenon Spivak has characterized as "a white men are saving brown women from brown men," albeit primarily in reference to the excess of critical desire evident in subaltern studies (Spivak 1988). (In the case of Odzer, the phenomenon might be described as "a white woman saving brown women from white men while keeping brown men for herself.") In short, postcolonial discourse has warned against positioning the legacy of imperialism as "historically progressive" for women in the same way that one could caution against locating immigration to the West as an escape from gender constraint. But the question at hand does not concern the truth value of distinctions between East and West, distinctions that often take on a reductive competitive structure (who is more oppressed and where) and that lead to futile attempts to sift "authentic lived experience" from impositions of Western bias. Rather, what does the narratival rendering of the distinction—the West as gender-enlightened against a prefeminist Asia—reveal about the conflictual interaction between race and gender discourses and about a specific moment in which ethnic women's texts circulate with greater cultural capital than ever before?

Contemporary criticism often seeks to claim for race and gender identical political valences, eliding the contradictory cultural work their intersection performs.[3] Following the conflictual nature of race and gender discourses initiated in chapter 1, I want to investigate what messages feminist narratives produce about race. Do they betray collective racial interests in the same way that women of color were said to betray the race in favor of women's solidarity during the women's movement? Does liberal feminism displace potentially radical expressions of ethnic collectivity by reconciling racial difference to a progressive, national conception of history? By implicitly tracing a genealogy of increasing equality, specific feminist narratives might enable not only a testimony of "otherness," but a simultaneous reassurance of sameness as well, a reassurance opened within the space of—in particular—white women's identification.

To provide difference and reassurance simultaneously as an implicit demand of "multicultural" testimony is specifically fraught for ethnic American literature, in whose roots lies a commitment to realism. This dual and seemingly contradictory pressure placed on the testimony of the literary "native" at home both parallels and contrasts that of anthropology's native informant, whose use value lies in her absolute difference. As Rey Chow notes, the project of the white feminist social scientist

> is to use Chinese women—and the more remote they are from Western urban civilization, the better—for the production of the types of explanations that are intelligible (valuable) to feminism in the West, including, in particular, those types that extend pluralism to "woman" through "race" and "class." (Chow 1991, 93)

Yet in the United States, the demand for a cultural product produced by a native with whom one can also identify establishes another criterion for authenticity. While "remoteness" is the catalyst for voyeuristic interest, an unintelligible native is nonetheless of no use, nor is one who remains absolutely (in)different. To function as "knowable," the ethnic specimen must undergo a dual process, one through which difference is established as a measure of authenticity, and another through which difference can become translated into the idiom of her audience. The demands of such an inscription are simultaneous: the defamiliarizing of American like-nesses, as well as the familiarizing of ethnic difference.

I am interested, then, in the ways that liberal feminist discourse can produce an intelligible racial subject and in the cultural work that the image of the prefeminist Chinese woman might perform. Two popular books by Chinese American women, one re-released and the other pub-lished in 1989, provide case studies of the way in which narratives of women's resistance to gender oppression are also the vehicles for narra-tives of racial and economic progress. Jade Snow Wong's *Fifth Chinese Daughter* has marked her in the lingua franca of cultural nationalism as a race traitor or, as recounted by Merle Woo, a sentiment more colorfully described as "Jade Snow Wong Pochahontas yellow" (Woo 1981). By affirming American culture as the site of gender equality, Wong's liberal feminism works in concert with her racial politics. Satisfying the desire for a familiar "celestial," the work reinforced a representation of the good Chinese as capitalist entrepreneur that could be exported to Asia during the Cold War. Similarly, as *The Joy Luck Club* has become synon-ymous with middlebrow feminism, Amy Tan has been labeled a sellout. Both texts enact a division between tradition and modernization through gender; in marking self-fulfillment as the logical and inevitable result of Westernization, both locate ethnic difference within an implicitly liberal racial agenda and a chronology of collective self-improvement.

This chapter explores the ways in which embedded racial discourses endemic to certain feminist plot structures potentially service national agendas by reproducing ideas of collectivity easily reconciled to individ-ual difference, in other words, how sentimentality itself may allow for the qualified inclusion of multicultural texts based on concepts of women's culture. The liberalism underlying the texts' engagement with feminism indicates a specific, hierarchical model of the interaction between axes of group affiliation. My intention is not to reduce Asian American women's narratives to a single ideological function or to suggest that all writing that reflects this broad emplotment—even the texts I have listed above—uncritically affirms the West as the site of women's freedom. The liberal feminist narratives in *Fifth Chinese Daughter* and *The Joy Luck Club* also produce their own contradictions, perhaps to reveal what Foucault would call "ruptural effects of conflict and struggle," effects that unmask beliefs—such as the belief in women's equality—as forms of common cul-tural consensus and systematizing thought (Foucault 1980, 82). As a point of contrast, I look at Sky Lee's Canadian novel, *Disappearing Moon Cafe* (1990), to suggest how a narrative about feminist empower-ment might produce these "ruptural effects" in ways that queer the frame I establish here.

The Celestial in Our Midst:
Jade Snow Wong's *Fifth Chinese Daughter*

"My parents demand unquestioning obedience.
Older Brother demands unquestioning obedience.
By what right? I am an individual besides being a
Chinese daughter. I have rights too." Could it be
that Daddy and Mama, although they were living
in San Francisco in the year 1938, actually had not
left the Chinese world of thirty years ago? Could
it be that they were forgetting that Jade Snow
would soon become a woman in a new America,
not a woman in old China?
  (*Fifth Chinese Daughter*)

6. What is the author's tone? Does she sound bit-
ter to you? Is she talking about "bad parenting?"
  (Questions for discussion on "Fifth Chinese
  Daughter" in *American Voices: Multicultural
  Literacy and Critical Thinking*)

"I do not think of myself as a writer," Jade Snow Wong wrote in 1951,
six years after her autobiography, *Fifth Chinese Daughter*, was published
(J. S. Wong 1951, 440). By then, her attitude of modest denial had been
undermined by the success of the book and the responses of charmed
postwar critics. Her writing, the *New York Times Book Review* noted,
"exudes the delicate femininity only the Asiatic women possess" (Joyce
Geary, *New York Times Book Review*, 29 October 1950, 27). An "en-
chanting record of Chinese customs and celebrations," this children's
book with crossover appeal was taken as a testimony of "happy" bicultural adjustment (May Hill Arbuthnot, *Children's Reading in the Home*
[Scott, Foresman and Co., 1969], n.p.).

What is notable about the work's original reception is not only, as
post–civil rights critics have pointed out, that reviewers failed to assess
the work with historical accountability to the Chinese American experience. What is more intriguing is that reviewers could so easily misread the
tone and tenor of the work, finding delight and enchantment in what is an
essentially bleak story of one who substitutes ambition for affection and
recognizes the difference, who accepts recognition garnered from small
achievements in lieu of real understanding and connection with others.
Jade Snow Wong's autobiography follows a familiar narrative trajectory
in its portrayal of an adolescent's struggle to rise out of obscurity and

poverty, but in spite of textual assurances to the contrary, Jade Snow's position in the world at the end of the narrative is neither secure nor settled. In light of this, the text's reception in 1950 may suggest something about the ease with which racial difference could become sentimentalized in the postwar period, transforming a work rife with contradictions that continually ripple the surface harmony of its overt premise into a seamless coming of age tale with an ethnic twist.

This overt premise, Wong's intention to write as a cultural informant "with the purpose of creating better understanding of the Chinese culture on the part of Americans" (vii), has since been called into question for endorsing an American ideology based on a belief in meritocracy. In its message that racial prejudice serves merely as an excuse for "individual failure," *Fifth Chinese Daughter*, has earned a controversial place in Asian American literature as a foundational work that nonetheless appears to counter the goals of collective activism, an accommodationist form of "propaganda-as-autobiography."[4] One 1976 review noted that as an "insider's guide" to Chinatown for tourists, *Fifth Chinese Daughter* merely "presents the safe and acceptable aspects of the author's life that are compatible with America's sensitivity regarding its treatment of minorities" ("Book Reviews: *Fifth Chinese Daughter,*" *Interracial Books for Children Bulletin* 7:2/3 (1976): 13). The most "safe and acceptable" aspect of Chinese American culture the autobiography presents has been acknowledged to be Chinese food. Following Chin's coining of the term "food pornography" to describe the exploitation of the "'exotic' aspects of one's ethnic foodways," critic Sau-ling Wong locates the text among a genre of autobiographical Chinatown "tour-guiding" works that capitalize off American interest in Chinese cooking by taking "the white reader on a verbal gastronomic tour" (Sau-ling Wong 1993, 63). In this case, what is intended to be a figurative assessment of textual politics is, in fact, literally accurate: from 1953 to the late 1980s, Wong has guided tours of Asia and run a business in San Francisco under the name "Jade Snow Wong's Giftshop and Travel Service." Because Wong has proudly (even defiantly) claimed roles as travel agent and "goodwill ambassador," her reassessment as cultural hustler would no doubt surprise her. Both roles situate her as a willing native informant, an insider to local culture whose knowledge must assume an aura of authenticity in order to function as a commodity.

While Wong's benign descriptions of ethnic traditions in *Fifth Chinese Daughter* establish this authenticity by testifying to her difference, her testimony requires that she be located *outside* Chinatown as well. If an inauthentic native insider is of no use, neither is one who remains unintelligible; as Rey Chow notes, "natives, like commodities, become knowable only through routes that diverge from their original 'homes'" (Chow 1993, 42).[5] Wong's chosen location as performed within the text (and quite materially outside it) demands the simultaneous defamiliarizing of her American likenesses requisite to establishing ethnic authenticity, and the rendering of her ethnic difference accessible. The title of the autobiography's sequel, *No Chinese Stranger* (1975), speaks to the anxiety underlying this dual process, conveying that she is, on one hand, no stranger to China; she is "like" China rather than alien to it. But it also implies that although she is ethnically Chinese, she is not alien to the United States, an assurance that only highlights the need for such assurance.

If Wong's descriptions of daily life spiced with ethnic flavor succeed in performing difference, it is the text's feminist narrative that renders Jade Snow knowable to her postwar audience. Highlighting the convergence between American individualism and the advocation of women's autonomy, equal rights, and access to education allows Jade Snow to constitute her "unfilial piety"—the break she makes with her Chinese family—as gendered (if not exactly feminist) resistance.[6] If *Fifth Chinese Daughter* mirrors an American mythos, it does so not only by soft-pedaling race and class oppression, but by advocating equal opportunity for women within a liberal feminist melodrama at a moment in which domestic representations of working women and international representations of the Chinese reflected larger cultural shifts.

Yet there is much within the text that is irreconcilable to its overtly liberal message; these moments come in the form of repressed histories that threaten to rupture the surface narrative and force the text to reveal its ideological contradictions. In highlighting these repressions, my point is not to perform a revisionist reading, seeking for Wong some status as "unduped" native against the accommodationist Jade Snow of the text.[7] Rather, the goal is to examine the ways in which the feminist narrative manages, in Chow's terms, "to make the native more like us," and in doing so deliberately obscures the less than delightful side of "bicultural adjustment." A central concern then becomes, how does the feminist narrative that structures these ethnic "slices of life" interact with what can now be taken as the text's essentially conservative message?

What gives Jade Snow's story emotional resonance is the portrayal of a repression/liberation scenario in which an autocratic yet benevolent father stands against his daughter as the impediment to her progress. Jade Snow's first feminist recognition early in the narrative, like her first awareness of cultural differences between the Chinese and Americans, makes her question the family hierarchy and evaluate her position as "unalterably less significant than the new son in their family" (27). Upon being denied the funds for a college education granted to her older brother, Jade Snow develops a mistrust of the authority she has accepted as a matter of "the right order of things." In appearing both unreasonable and extreme, accounts of her Confucius-quoting father's excesses mark an ethnographic awareness of an external gaze, mirroring moments that describe ethnic traditions with prefaces such as "and then came a strange sight." Glimpses of life outside the family's factory home become occasions for American ethnographic analysis that end up pointing to the limitations of her Chinese family. Depictions of her experiences as a live-in domestic to a white family with the overdetermined pseudonym, the Kaisers, result in the conclusion that in American families, "each member, even down to and including the dog, appeared to have the inalienable right to assert his individuality" (114). While the statement unwittingly locates her status in the Chinese family as less than the dog's, it is intended as an exaggerated affirmation of the democratizing American tendency to accord even pets status. Borrowing the rhetoric of the Founding Fathers to make a stand for the assertion of individuality as an "inalienable right" is posited against the submersion of individuality implied by membership in a degraded group identity, that of women.

The conflict comes to a head in the middle of the autobiography when Jade Snow challenges parental authority by delivering a "declaration of independence": "I am an individual besides being your fifth daughter." In resisting patriarchal authority, Jade Snow's cultural negotiation is put in terms of struggle for women's rights within her own family, which is characterized as the singular locus of her oppression as a woman. By positioning her father as representative of Chinese culture and locating American culture outside the family's domestic sphere, Wong sets up a cultural division predicated on a public/private dichotomy that codes individuality and opportunity for women as American and public, while casting submergence of self through filial piety as Chinese and private.

Thus *Fifth Chinese Daughter*'s narrative suspense centers around a conflict over her family's recognition of her individuality; her stand for fairness and a voice within the family is cast in terms of a liberal feminist argument for equality as she rallies for just treatment in spite of "being born a girl." In seeking greater acknowledgment and dignity than her lowly placement as fifth daughter would indicate, Jade Snow does not question the necessity of the hierarchy as much as she does her place within it. The text positions women's autonomous selfhood as something to be individually earned: equality is not necessarily open to all women, but only to those who prove themselves as equal to men through their achievements. Wong's belief in meritocracy underlies her depiction of

growing seeds, transforming an innocent lesson into a metaphor for acculturation that Americanizes Darwin's concept of natural selection:

> Grandmother continued her lesson, "Now you can see that, when conditions
> change some will adjust readily and come out first, while others may still be left
> behind."
>   Jade Snow nodded. She could see again that handful of all alike seeds lying
> in Grandmother's open palm, and she reflected on the wonders which water
> and soil could accomplish for those which would try. (33)

Given an equal opportunity to develop, it is not a predetermined fitness,
but the seeds' effort that makes the difference. Easily reconciled to the
text's racial argument that casts group difference as individual distinctive-
ness, the analogy implies that transplantation to an alien environment is
no excuse for a failure to advance, that is, like "coming out first," attributed to the individual. Critics have noted the dissonance produced by
passages in which Wong bypasses evidence that conflicts with the work's
racial politics; as Elaine Kim points out, Jade Snow remarks that the
kitchen staff in the Mills College dorm is entirely Chinese precisely at the
moment she praises the college's democratic living. Wong's text attempts
to harmonize other such instances of race segregation—such as ethnic
ghettoization—by giving them the appearance of individual volition. For
example, while the women's dorms are apparently not racially segregated, Wong unwittingly introduces evidence of de facto segregation:
with one exception, her friends are all Asian yet this has the appearance
of voluntary association rather than being attributed to the exclusionary
practices of the largely white, female student body.

However, the handicap establishing that all "seeds" are not, in fact,
identical is largely represented in the narrative as gender, not race. The
blow for justice, then, is struck against a sexist family rather than a racially stratified society. Such a displacement might have been influenced
by the text's historical moment: the book was completed in 1946, when
a wartime economy opened opportunities for women. The sudden influx
of women into the labor force created a potential space for liberal feminism: Wong's call for equal opportunity and women's "independence"—
both marked as liberating American influences—reflects the rhetoric of
women's recruitment into war-related industries that portrayed labor as
a form of national duty. As a result, women made up a third of the
workforce between 1941 and 1945, and their success in heretofore male-
dominated fields necessarily raised questions about equal pay and equal
opportunity (Gregory 1974).

But by the time of the book's publication in 1950, these opportunities
had ceased, as demobilization resulted in massive layoffs of women despite their desire to keep high-paying industrial jobs. Jade Snow's advice

from the unsympathetic boss—"as long as you are a woman, you can't compete for an equal salary in a man's world"—reflects the attitudes of postwar industrial management that preferred to hire men even though women represented cheaper labor for equal productivity. Historian Ruth Milkman has noted that management's adherence to what seemed an irrational policy testified to the strength of gender bias and explained the resurgence of domesticity after the war. Women's nonvoluntary reincorporation into the labor-norms of the prewar period—into low-paying, gender-segregated employment—after having proven themselves in traditional "men's jobs" challenged the American ideology of meritocracy by demonstrating that employment was not based on job performance.[8] Such a circumstance reflects Wong's structuring premise that being female does not make for a level playing field. Her autobiography may have met with an audience receptive to her brand of feminism, but also potentially ambivalent about it: once afforded opportunities as a result of labor shortages, women were forced to return to the domestic sphere or to gender-defined labor.

Wong's stance is in keeping with the resurgence of domesticity following the war: she does not see traditional "woman's work" as limiting; rather, domestic and secretarial work are catalysts for her entry into the white world. As Wong has stated, "Though I don't think being a woman has been any problem, I give priority to women's responsibility for a good home life; here, I put my husband and four children before my writing or ceramics" (cited in *Contemporary Authors* 109: 536).[9] Her text not only associates domestic tasks with duty and maturity, but with pleasure. Wong's emphasis on Chinese cooking both satisfies the need for ethnic specificity *and* affirms women's work; in this sense, ethnicity becomes mediated by gendered universality.

Wong's dual testimony is only plausible in relation to herself: for a narrative whose overt theme lies in women's recognition, portrayals of Jade Snow's mother are markedly absent. Not only do they threaten the text's thematic coherence by centering on her father, they challenge her affirmation of the free movement between Chinese and American spheres. Wong's repression of the historical reality of her own position—tenement living, racial discrimination, struggle for education, and bleak emotional life—is momentarily suggested through the figure of her mother, unexpectedly pregnant near the end of her childbearing years:

> Whatever was in her mind, whatever the feelings that Mama and Daddy shared about another child expected now fourteen years after the last one had been born, Jade Snow was not told, and she felt no right to pry. But now, as a young woman of twenty, she suddenly felt pity for another woman who was working away her life almost by compulsion, who was receiving little affection from the

very children for whose welfare she was working, because affection had not been part of her training, and she did not give it in training her own. As if a veil separating her from her mother were lifted for a moment, Jade Snow saw clearly that at this time Mama did not need from her grown daughter the respect which she had fostered in all her children so much as she needed the companionship which only one woman can give another. (184)

This glimpse into her mother's life from the position of woman, not daughter, momentarily threatens Wong's overt textual message: as an immigrant Chinese woman speaking little English, economically dependent on her husband, and pregnant with what we are led to believe is her ninth child, her mother does not have the "American" privilege to choose her Chineseness when appropriate. The fact that Jade Snow's mother's limited chances for mobility lie in stark contrast to her own disrupts Wong's argument that sees racial and cultural difference as a means of soliciting "favorable interest."

Jade Snow transcends her position as fifth daughter—thereby satisfying the underlying trajectory of the narrative—when she is able to see "Mama" as others would see her: disempowered. Yet she does not associate her mother's disempowerment with her status as a Chinese American woman, but sees only the diminishment of an authority figure:

Here for the first time was a defenseless, criticized, bewildered, intimidated Mama, unburdening herself to her daughter. The Mama who wielded the clothes hanger, the Mama who seldom approved of anything that was fun, the Mama who laid down exacting housework requirements, the Mama who criticized with stern words, was suddenly seen in a new light. (81)

What the twenty-four-year-old writer is singularly concerned with is the erosion of the family hierarchy that provides evidence of her novel adult status. Aside from providing this glimpse of her mother's vulnerability, Wong does not push her analysis toward a collective identification that would undermine her argument about women's equality through individual distinction. Representations of Jade Snow's older sisters are similarly absent, a gap the text explains in terms of culture: her parents have discouraged visits because they "might undermine respect" (88) and her sister's marriage has exiled her from the clan per the convention of exogamy. There are perhaps other reasons for the absence of portrayals of these Chinese American women closer to Jade Snow in generation; the fact that one sister has already completed a college degree might have bolstered Wong's liberal feminist argument, but by revealing that Jade Snow is not the first daughter to test boundaries, the information deflates the significance and singularity of her own resistance to tradition-bound patriarchy. A second reason may be that these are her half sisters.

Through a cross-textual reading of dates and scenes in *Fifth Chinese Daughter* and Wong's second book, *No Chinese Stranger*, it becomes clear that Wong's mother is not her father's first wife and that Wong has manipulated immigration dates to obscure the possibility of her father's bigamy. This repressed maternal presence momentarily surfaces in a letter in which "Daddy" refers to his wife in China, "who had little, two-and-a-half-inch, bound feet" (72). Yet in the next scene, Wong discusses Mama's Sunday walks that take them all over San Francisco, a regular outing that would prove incredibly painful, if at all possible, on bound feet. Moreover, Wong's portrayal of her mother's pregnancy is startling because it occurs as her father approaches seventy, indicating a disparity in their ages. *No Chinese Stranger* locates her mother's date of immigration at 1919 while *Fifth Chinese Daughter* puts the family's immigration within "the opening decade of this century."

This subtextual presence indicates the repression of historical information that challenges the individualist premise of the work. The practice of bigamy was not unusual nor particularly taboo given the circumstances of Chinese immigration, but revelation of the historic reality of racist and ethnocentric exclusion laws that fostered it would criticize the country whose opportunities Wong extols.[10] Reference to this first wife emerges at precisely the point at which Wong connects her father's belief in liberal feminism to his Christian conversion and ordination as a minister. The presence of another wife would put into question his newfound feminist philosophy, his moral authority, and his credibility as a model of propriety sufficient to "bear God's closest scrutiny." Signaled only in the muted form of textual contradictions, this aspect of Chinese American history does not harmonize with Wong's presentation of a benignly exotic Chinatown consisting of herbalist shops and wonderful restaurants. This is not to say, however, that this history indicates a more authentic Chinese woman struggling beneath the surface text akin to Charlotte Perkins Gilman's phantom woman trapped inside the yellow wallpaper. Rather, like the simultaneously present and obscured intrusions of imperialist and racially stratified labor history in the autobiography that Karen Su and Elaine Kim have pointed out, this "other mother" marks a challenge to *Fifth* as a testimony to American altruism. Between her two autobiographies, Wong succeeds in controlling, but not erasing, a Chinese woman who bears with her a history of exclusion. A mute witness like Spivak's subaltern woman, she exists as excess, what cannot be brought to heel within the prevailing narrative of an ethnic family's ultimately triumphant story of perseverance, thrift, hard work, and discipline.

Having set up a feminist conflict as the tension needing resolution, *Fifth Chinese Daughter* achieves a happy ending by linking paternal respect and American business success, a success the work marks as a sign of female equality. The opposition between what is Chinese and what is

American is thus bridged through the convergence of Christian ethics and Chinese American capitalism. While I have previously noted that Wong's liberal feminist message was put forth in a period which saw an influx of women into wage-labor, the work's 1950 publication also saw a shift in the State Department's policy on China, a policy consistent with Wong's assurances about the Chinese in the United States. The text's underlying support of entrepreneurship reconciles liberal feminism and foreign policy dictates of the time.

Jade Snow's father invokes China's "superior" culture and a strict hierarchy of ancestral descent to substantiate his authority when it suits him. Adamant about his family's difference from "foreigners," he resists his daughter's attempt to justify her rebellion with a conservative appeal to Chinese essence in the wonderfully melodramatic statement, "You are shameless. Your skin is yellow. Your features are forever Chinese. We are content with our proven ways. Do not try to force foreign ideas into my home. Go. You will one day tell us sorrowfully that you have been mistaken" (130). However, her father dismisses the contradictions that arise in adhering to Confucian filial piety and "New World" necessities through his ability to reconcile them with Christian values: if he must put women—his wife and the seamstresses in his factory—to work outside the home in order to make a living upon immigration, he finds his new beliefs validated "according to New-World Christian ideals [in which] women had a right to work to improve the economic status of their family" (5). Likewise, he justifies sending his daughters to Chinese school by tying it to his own anti-imperialist nationalism: "If nobody educates his daughters, how can we have intelligent mothers for our sons? If we do not have good family training, how can China be a strong nation?" (15). "Daddy's" ease in modifying his philosophy when presented with conflicting values underscores the coherence between liberal feminism and capitalism; while Jade Snow's "unfilial" transgressions and defiance of ancestral authority represent a challenge to her parents' "Chinese" way of thinking, their reconciliation reflects the values the elder Wongs have previously held or have internalized upon immigration.

Because the text is structured as a chronology of Jade Snow's progressively greater contact with the world outside Chinatown and because her narrative conflict hinges on whether or not she will "be a person respected and honored by [her] family when [she grows] up" (93), the moments of her achievement in the Caucasian public sphere—her graduating, winning an essay contest, and succeeding in business—have only to be recognized by her parents as significant to enable the text to come to resolution. This resolution depends on her parents' eventual acceptance of "Western" ways. When Jade Snow christens a ship as a result of winning an essay contest on increasing war productivity, the Wongs receive a "fellow countrymen's" congratulations: " 'We are reading in the papers that your fifth daughter has won great honor in the American world. You must be very satisfied to have your family name so glorified by a female'" (196). Jade Snow's father shakes her hand in a gesture of respect punctuated by its Western connotations. By the end of the autobiography, her parents seem to accept their daughter's "foreign" recognition as somehow more honorable than achievements within the family or community sphere, the locus of "Daddy's" not inconsiderable influence. Jade Snow's ultimate achievement, the success of her pottery business, is shown to be coherent with her parents' values as owners of a community-based small business. Her father's pride in her college graduation stems not so much from her scholarship or her "art," but from the fact that she has learned a marketable trade. The bridge or "middle way" between cultures Jade Snow finds by the end of the book rests on a similarity between economic ideologies and the tacit acknowledgment that contact with Caucasians can lead to business opportunities.

The text's implicit endorsement of capitalism performs an ethnic normalizing function by testifying to Chinese American adherence to a fundamental aspect of American norms and attitudes. But the text bolstered more than domestic ideology; the autobiography served the interests of foreign policy by lending credibility to a historically necessary representation: the good Chinese as capitalist. Wong wrote her autobiography in a period of Chinese alliance with the United States during the Second World War—a time during which *Japanese* Americans were interned. The year of the autobiography's publication, 1950, witnessed a shift in the State Department's China policy, a shift explained in the August 1949 release of "The China White Paper." In attempting to justify the Truman–Acheson policy against continuing aid to the Chinese Nationalists, "The China White Paper" reflected the belief that the United States had done all it could to support Chiang Kai-shek and the Kuomintang (KMT), implying that the KMT had failed to retain control of the mainland because of its own inadequacies and military defeats at the hands of the Communist Party. Interestingly, the State Department's justification for withdrawing foreign aid dovetails with Wong's own message: failure, like success, is neither preconditioned nor systemic, but is an individual matter; when denied (educational) aid, Jade Snow is forced to make it on her own and comes out the better for it.

This convergence—neither a simple validation of American allies nor a vilification of its enemies, but a general affirmation of self-reliance—did not go unnoticed by the State Department, which negotiated the rights to foreign editions of *Fifth Chinese Daughter* and sent Wong on a 1953 speaking tour of Asia. Wong's chronicle of the tour in the autobiography's sequel reveals little consciousness about the State Department's agenda, attributing its interest to a financial stake in sales. However,

Wong is not naive about what she later calls "the no-no American word 'Communist'"; given the tense state of international affairs as the Cold War escalated, she encounters anti-American sentiment on the tour, particularly in Burma where, she implies, it had just come to light that CIA operatives were caught aiding KMT troops on Burma's border with the People's Republic of China. Having her picture taken with one identified as a KMT leader in Rangoon is thus "embarrassing," but not necessarily more fraught than meeting with other Rangoon Chinese who identify with their now communist homeland. True to her moderate liberalism, the sequel questions Cold War logic on the grounds that, communist or not, the Chinese are hardworking individuals: the Chinese Communist, she writes, "might in reality prove to be a flesh-and-blood young man trying to make his social contribution" (*NCS* 92).

Seeing "communist" as a scapegoat term in 1975, however, is not an indication of pro-Maoist leanings; more likely than not, Wong's views deviated from those of the 1953 State Department for the simple reason that its refusal to recognize the People's Republic was for her, a tour operator, allowing politics to interfere with business. Still, while trying assiduously not to "talk politics," she could not help but serve a political agenda; she and her book were no doubt deployed in Asia to validate underlying American values and the "timeless" Chinese virtues that arguably only existed among the diasporic Chinese, if at all.[11] Wong's work may have thus caught an American public looking for evidence of the ethnic specimens they had always known, a sentiment expressed in a 1966 history: "The Communist revolution has confronted us with a China so different from the China we once knew that we are still groping to comprehend it. It is plain to see that some of our fondest assumptions about the celestial land are no longer valid" (A. T. Steele, *The American People and China*. [New York: McGraw-Hill, 1966], 57). *Fifth Chinese Daughter* assured Americans that our fondest assumptions about celestials could remain valid if only in our own backyard.

Wong's confirmation of these assumptions about "celestials" appears not necessarily as a testimony to absolute "otherness," but to quaint Chinese convention. In one instance, this need to satisfy an appetite for difference-with-charm justifies her choice of narrative voice:

> Although a "first person singular" book, this story is written in the third person from Chinese habit. The submergence of the individual is literally practiced. In written Chinese, prose or poetry, the word "I" almost never appears, but is understood. In corresponding with an older person like my father, I would write in words half the size of the regular ideographs, "small daughter Jade Snow" when referring to myself. . . . Even written in English, an "I" book by

a Chinese would seem outrageously immodest to anyone raised in the spirit of
Chinese propriety. (xiii)

Superficially, the use of the third person satisfies the underlying purpose
of the book, the substantiation of American ideas of Chinese modesty, by
producing the illusion of a charming filial deference. Wong's decision to
render her name in its English translation, Jade Snow, rather than its
Chinese phonetic equivalent, contributes to this effect. Both the refusal to
assert "I" and her choice of translation can be read as pandering to white
expectation by reinforcing the belief that submergence of self is typically
Asian. Yet the ostensible cultural convention that she gives as a reason for
her use of the third person seems to be a textual fiction. Wong notes that
she labors over childhood Chinese compositions; because she writes primarily in English, she is presumably comfortable with the conventional
use of the first-person pronoun. The fact that she gives an ethnic, cultural
reason for her choice of voice contradicts a note prefacing her shift to the
first person in the sequel: "After Daddy's death the habit of referring to
myself in the third person could gradually be changed to the use of the
first person" (13). Wong's choice of voice distances her from Jade Snow's
unfilial behavior; she uses the third person not out of deference to Chinese
written convention or Chinese modesty, but potentially out of an inability
to see herself as a subject. Wong's two explanations for her use of the
third person, one that points to ethnic convention, and the other to female submersion of self in the face of patriarchy, indicates, once again,
the tension between performing ethnic authenticity and gendered
universality.

The "conversion" of Jade Snow's father into a feminist himself is necessary to the text's narrative resolution. Their reconciliation is figured not
in terms of converging economic philosophies but in terms of Jade Snow's
desire for recognition "as a female." In the end, her father recounts a
story that shows her achievements to be the fulfillment of a prophecy:

> When I first came to America, my cousin wrote me from China and asked me
> to return. That was before I can even tell you where you were. But I still have
> the carbon copy of the letter I wrote him in reply. I said, "You do not realize the
> shameful and degraded position into which the Chinese culture has pushed its
> women. Here in America, the Christian concept allows women their freedom
> and individuality. I wish my daughters to have this Christian opportunity. I am
> hoping that some day I may be able to claim that by my stand I have washed
> away the former disgraces suffered by the women of our family." (246)

The letter writes Jade Snow into the family lineage through her achievements *as a daughter* according to the dictates of the narrative's need for
conflict resolution while simultaneously underscoring the limits of its
feminist stance: the letter positions the father as the primary agent against

injustice. Like the dissonant emergence of a lost letter in conventional melodrama, the letter sets right a mistaken identity: the figure who resisted change is revealed to have advocated change all along. The sentiment revealed in the text's final lines is equally unconvincing: "And when she came home now, it was to see Mama and Daddy look up from their work, and smile at her, and say, 'It is good to have you home again!'" (246). Such an ending asks the reader to imagine that parental indifference is transformed into affection through the events of the autobiography—a description of the achievements through which Jade Snow earns their respect. *Fifth*'s forced ending, along with the discomfort of its narrative voice and historical repressions, mark it as a profoundly ambivalent text. To read Jade Snow as one who has negotiated an acceptable "middle way" between Chinese and American cultures is to ignore the discomfort of this voice and the repressive structures this discomfort uncovers.

Yet this ambivalence does not necessarily contest Wong's message that racial or gender prejudice is not an excuse for personal failure. In marking this "other" mother as a function of the text's historical repression, I do not mean to suggest there exists a more authentic feminist struggle subordinated to the text's overtly liberal feminist politics. Any unequivocal attempt at feminist revisionism may reflect the critical desire to recuperate an oppositional standpoint for Wong, one that, while testifying to the inability to harmonize social reality with an overt liberalism, nonetheless runs the risk of privileging what is *not* said at the expense of eliding what is. While this ability to read gaps in phallogocentric discourse may be a cornerstone to feminist theory, it may also be a function of what Jane Marcus has self-reflexively analyzed as the need to construct an angry foremother to fuel the feminist critical enterprise.[12] Transposed to an ethnic context, it is this method of reading that makes so tantalizing Wong's comment that two-thirds of the original manuscript was excised by her editor. The missing pages may fuel speculation that Wong's editor refused portions of the manuscript not in keeping with the racial liberalism of what was eventually published (Chin et. al. 1974). But this speculation may be unwarranted; Wong herself frustrates any desire to create in her the properly abject object of feminist or ethnic recuperation. While the text served as a role model for writers like Maxine Hong Kingston, not only has Wong failed to die, like Woolf's Judith Shakespeare, "young, cramped and thwarted," but she is largely unsympathetic to the culturally nationalist views of succeeding generations.[13] In her steadfast adherence to a point of view developed as a twenty-four-year-old, Wong is the native who refuses to shift into her proper critical frame.

The question remains whether *Fifth*'s internal dissonance undermines its overt political message or whether it remains, as a document of Asian American experience, a "snow job." Are its contradictions sufficient to counter the affirmation of meritocracy that has been the source of its critical scrutiny, especially given that it is used, almost a half century later, to serve what Karen Su notes as the neoconservative agenda of multiculturalism? The question may be moot if, as my epigraph taken from a multicultural textbook shows, class, race, or gender issues can become interiorized as a function of pop psychology. Or is the anxiety about the text and others like it over the fact that capitalist entrepreneurship continues to be supported by many within the Chinese American community? Such questions speak to the problem of a wholly recuperative feminist enterprise or a cultural nationalist denunciation as critics in related fields have shown. For example, Claudia Tate recuperates black women's novels at the turn of the century that promoted a vision of black middle-class self-improvement. While Tate acknowledges that the economic and social reality for blacks in the post-Reconstruction era countered the novels' portrayal of middle-class domesticity, she attempts to reclaim for these writers a measure of social progressivism by reading their fiction as "allegories of political desire," situating the authors' contribution to racial uplift as the envisioning of an idealized domestic sphere. Is it possible to claim such an allegory for Wong? Jade Snow's ability to finance her way through college and start a business are achievements not to be dismissed; however, Wong fails to attribute them to the opening up of women's opportunities during wartime production, preferring instead to attribute them to her own hard work and the kindness of strangers.

Wong's original intention "to contribute in bringing better understanding of the Chinese people so that in the Western world they would be recognized for their achievements" (235) may have been laudable in 1950, but it now seems dated for its "just as good as" stance, a gaze that turns Chinese American culture, and herself along with it, into spectacle. The limitations of an "I'm just like you but different" position are currently suggested by specific lesbian and gay movements, where the very strategy for supporting antidiscriminatory legislation may counter long-term aims. *Fifth Chinese Daughter* will remain problematic for its overt accommodationist message and confirmation of American values of self-reliance and careerism. Yet what remains undecidable about the text is how successfully its narrator convinces us of her resolution that being Chinese in America is not a matter of being handicapped by prejudice, but is a source of "cultural enrichment" that creates "favorable interest" in one's life. The "middle way" that Jade Snow desires to find as a Chinese and an American is only uneasily presented at the end of the text as the attainment of paternal respect through American business success. For the sake of textual coherence, facts that challenge this message seem to be absent or repressed. Nowhere in the original text is the historical specificity of her life in an ethnic ghetto revealed with the clarity of the preface to the 1989 edition: "Who would be interested in the story of a poverty-stricken, undistinguished Chinese girl who had spent half of her life working and living, without romance, in a Chinatown basement?" (vii).

The question is disingenuous almost to the point of being "outrageously immodest"; readers find romance in *Fifth Chinese Daughter*'s plot of heroic feminism and adolescent culture clash. While others have argued that Wong's ethnic commodification fed white appetite for difference, what also bears scrutiny is the text's feminist narration as it provides a normalizing counterpoint to ethnic differentiation. As Wong's feminist resistance stands in for overt resistance to American culture, the text suggests one effect of racial and gendered discursive interaction: while representations of race and ethnicity may resist decontextualization, narratives of gender oppression often assume an air of timelessness, particularly in cases where thwarted self-actualization is situated within a narrative of parent/child conflict.

If plotlines of self-actualization thwarted by one's *husband* are intrinsic to the "canon" of women's literature, Amy Tan's 1989 *The Joy Luck Club* combines elements of both narratives as spousal and parental figures are constructed as impediments (or catalysts) to fulfilling individual potential. The narrative of the daughter's putative triumph over (and eventual reintegration into) ethnic family moves from a postwar context that saw a need for a familiar celestial to the context of the early 1990s, where the celestial has remained unrepentantly communist. The sentimental plotline nevertheless accommodates the shift in national desires: no longer responding to the irreducibly different native without, the American public demonstrated an increasing interest in the native within, an interest that corresponds to a shift in national self-conception from melting pot to multicultural mosaic. The prefeminist Chinese woman might not perform identically in both historical contexts, but one aspect of witnessing her trauma might remain constant: she becomes a means of accessing alterity within the safe confines of affect. Lauren Berlant reveals the nationalist function of sentimentality in noting, "in the United States a particular form of liberal sentimentality that promotes individual acts of identification based on collective group memberships has been conventionally deployed to bind persons to the nation through a universalist rhetoric not of citizenship per se but of the capacity for suffering and trauma at the citizen's core"[14] (Berlant 1998, 636). My own point is not so much that the process of identifying with sentimental representations of prefeminist Chinese women binds the citizen to the nation as much as it serves another function: it universalizes difference through women's oppression, building what Berlant would call "pain alliances from all imaginable positions within U.S. hierarchies of value." What better text, then, to witness pain alliance than Amy Tan's *The Joy Luck Club*?

Landscape of Emotions?: Amy Tan's *The Joy Luck Club*

In its emphasis on family nostalgia culminating in a message of empowerment and reconciliation, Tan's fiction met what seemed to be the new
criterion for ethnic bestsellers; as one New York editor cynically put it,
"let's have more Grandma" (cited in Richard Rodriguez, *Hunger of
Memory: The Education of Richard Rodriguez* [New York: Bantam,
1982], 7). *The Joy Luck Club* served up, if not ethnic grandma, then
ethnic matrilineal inheritance to feed the growing interest in the experiences of women of color, an interest significant enough to warrant a
reported advance of $4 million for *The Kitchen God's Wife* in 1991. *The
Joy Luck Club* both came at a moment—and helped *produce* a moment—of mainstream interest in literary treatments of the ethnic experience as women's experience. In linking Tan's popularity to a specific race
and gender discursive interaction, I would highlight Hayden White's
analysis of the relationship between formal qualities of historical narration and the historian's reception. "[T]he prestige enjoyed by a given
historian or philosopher of history within a specific public," he writes,
"is referable to the precritically provided linguistic ground on which the
prefiguration of the historical field is carried out" (White 1973, 429).
One of the lines from *The Joy Luck Club* quoted in early reviews speaks
to the linguistic ground established by the civil rights and women's
movements: "Once you are born Chinese, you cannot help but feel and
think Chinese." Thus before ever picking up the novel I wondered if
what it promised was a tour of the mysteries of the Far East within a
reassuring narrative about one's atavistic connection to homeland. This
intuition was perhaps only partly correct; *The Joy Luck Club* offers a
tour, not of China or Chinatown, but, as another review put it, through
a landscape of *emotions*.[15] What makes China "different" may be rendered intelligible by the identificatory possibilities of gendered sentiment, a dynamic perhaps not so different from that of *Fifth Chinese
Daughter*.

Reviewers often invoke the "universal mother/daughter bond" or "the
generation gap" as if in an effort to assure us that ethnic particularity is
both fascinating and irrelevant precisely because it can be transcended.
To wit: "When I finished reading *The Joy Luck Club* and *Seventeen Syllables*, I found myself weeping about the chasm between my own immigrant mother and her lost ancestors and descendants" (Valerie Miner,
"The Joy Luck Club," *The Nation* 24 April 1989, 566). Another reviewer
praised the novel for representing ethnic experiences that "could belong
to any immigrant group" (Julie Lew, "How Stories Written for Mother
Became Amy Tan's Best Seller," *New York Times*, 4 July 1989, 23). This

reaction testifies to the power of sentimentality but also to a belief in the transferability of certain types of experiences of certain types of people. What does it mean that identification with ethnic America is expressly marked as *women's* capacity to enter the lives of others, particularly through narratives of trauma?

The Joy Luck Club invites such responses, in effect, by performing them. It is fair to say that in the novel conflicts between the Chinese mothers and Chinese American daughters are resolved through their recognition of a commonality of experience based on their subordination as women; the cultural distance between immigrant mothers and American-born daughters is therefore bridged not through the characters' confrontation with contrasting cultural values but through their recognition that matrilineal heritage transcends the gap caused by the daughters' greater cultural enfranchisement. The emphasis on the female bond works to privilege gender sameness over differences based on class position, mobility, and generation; as I have argued in the case of *Fifth Chinese Daughter*, this privileging also mediates testimonies of ethnic difference. The mother/daughter pairs are structured according to two paradigms: June and Waverly must reconcile their belief that they cannot live up to their mothers' expectations whereas Lena and Rose must learn strength from their maternal inheritance. June struggles toward a positive interpretation of herself and accepts it as her mother's interpretation, to reconcile the fact that there is no "better self" seeking to overwhelm her by reminding her of her own limitations. Waverly's stories likewise reveal a dependence on her mother's approval as a source of self-esteem and, like June, her reconciliation comes through the recognition that she is more like her mother than she realized. Maternal reconciliation for both is based on their ability to reorient interpretation toward likeness and identification. Lena's and Rose's stories operate on a related paradigm of mirroring: they are shown to be overly dependent on their husbands and lacking the will to stand up for themselves, a point both their mothers see as a consequence of maternal inheritance. The resulting narrative trajectory of Lena's and Rose's stories is simply their mothers' desire to pass on lessons of strength learned through their own losses and suffering as women. The narrative movement in *The Kitchen God's Wife* is virtually identical: Winnie narrates the "tragedy of her life," namely, a "bad marriage" in China, to heal her daughter's multiple-sclerosis-as-multiple-neurosis. In both works, generational transmission, what Kingston's narrator calls "ancestral help," hinges on the recognition of both positively and negatively coded likeness.

The theme of women's endurance in narratives of privation and hardship appears across Asian ethnic texts. Helie Lee's *Still Life with Rice*, Julie Shigekuni's *A Bridge Between Us*, Akemi Kikimura's *Through*

Harsh Winters, Ronyoung Kim's *Clay Walls*, and Sky Lee's *Disappearing Moon Cafe* all reveal the harsh material conditions on which the middle class present or middle class in-the-making is founded. These texts also imply a subject for whom narratives of the past are intended; stories of trauma are offered as a corrective to the present—as instructive, healing, and ultimately empowering. Tan's novels exemplify this structure; a daughter self-consciously engages in a recuperative project that replaces an overly critical, authoritative parental voice with that of an oppressed woman. By identifying with this voice, she establishes gendered likeness as a means of self-help: narration excavates a past wherein oppression is latent until a strategic moment when it rises up to resolve (or fail to resolve) a contemporary situation.

As I have mentioned, the predominance of this treatment of women's stories in fiction and autobiography follows feminist literary critical practices of the 1970s and 1980s, when feminist identification, "the intertexuality of ourselves with women writers' texts," was acknowledged as a cornerstone to feminist criticism (Marcus 1988; Kaplan 1996). Both projects of foregrounding women's connectedness may derive from a contemporary critical desire to see in women's community (and later, racial collectivity) an antidote to stultifying individuality. Nancy Chodorow's influential "Family Structure and Feminine Personality" that situates "embedded" feminine personality in practices of mothering is a case in point. According to Chodorow, because as primary caretakers mothers tend to "identify more with daughters and help them differentiate less," women are less individuated and more communally invested (Chodorow 1974, 48). But as Wendy Brown has noted, the appeal of Chodorow's theory lies in the belief that "women inhabit a different moral, cultural and nascently political universe than men, with different (and better) guiding values" (Brown 1991, 1–2). This substantiation of gender embeddedness is part of *The Joy Luck Club*'s appeal; significantly, the desire to seek different (and better) alternatives to monadism is also reflected in critical orientations toward ethnic American and Third World literatures. For example, Malini Johar Schueller reads *The Woman Warrior* as a Marxist intervention, a radical narrative that, in its inscription of voice within a community of voices, "questions the unified and autonomous subject of liberal capitalism" (Schueller 1992, 143). For anthropologist Michael Fischer, ethnicity assumes the cachet of the collective and is posited as a cure to modern-day alienation. In regard to Native American autobiography he writes,

> The techniques of transference, talk-stories, multiple voices or perspectives, and alternative selves are all given depth or expanding resonances through ironic twists. Thus talk-stories or narrative connections to the past, to the ani-

mated cosmos, and to the present are presented as the healing medicine not only for Indians but for Americans and modern folk at large. (Fischer 1986, 224)

Cast in Freudian terms, anxiety stems from a sense of alienation in autonomy; ethnic autobiography mirrors back a "cure" by making conscious the process through which the individual is reintegrated into a collective whole. This view of ethnicity echoes somewhat Fredric Jameson's romanticization of a tribal subjectivity that predates the emergence of the individual and of myth as the ideal form of narrative insofar as it refuses "later categories of the subject, such as the 'character'" (Jameson 1981, 124). Jameson's validation of "Third World Literature" for its refusal to psychologize character reflects the hope that in the Third World one sees the potential "emergence of a post-individualist social world," where "the reinvention of the collective and the associative, can concretely achieve the 'decentering' of the individual subject" (Jameson 1986, 125).

The point is not to reduce nuances in these critics' treatment of collectivity, but to point out parallels between critical desires, the somewhat utopian impulses of critical projects toward ethnic and women's literature that seek oppositionality in communalism as a potential challenge to the bourgeois (and patriarchal) humanist subject by postulating the existence of an alternative, nonindividuated concept of social being. Tan's novel raises the question of whether the emphasis on gender collectivity represents an assault on the modern subject. What is interesting about the paradigmatic structure of Tan's writing is that, whether located in ethnic-racial or women's community, affirmations of collective integration culminate in individual self-actualization in ways that harmonize it with the prevailing ideology of American individualism. In other words, what appears to counter autonomous selfhood through genealogical connection might merely enable individual empowerment in the name of the collective. In *The Joy Luck Club* faith in the transference of experience is attributed to the blood tie: "Your mother is in your bones!" An-mei's comment, "A mother knows what is inside you," derives from her belief that one's own true nature, "what was beneath my skin. Inside my bones," lies within "her mother and her mother before her." Throughout *The Joy Luck Club*, the maternal connection is mystified as a genetic inheritance, what is passed down as a bodily memory in the same way Chineseness is essentialized as being "in our blood." This naturalization, unlike Chodorow's attribution of feminine embeddedness to social practices, employs what is usually a racialized discourse of genetics to explain, I would argue, *women's* connection. The blood tie reconciles the mother/daughter conflict, giving the novel its overly neat, feminist ending; the battle for autonomy from one's mother, one's difference from her, is replaced with the recognition of one's sameness to her.

This ending can only be achieved if the daughters' racial difference does not at first appear as their own but is externalized as representative of their mothers' Chineseness. For example, in realizing that she has "never really known what it means to be Chinese," June muses that her race is constituted by "a cluster of telltale Chinese behaviors, all those things my mother did to embarrass me—haggling with store owners, pecking her mouth with a toothpick in public, being color-blind to the fact that lemon yellow and pale pink are not good combinations for winter clothes." In other cases, Chineseness appears as a flexible, external marking: as half-Chinese Lena can pass as white but is pleased that the women in her aerobics class tell her she looks "exotic." After a lifetime of disassociating herself from ethnicity, Waverly appears to want "to be Chinese, it is so fashionable," implying that she has the power to claim or downplay her race according to dominant trends in the same way that Jade Snow Wong shuttles in and out of Chinatown. While their "American" subject positioning remains intact, it is their racial and cultural difference that they experience as their own "otherness" and because they displace this negatively coded difference onto their mothers, the novel suggests, they cannot embrace ethnicity as part of themselves until they are able to valorize it as positive.

Throughout *The Joy Luck Club*, the mother/daughter distance takes the form of the daughters' devaluation of what they perceive as foreign in their mothers as a means of substantiating their own American-ness. The disassociation they effect is not only in terms of individuation of the child from the mother but also in terms of the formation of the daughters' national identity through their disassociation from immigrant parents. The daughters' racial consciousness, "what it means to be Chinese," occurs not necessarily as their ability to claim racial identity through the recognition of how it is constituted as Other within the dominant culture, but as their new ability to valorize what is Chinese in their mothers and to claim it as their own. Yet in Tan's novel, the reconciliation of a cultural dichotomy is effected through a recognition of *feminine* strength as a "natural" maternal inheritance and as a point of identificatory sameness.

In *The Woman Warrior*, the narrator actively constructs ethnic identity out of her mother's stories that offer her conflicting models of feminine strength and powerlessness in the figures of the woman warrior and Brave Orchid versus the No Name Aunt and Moon Orchid. Similarly, American culture offers competing dictates for femininity—while American girls are expected to whisper to "make their voices American feminine," outside the narrator's Chinese family, America yet offers her the opportunity "to chop down trees in the daytime and write about timber at night." While Kingston's narrator constructs identity out of a simultaneously presented multiplicity of competing discourses, *The Joy Luck Club* presents the competition between gender and racial discourses less complexly; China is the location of woman's suffering and America embodies the opportunity for women's choices ("That was China. That was what people did back then. They had no choice. They could not speak up. They could not run away. That was their fate").[16] Based on this dichotomy, ethnic consciousness is achievable through the following: until the daughters accept their Chinese mothers' lessons about womanhood, they will not understand what it means to be Chinese. Tan's feminist resolution requires that femininity be associated with ethnicity, that characteristics of femininity and "Chineseness" operate along the same paradigm of embeddedness.

Rather than reflecting Chodorow's theory, which would posit self-effacing personality as a consequence of femininity,[17] Rose perceives it to be culturally Chinese and a condition that she unfortunately inherits as a Chinese American: "when you're Chinese you're supposed to accept everything, flow with the Tao and not make waves." Weighed against standards of American/masculine autonomy, Chinese culture is feminized through its association with qualities of embeddedness. Rose comments, "I have to admit that what I initially found attractive in Ted were precisely the things that make him different from my brothers and the Chinese boys I had dated: his brashness; the assuredness in which he asked for things and expected to get them; his opinionated manner." The dichotomy—individuality as American and embeddedness as Chinese—supports the separation between external American action and internal Chinese being. Lindo's comment—"I wanted my children to have the best combination: American circumstances and Chinese character"—represents ethnicity as a given attribute of individual being, an attribute that, for June, remains latent until it rises to the surface through maternal reconciliation.

The mothers support this distinction by privileging America as the land of opportunity, "where you could be anything you wanted to be," against a China oppressive to women's choices, a New World of options against a "back then" bound by fate. As in *Fifth Chinese Daughter*, America embodies the promise of the daughters' individualism, what is revealed to be denied the mothers' generation. The mothers' dilemma in view of this assimilation is that, while it distances them from what they perceive as proper Chinese respect for parents, it yet offers their daughters the luxury of choices they never had as women in China. Yet while their ambivalence toward their daughters' Americanization seems to be rooted in this incommensurability between maternal influence and self-determination, what surprises them is the daughters' reluctance (Rose's and Lena's in particular) to act as Americans, which is to say, to act in their own self-interest in the apparent absence of gender impediments. The distinction between the capacity to act and socially controlled passivity is signaled in Tan's repeated use of the words "choice" and "fate," not only throughout *The Joy Luck Club*, but *The Kitchen God's Wife* as well. Invoked primarily to draw distinctions between China and the United States over gender issues, the terms signal Tan's ideological bias by setting up an explicit national hierarchy resonant of differences between tradition and modernization.

These differences are enforced by Tan's biographical comments; she reveals that her mother Daisy's ambitions for her did not arise out of a desire to live vicariously through her daughter but out of what she saw as Amy's reluctance to take advantage of opportunities denied Daisy Tan in China: "Here we were, with all these opportunities, and we were focused on pizza and thin noses and miniskirts" (cited in Susan Kepner, "The Amazing Adventures of Amy Tan," *San Francisco Focus Magazine* 36:5 (1989): 60). What could be seen as an indictment of American consumerism and dominant standards of beauty is, I think, more accurately a criticism of the triviality of interests that draw energy away from personal enrichment or attempts at class advancement. Thus in the novel, the conflicts over the mothers' gender expectations for their daughters do not necessarily indicate a generational gap caused by the daughters' assimilation into American culture away from Chinese culture but, rather, the opposite. In spite of the mothers' laments about daughters who swallow "more Coca-Cola than sorrow," tensions arise between generations ironically because the mothers do not perceive the daughters to be American enough.

In spite of their rise into the middle class through education or marriage, the daughters have failed to live up to models of strong, independent womanhood that appear to the mothers as their birthright as American citizens. An-mei and Ying-ying do not necessarily object to their daughters' marriages to white men but to the fact that despite their freedom, not only did they choose wrongly, but they seem to accept their fates passively. The narrative trajectory conforms to that in *Fifth Chinese Daughter* but with a subtle difference: *The Joy Luck Club's* feminist narrative does not simply advocate class advancement (What good is a fur coat or a fancy house if they don't make you happy or equal to men?) but in effect validates a progressive notion of history by situating degrees of gender freedom as the chief indicator of differences between China and the United States, "back then" and now, "feudal" and modern thinking.

While the novel's reception can be tied to a moment of popularizing narratives of women's trauma—particularly those that give this trauma the valence of pastness—it might also be tied to generational issues arising within a specific historical moment. The novel was written directly after a period in which Tan "connected" with her Chinese heritage in a tangible way: "When my feet touched China," she notes, "I became Chinese" (cited in Lew). Such a sentiment reflects the *Roots* era of "rediscovered" ethnic pride or, as critic Sau-ling Wong puts it, "post-civil rights ethnic soul-searching" (Sau-ling Wong 1995, 202). However, the novel's emphasis on family reconciliation places it within a more generic moment; Tan attributes the novel's success in part to its addressing "baby boomer" issues:

> I think I wrote about something that hit a lot of baby boomer women whose mothers have either just recently died or may die in the near future. They felt that their misunderstandings, things that had not been talked about for years, were expressed in the book. There are so many mothers I know who gave the book to their daughters, and daughters who gave the book to their mothers, and marked passages of things they wanted to say. (Cited in Barbara Somogyi and David Stanton, "Amy Tan: An Interview," *Poets & Writers Magazine*, September/October 1991, 24–32.)

Her comment situates the work as a medium channeling repressed interpersonal communication; sharing the book literalizes the symbolic transmission of experience depicted within the work. Yet Tan's apprehension of the novel's appeal to her American generation locates it within the realm of the intensely personal, as ultimately concerned with self-healing, in short, with therapy. (Tan has, in fact, jokingly referred to her writing as "bad psychiatry" and turned to writing fiction as a means of curing work addiction after her psychiatrist fell asleep during one of her sessions; cited in Elaine Woo, "Striking Cultural Sparks: Once Pained by her Heritage, Amy Tan has Tapped it for a Piercing First Novel," *Los Angeles Times*, 12 March 1989, 1.) While her comment appears to historicize the novel as the coming of age story of a specific generation, such a contextualization redirects the novel's popularity away from its ethnic content; Tan situates the work among female baby boomers as a correction to a question about the novel's interest among Americans seeking to connect with ethnic roots.

The link between privatization and generational progression as class progression produces a similar message about the relation between racial history and self-help in Holly Uyemoto's novel, *Go*. There, the issei are agricultural workers, the nisei are math professors and homemakers, and the sansei are represented by the narrator, a college student recovering from a nervous breakdown. The novel suggests that excavating racial history (the narrator is a history major) might intervene in the personal crises of subsequent generations. While such plotlines might suggest that self-reflection is, as an outgrowth of bourgeois self-absorption, a luxury, they mark past oppression as usable potentially only to heal middle-class individuals who do not feel worthy (or loved) enough. Lowe argues against such privatization in one local textual instance in *The Joy Luck Club* while acknowledging that such a tendency is possible in regard to the novel's cultural circulation (Lowe 1991). Certainly what seemed to resonate most forcefully in the cultural moment of the late 1980s were narratives implicitly or explicitly about self-esteem or self-fulfillment, particularly those that could dovetail with sociologically inflected interests in, for example, "bad parenting."

This emphasis on identity often fails to be reconciled with contemporary politics within a global frame. For example, can the version of China essential to "growing up ethnic" stories ever be reconciled with the China of the Maoist revolution? *The Joy Luck Club*'s release in the spring of 1989 came only a few months before the massacre in Tiananmen Square, an event that broadcast an image of China into American homes that seemed to bear little relationship to representations of upper-class domesticity offered in Tan's work. Upon being asked to comment on the recent events in China, Tan said, "The first thing I would like to emphasize—because these events are so sensitive—is that my feelings are strictly personal. My relatives represent all sides of the situation. My uncle is a high Communist official, and my sister is a member of the Communist party, which is a very small elite in China. I also have relatives who are students and professors. The media was so one-dimensional, the evil villains versus the noble student heroes. But this wasn't a football game, it was my family!" (Cited in Joan Chatfield-Taylor, "Cosmo Talks to Amy Tan," *Cosmopolitan*, November 1989: 178.) Personalizing politics as a matter of family loyalty and invoking China's political spectrum through the rhetoric of intimate connection allows Tan to avoid rendering a judgment as a method of political intervention. The sentimental strain here, like that of the novel, cannot answer to the material world much less soothe its political ruptures. After all, love means not taking sides.

The question raised by this inquiry is whether narratives that rely on woman's identification with her prefeminist Other can serve more a radical function. Marking a shift in my argument, I turn to Sky Lee's *Disappearing Moon Cafe*.

Queer Sentiment: *Disappearing Moon Cafe*'s Incestral Help

The novel finds Kae, the narrator of her family history, estranged from both her newborn and her work and in the middle of thirty-something yuppie angst. A Vancouver "investment research analyst" contemplating a new job offer, an alienated Kae finds herself reassessing the direction of her life. Her job has forced her to figure aspects of her identity as marketable commodities, to be "the token, pregnant, ethnic woman" (123) in the interest of somebody else's profit. This crisis in the dual concept of her labor—her job and the delivery of her son—is compounded by another "identity crisis": she learns that she may be the product of brother/sister incest. This revelation of family secrets provokes Kae into narrating four generations of her family's history, self-consciously re-creating (as does the narrator in *The Woman Warrior*) scenarios that delve into the passions and motivations of her ancestors as a means of coming to terms with her own life. *Disappearing Moon Cafe*'s plot trajectory is thus similar to that of *The Joy Luck Club* and other novels I named earlier in the chapter as the unveiling of family history intervenes to resolve a contemporary personal crisis. The narration of women's oppression in particular, of how three generations of women negotiate a "woman-hating world," is intended as a salutary lesson about the subsequent generation's individual self-fulfillment. As I have been arguing, such outcomes risk romanticizing agency and imbuing an evolutionary account of history with First and Third World resonance. Nevertheless, this same narrative structure might have a different outcome, an outcome that, in effect, queers that plot. In contrast to Wong's and Tan's texts, *Disappearing Moon Cafe* inscribes an alternative feminist genealogy precisely in its lesbian resolution.

A fourth-generation Chinese Canadian, Kae challenges compulsory heterosexuality as a result of uncovering incest in her ancestral line: the novel portrays her transgression as both the betrayal of family secrets and the betrayal of repressive social dictates. By imbibing as lessons the individual stories that coalesce into a collective "tragedy," Kae breaks through her current alienation to pursue more consciously the life she desires—that of a writer and a lover of women. Her initial estrangement from life is a motif echoed in the situations of the other characters and is articulated through a specific trope—that of being an orphan. While the term "alienation" implies the subordination of human life to its capacity to labor intrinsic to Marxist philosophy, it takes on a more specific resonance in *Disappearing Moon Cafe*, where the state of being an orphan not only refers to children left parentless by death, but to concepts of legitimacy and illegitimacy, as well as to groups of people systematically excluded from larger collectivities—the Chinese diasporic community in the "wilderness" of Canada, the bachelor society cut off from women by exclusion acts, women whose bonds with other women are subordinated within patriarchy. As Kae's potential lover, Hermia, notes, "Grown women are orphan children, are we not? We have been broken from our mothers' arms too soon and made to cling to a man's world—which refuses to accept us—as best we can, any how we can" (138). The state of being lost, exiled, or orphaned from a nurturing or supportive community is revealed to have roots in systematic causes—the abdication of parental duty in favor of social standing, the racist and economic motivations behind immigration laws and public policy, and the uncritical adherence to patriarchal norms that establish lines of descent and laws of inheritance. The novel thus opens with Kae "waiting for enlightenment" and in need of, to echo Kingston, "ancestral help."

In "channeling" her ancestors to intervene in her contemporary crisis, Kae discovers that their alienated lives are the consequence of events that take place three generations before her birth. Briefly, Kae's great-grandmother, Mui-Lan arranges for a surrogate "wife" to bear a child with her son, Choy Fuk, who has failed to produce a male heir to guarantee the Wong lineage. The surrogate, waitress Song An, ultimately bears a son at the same time that his legal wife, Fong Mei, gives birth to a girl as a result of an affair. Because the paternity of the two children is kept secret, the conspiracy to produce Wong descendants comes to a crisis at the moment the putative half brother and sister, Kae's parents, decide to marry. Paralleling this chain of events, the illegitimate and unrecognized son of the Wong patriarch bears a son, Morgan, who falls in love with— unbeknownst to him—his half sister. Kae stumbles on this repressed history after she herself has had an affair with Morgan, who accurately claims to be her uncle. The convoluted genealogy is bound together not only through its relevance to Kae's life, but by the underlying similarities of individual circumstances. All of Kae's ancestors' "illegitimate" liasons are enacted out of an irrepressible passion that threatens social boundaries defined by gender, race, and class: Gwei Chang falls in love with someone of the "wrong" race, Fong-mei of the "wrong" class, Morgan of the "w(r)ong" lineage, and, finally, Kae of the "wrong" gender.

Lee suggests that her characters' failures lie not in their participation in sexual acts outside the bounds of socially sanctioned heterosexual, monogamous, same-race marriage but in their cowardice. They ultimately refuse to flout propriety and eventually give up the loves of their lives for security, duty, and social position. These renunciations have consequences for the entire Wong family, not the least of which is the imposition of a kind of double life: each case of ancestral excess—of miscegenation, reproductive interference, adultery, and incest—results in estranged or "orphaned" lives characterized by sexual repression and unfulfillment. I would argue, then, that the novel's point is not merely to lead Kae to an individual catharsis as a result of narrating her muddled family history but to expose the ways that cultural forces impel her ancestors to channel passion toward a "proper" love-object. In effect, it analyzes the ways in which the dictates of capitalism, racial segregation, and patriarchy regulate sexual behavior. While the novel does tend to naturalize desire in portraying characters at odds with libidoes yearning to break free from social constraint, it nonetheless also exposes the way that desire is channeled to serve a social function.

In portraying its characters as sexual dissidents (who ultimately lose their nerve), *Disappearing Moon* implicitly challenges the ways that specific sexual practices become placed in a hierarchy of descending privilege, what Gayle Rubin has noted as modern Western society's appraisal of "sex acts according to a hierarchical system of sexual value" (Rubin 1993, 11). Her argument in "Thinking Sex" recognizes that "[m]arital, reproductive heterosexuals are alone at the top of the erotic pyramid" (11), consigning those whose sexual practices do not fall within this heterosexual, monogamous, procreative fold to the "lower depths" of the sexual hierarchy, where they occupy the space of "bad, abnormal, unnatural, damned sexuality." The novel comments on the consequences of redirecting desire, on the social pressures that cause one to renounce those love-objects deemed inappropriate by, in the order in which the novel presents them, race, marital status, lineage, or gender. Throughout *Disappearing Moon*, Kae's analysis of the reasons behind the cycles of renunciation and cowardice in her lineage takes the form of a cultural critique; reading the impact of racism, patriarchy, and middle-class pursuit on the sexual lives of her ancestors—particularly the prefeminist women—allows her to question the structures that support a rigid hierarchy of sexual value and act on it.

Miscegenation is the first taboo to be challenged in the Wong lineage. After marrying a half-Chinese, half-Indian woman, producing a son, and living a "natural" tribal life, Kae's great-grandfather, Gwei Chang, heeds the call of duty and returns to China, where he marries a second time. The novel's initial 1894 narrative also ends it; the final sequences explain why Gwei Chang deserts his Indian wife, instigating the genealogy of renunciation. His idyll is tempered by his sudden recognition of the distance between them; an Indian, she represents the barbarity and uncertainty of living in the wilderness: "In the next instant he looked at Kelora, and saw animal" (234). By leaving Kelora (and later refusing to acknowledge their son) to secure his social standing, he loses himself to the pursuit of capital and to a fantasy life of nostalgia. This end sequence marks Gwei Chang's second thoughts about his miscegenation as the originary moment of the Wong cycle of repudiation and loss. Lee's fictionalization of the fallout from the murder of Janet Smith in Vancouver, a case in which a Chinese houseboy was accused of murdering a white woman, reveals how the fear of miscegenation as a sexual taboo was manipulated to serve the state's economic interests in regard to a minority population. Touted as a safeguard to morality, the resulting Janet Smith Law prohibited white women from working in close proximity with Chinese men and had economic consequences for Chinatown, especially for those businesses that employed white waitresses. As Canada's later embrace of multiculturalism as a distinct national ethos later encouraged unofficial segregation, here Lee reveals how sexual prohibitions divided racial communities.[18]

The second "test" that the Wong ancestors fail lies in Kae's great-grandmother Mui Lan's capitulation to patriarchy; Lee's portrayal of women's opppression in China, however, reverses the association of the New World as the site of Chinese women's potential liberation at play in Tan's novel. Ironically, Chinese "feudalism" in the form of the separation of spheres in the Confucian household is portrayed as encouraging women's autonomy, an autonomy lost upon immigration as a result of the state's regulation of the Chinese Canadian community:

> And Mui Lan's nightmare was loneliness. She arrived and found only silence. A stone silence that tripped her up when she tried to reach out. Gold Mountain men were like stone. She looked around for women to tell her what was happening, but there were none. By herself, she lacked the means to know what to do next. Without her society of women, Mui Lan lost substance. (26)

Unlike the excessively genderist Old World depicted in *The Joy Luck Club*, China here is portrayed as the source of an empowering and sustaining women's community. Lee implies that Mui Lan mistakenly responds to her isolation not by trying to recover a woman-centered community, an endeavor hindered by Canadian immigration policies, but by mimicking the money-conscious values of the male-dominated "wilderness" of the New World: "Having never been in control of her own life, she suddenly found herself in charge of many people's lives. Frustrated and isolated from the secluded life she understood, Mui Lan had to swallow bitterness, so she made her suffering felt far and wide" (31). As the domestic sphere becomes the limited arena of her influence, she ends up manipulating those with whom she could have found connection—other women. In her attempt to control her daughter-in-law, Fong Mei, and exploit waitress Song An for her reproductive capacity, she enacts women's oppression, wielding her class status. Through Kae, the novel self-consciously represents its characters' failings as a form of misguided ideological consent: Mui Lan and Fong Mei are both victims of and participants in women's "common debasement."

However anachronistically, Kae's narration likewise attempts to bring feminist cultural analysis to her grandmother's story. Brought from China to secure the Wong lineage yet unable to conceive as a result of her husband's undisclosed infertility, Fong Mei is lambasted for being a flawed and very expensive commodity and threatened with social disgrace, the dissolution of her marriage, and deportation. Out of fear of "being with an orphan" with no economic standing, Fong Mei nonetheless refuses to give up the "property and respectability" that come with her marriage after she becomes pregnant as a result of her ongoing adultery. Kae thus has Fong Mei come to a belated feminist regret of her decision to renounce her lover, Ting An, keep her children's paternity secret, and remain in a loveless marriage:

> I once thought it was funny that I could take my revenge on the old bitch and her turtle son. Another man's children to inherit the precious Wong name, all their money and power. I forgot that they were my children! I forgot that I didn't need to align them with male authority, as if they would be lesser human beings without it. . . . I sold them, each and every one, for property and respectability. (189)

Kae's gender analysis in the form of "channeling" the voices of her ancestors emphasizes women's capitulation to the status quo. But her narration also marks women as agents with other choices, prefiguring Kae's resolution to depart from the cycle inscribed by this history. *Disappearing Moon's* feminist sensibility contrasts the liberalism of *Fifth Chinese Daughter* and *The Joy Luck Club*:

> In each of their women-hating worlds, each did what she could. If there is a simple truth beneath their survival stories, then it must be that women's lives, being what they are, are linked together. Mother to daughter, sister to sister. Sooner or later, we get lost or separated from each other; then we have a bigger chance of falling into the same holes over and over again. Then again, we may find each other, and together, we may be able to form a bridge over the abyss. (145)

The novel validates a sentimental, almost utopian view of women's community as an alternative culture characterized by, as Wendy Brown has noted, "different (and better) guiding values" (W. Brown 1991, 1–2). But it also depicts collectivity as a form of horizontal comradeship and a logical response to divisions created by social hierarchy. This is the "lesson" that Kae imbibes; the familial and privatized story of her ancestry provides the text by which she reads culture and can abstract from the individual life a political critique. Lee's emphasis on Kae's self-search as a process of coming to multiple collective identifications echoes Stuart Hall's reading of Gramsci, who "argues that this multi-faceted nature of consciousness is not an individual but a collective phenomenon, a consequence of the relationship between 'the self' and the ideological discourses which compose the cultural terrain of a society" (Hall 1986, 22). Analyzing the impact of racism, patriarchy, and class-striving on the lives of her ancestors, Kae uncovers and begins to interrogate the ideological structures that systematically reduce the lives of individuals. This knowledge frees her to seek an erotic connection with her friend, Hermia Chow.

Love Free from Restraint: *Disappearing Moon's* Lesbian Resolution

This erotic connection forms the resolution to Kae's identification with the Chinese Canadian community, her ancestors, and women. She transcends her individual identity crisis by understanding the tragic results of allowing repressive social convention to circumscribe sexual lives, of bowing to profit rather than pleasure, to propriety rather than passion. The first test of Kae's willingness to act on desire occurs in the form of a handsome, older, working class, Eurasian man who excites her teenage sensibility. Not incoincidentally, he also claims to be her uncle. Their incestuous, one-time coupling is unfulfilling but revelatory. Kae gushes, "I had managed one small glimpse into what it was like to release one's being, to let it slip into the other realm where all the senses explode. And that was enough to set me off on a lifetime quest for more of the same" (162). Her reaction appears rather overblown, given the description of the desperate sex that initiates it; nevertheless, the incident foreshadows the novel's ending in which she chooses desire over "hoarding integrity" as a safeguard against being seduced. Kae's Hong Kong friend, Hermia, represents another "enticing lure" toward what Rubin would call "erotic non-conformity" (22), as both Morgan and Hermia embody the taboo love-object. In this sense, the novel places consanguineous sex and homosexuality on the same continuum; it does, however, avoid linking incest with abuse even though Kae is only seventeen during her first affair.

While the nature of their relationship is left ambiguous, their interactions are characterized by playful, romantic, and insinuating language. Kae's "intoxication" over Hermia is apparently reciprocated:

> Kae, I see it in your eyes . . . that drive to love and create. Why do you want to deny? Women's strength is in the bonds they form with each other. Say that you'll love me forever! The bond between true sisters can't be broken by time or distance apart! Say that, Kae . . . tell me! (39)

While Hermia's plea for a connection with Kae does not literally express sexual desire, her passion implies something more than sorority. Likewise, Kae's response indicates that she reads a message beneath the expression of enduring friendship, a message that she sees as vaguely illicit. In suggesting that Kae's story ends with a lesbian resolution, my reading self-consciously echoes Barbara Smith's reading of *Sula* as a lesbian novel. Her "Towards a Black Feminist Criticism" defines a literary work as lesbian "[n]ot because women are 'lovers,' but because they are the central figures, are positively portrayed and have pivotal relationships with one another" (Smith 1982, 164). Her positioning reflects that of

Bettina Aptheker, who defines lesbians "as women whose primary emotional, intellectual, and erotic relationships are with other women" (Aptheker 1989, 87) and who places sexuality as a specific criterion for "lesbian" within a historical context. *Disappearing Moon*'s ending in which Kae assents to Hermia's cryptic challenge, "would you rather live a great novel or write one," affirms both Smith's and Aptheker's emphasis on women's emotional bonds as a facet of lesbianism. Lee herself expands the concept of "women love" that is "a little bit larger than lesbianism" (S. Lee 1990, 122).[19]

I would nonetheless suggest that the novel's ending in which Kae prepares to meet Hermia in Hong Kong represents Kae's choice of a lesbian relationship over her heterosexual marriage, not because the novel leaves no room for interpretation, but because this choice forms a logical conclusion to the novel's thematic focus: her "enlightenment" lies in the realization that her ancestors have renounced desire that cannot be channeled toward a socially appropriate love-object. Lesbian sexuality initially operates on the same contiuum as uncle-niece incest, as it comes to represent a challenge to Kae's sense of legitimacy and order. Complementing Hermia's representation as a sexual risk-taker is her challenge to Kae's loyalty to the business world over her writing career; throughout the novel, Hermia is figured as Kae's foil—one who pushes her sexually, artistically, and, especially in regard to feminist thought, politically. Hermia's counsel, "Think of love as something free from remorse and restraints . . . Genitalia coming together because it feels good" (187), forms an appropriate resolution to Kae's genealogical narration, lending the novel a clear aesthetic unity as well. In the process of affirming her connection to her ancestors, there is not only a reconciliation with the past, as in Tan's novel, but a transformation of consciousness culminating in the realization that "love makes us expand in our relationship to life, and to each other" (215).

In the larger scheme of things, it could be said that Kae's resolution to pursue the life of a writer and a lover of women does not qualify as evidence of radical consciousness but merely indicates a choice of lifestyle. In this, the novel's resolution is not so different from *The Joy Luck Club*'s. However, Kae's "crisis" is ultimately revealed to be more than postpartum depression, suburban angst, or a need to recover ethnic roots. In recognizing the consequences of acceding to the cultural restraints put on desire, to false taxonomies of legitimacy and illegitimacy, the novel suggests that what produces and sustains the characters' states of alienation, their inability to read the structures that prevent connection with one another, is the subordination of human desire to its social function—the accumulation of capital, the maintainance of patriarchal lines of descent, the "ownership" of women within family and clan, and the enforcement of compulsory heterosexuality. The novel's appeal does lie in a plot structure that mirrors that of *The Joy Luck Club* in portraying diasporic Chinese experience as progressively freeing and ultimately salutary for their female protagonists. However, against the grain of my previous argument on both Wong and Tan, the seemingly individual and privatized genealogy narrated in *Disappearing Moon* initiates an understanding of how racism and misogyny have delimited life, the costs of capitulating to (primarily sexual) social norms. Femininst narratives of empowerment do not necessarily serve to harmonize racial difference but can also expose culture's investment in both the homosocial bond and a sexual hierarchy.

What makes the difference between *Disappearing Moon*'s and *The Joy Luck Club*'s treatment of women's bonding is no doubt Lee's activist feminist commitment as well as the fact that she published with a small feminist press, a move that did not produce instant bestseller status or result in a major motion picture. To compare the circumstances of both novels' writing, however, implies that such circumstances produce specific ideological effects, that a book's content is compromised by its method of production and distribution. One aspect of *The Joy Luck Club*'s publication history bears this out; the first segment of what would become the "novel" reads quite differently from the rest of the work in its unsentimental and ambiguous depiction of the mother/daughter bond. Begun in 1985, *The Joy Luck Club* was originally conceived as a collection of short stories. Significantly, Tan's publication of "Endgame" (what would later become "Rules of the Game") led to the "novel's" commission.[20] While this short story reflects the content of the novel, unlike the other sections, it takes interethnic conflict over class and racial integration as its center and can be read as a parable of ambivalent acculturation that challenges the ideological content of *The Joy Luck Club* as a whole.

"Rules of the Game" refers to chess and to the "rules" of acculturation that one must manipulate in order to "rise above one's circumstances" or transcend class position. Lindo's "teaching art of invisible strength" assumes a double meaning as chess strategy converges with strategies on how to negotiate racist immigration law:

> Every time people come out from foreign country, must know rules. You not know, judge say, Too bad, go back. They not telling you why so you can use their way go forward. They say, Don't know why, you find out yourself. But they knowing all the time. Better you take it, find out why yourself. (95)

Lindo's fears about Waverly's emerging distance from her ethnic family rise as chess tournaments cause her daughter to move both literally and figuratively farther away from home ("I no longer played in the alley of

Waverly Place" [100]) and to draw hierarchitizing cultural comparisons ("The chessmen were more powerful than old Li's magic herbs that cured ancestral curses" [94]). Game strategies of attack and escape are metaphoric of cultural movement as Lindo becomes the opponent who frustrates Waverly's construction of alternative "escape routes" from home.

The real losses that concern Lindo are the "pieces" of Chinese culture, including ties to family, that are potentially sacrificed in the process of acculturation:

> My mother placed my first trophy next to a new plastic chess set that the neighborhood Tao society had given to me. As she wiped each piece with a soft cloth, she said, "Next time win more, lose less."
>
> "Ma, it's not how many pieces you lose," I said. "Sometimes you need to lose pieces to get ahead."
>
> "Better to lose less, see if you really need." (98)

The quarrel here does not only concern parental pressure to create overachievers; rather, it raises a familiar question on integration: Do you need to lose ties to ethnicity to "go forward"? Waverly's participation in chess is also linked to change in its feminist connotations; her triumphs are figured as victories for women challenging the male grandmasters. Moreover her public recognitions reorder traditional gendered work roles within the family—her brothers have to wash the dishes, a change her mother champions. Yet Lindo appears to withdraw her support as communalism and meritocracy come in conflict: Waverly's question, "'If you want to show off, then why don't you learn to play chess?" outlines a fundamental difference between collective and individual achievement. Waverly's inability to disassociate herself from collective ties is signified by the remains of the family dinner, a fish whose head "was still connected to bones swimming upstream in vain escape." The end of the story finds Waverly dreaming of disembodied limbo; momentarily alienated from her family, she experiences herself as alone, rootless, and unconnected.

As an autonomously published story, "Endgame" suggests that the process of acculturation can result in the individual's alienation from a collective identity, a sense of self located in ethnic family and place. Yet as part of the novel, the ambivalent moment is reconciled in futurity, revealing the conflict to have been not so much related to class tension and the daughter's increasing cultural enfranchisement and mobility, but simply to childish growing pains surrounding individuation that necessitate the adult's attempt to regain self-esteem. The potentially provocative focus revealed by this initial writing seems to have been displaced in favor of a more interiorized, "universal" narrative on coming to terms with parenting. This displacement perhaps suggests that the material circumstances of the text's production, the necessity of publishing under a deadline and *as a novel* perhaps forced the need for narrative closure figured as multiple mother/daughter reconciliations.

As I have pointed out in reading contradictions and repressions in *Fifth Chinese Daughter*, no text is entirely compromised by its narrative resolution. Thus, this local instance in Tan's novel can be read against what I have argued to be the effect of its narrative trajectory, namely, that in a potentially depoliticizing gesture the work reconciles conflicts between women based on differences of class and levels of cultural enfranchisement to favor an ahistorical, transcultural belief in the commonality of women's experience. This "evidence" of a politically alternative *Joy Luck*, one prior to its wooing by mainstream presses, is one that other critics nevertheless see reflected in the entire work; Lisa Lowe has pointed out that novel historicizes "both privatized generational conflict and the 'feminized' relations between mothers and daughters" as both come to signify "the broader social shifts of Chinese immigrant formation" (Lowe 1991, 78). She notes,

> It is possible to read *Joy Luck Club* not as a novel that exclusively depicts "the mystery of the mother/daughter bond" among generations of Chinese American women but rather as a text that thematizes how the trope of the mother-daughter relationship comes to symbolize Asian American culture. That is, we can read the novel as commenting on the national public aestheticizing of mother-daughter relationships in its discourse about Asian Americans, by placing this construction within the context of the differences—of class and culturally specific definitions of gender—that are rendered invisible by the privileging of this trope. (Lowe 1991, 79)

Significantly, however, *The Joy Luck Club* does not merely comment on the way the trope of the mother/daughter relationship comes to symbolize Asian American culture but, in fact, participates in constructing this trope. Its success highlights the dual and contradictory work of multiculturalism, which is, as Lowe notes, "both a mode of pluralist containment and a vehicle for intervention in that containment" (Lowe 1996, 85).

Nevertheless, highlighting the incommensurability between political intervention and the uses of "multicultural" texts in the 1980s, Hazel Carby notes, "We need to ask why black or other nonwhite women are needed as cultural and political icons by the white middle-class at this particular moment" (Carby 1992, 11). Speculating that texts by black women are a guilt-relieving means of gaining knowledge of the Other and function as substitutes for desegregation activism, Carby's remarks are suggestive not of the content of the works, but of the ideological underpinnings of cultural consumption (Carby 1992, 342). Thus situated, cultural products not only respond to the needs of specific historical moments, but exert a normalizing effect on a status quo potentially threatened by contradiction; as the articulation of a desire for pluralist inclusion, multiculturalism, Carby suggests, arises precisely at a time in which society remains more trenchantly segregated. Her reading locates this effect among a necessarily homogenous group of white, middle-class students and academics as if to suggest that this is the only audience that matters; nor does her point speak to a motive other than guilt feeding the drive to know "otherness." Nevertheless, her comments reflect the wariness that Lauren Berlant recognizes about the turn to sentimental rhetoric at moments of social anxiety, a sentimentality that may sublimate "subaltern struggles into conventions of narrative satisfaction and redemptive fantasy" (Berlant 1998, 665). David Palumbo-Liu makes a similar point about how ethnic literature renders race relations manageable precisely through a reader's ability to "relate" to difference, but he acknowledges that an alternative pedagogy with regard to ethnic literature could be sought that would not merely "mimic and reproduce the ideological underpinnings of the dominant canon" (Palumbo-Liu 1995, 2).

bell hooks suggests an alternative motive to Carby's emphasis on guilt fueling interest in ethnic texts in naming ethnicity "the spice to white culture," an analogy that positions ethnic and racial difference as a positive, yet ancillary appendage to an unmarked norm or as a supplement existing purely as ornamentation (hooks 1992, 21). This idea of difference-as-supplement underlies Trinh T. Minh-ha's projection of what mainstream culture wants from its ethnic specimens:

> Now, i am not only given the permission to open up and talk, i am also encouraged to express my difference. My audience expects and demands it; otherwise people would feel as if they have been cheated: We did not come to hear a Third World member speak about the First (?) World, We came to listen to that voice of difference likely to bring us what we can't have and to divert us from the monotony of sameness. (Trinh 1989, 88)

Hazel Carby, bell hooks, and Trinh Minh-ha implicitly locate in liberal multiculturalism a desire to experience the Other—an increasing demographic necessity—in a distanced, safe medium. By focusing on the needs of a dominant consuming audience, they attribute this effect solely to form: both ethnic and gender content are relegated to performing identical functions in satisfying an appetite for "spice."

The use of the black woman as a cultural and political icon among critics in the 1980s has produced, in Ann duCille's words, a "traffic jam" in black feminist studies. DuCille suggests that the rush of white feminist critical interest in part stems from the perception that black women occupy the "quintessential site of difference" so that by the inverse logic of current theoretical developments, "the last shall be first" (duCille 1994,

592). DuCille thus links canonization to the level oppressed groups are seen to occupy in a hierarchy of oppressions, an institutionalization contingent on the potential promises and pleasures of "lastness." Elizabeth Abel implies as much in speculating that white feminist critics may seek in black women's literature "the text that promises resistance and integrity," a search that is "fueled by the perception of an increasingly compromised white feminist social position drained by success of oppositionality" (Abel, 1993, 494). In the context of Asian American literature, Rachel Lee has noted the difference in the extent of institutionalizing Maxine Hong Kingston's *The Woman Warrior*, which details a woman's coming to voice, and her next novel, *China Men*, focusing on the male immigrant's claiming America. In commenting on the former's successful incorporation into Women's Studies, she notes, "we value texts [in the academy] based upon the degree to which they remain marginal" (R. Lee 1995, 157). The desire for oppositionality as the reward for excavating the "quintessential site of difference" is only half of the story; as Carla Kaplan has pointed out, Anglo-American feminist criticism in the 1980s celebrated the critic's identification with "women's experience" as part of its recuperative project (Kaplan 1996). In this context, multiculturalism in the United States requires a subject distinct from the one necessary for postcolonial critical production—not merely one that "speaks," but one that testifies to notions of universality circulating in a particular culture at a given moment. I would argue that the concept of gender equality now functions as a potent trope precisely because it can circulate as a form of common sense. In Asian American women's writing, it surfaces through the idea that women have the right to make choices about their lives. The subsequent drama, then, lies in whether or not the prefeminist woman (or her daughter) will come to recognize and claim these rights.

"Multicultural" texts do perform a service parallel to the contributions of feminist scholars' recovery of women's writing. The process of recuperation—both as a critical practice and as a concern in literature—has the potential to shed light on the repressive politics of domination that inform women's experience as one example of "subjugated knowledge." As Foucault notes,

> The making visible of what was previously unseen can sometimes be the effect of using a magnifying instrument. . . . But to make visible the unseen can also mean a change of level, addressing oneself to a layer of material which had hitherto had no pertinence for history and which had not been recognised as having any moral, aesthetic, political or historical value." (Foucault 1980, 50)

Thus the significance of feminist history has been not only to "make visible the unseen," but as historian Joan W. Scott has noted, to "unmask all

claims to objectivity as an ideological cover for masculine bias by pointing out the shortcomings, incompleteness, and exclusiveness of 'mainstream' history" (Scott 1992, 30). Texts that participate in recuperating
the women-centered stories of an immigrant generation contribute to unmasking masculine bias as well as the exclusions and imperial endeavors
on which American history has been based.

Nevertheless, taking "lived experience" as a foundation that sanc-
tions these texts or histories runs the risk of fetishsizing the knowledge-
experience equation in ways that counter postmodernist claims about the
destabilizing effects of repressed "minority" viewpoints. As Scott writes,
the unfortunate consequence of treating marginalized histories as corrective add-ons is that "the project of making experience visible precludes
critical examination of the workings of the ideological system itself"
(Scott 1992, 25). Foucault addresses the dangers of reincorporation,
questioning, "is it not perhaps the case that these fragments of genealogies are no sooner brought to light, that the particular elements of the
knowledge that one seeks to disinter are no sooner accredited and put
into circulation, than they run the risk of re-codification, re-colonisa-
tion?" (Foucault 1980, 86). The question to be posed about texts that
incorporate the feminist narrative structures found in *Fifth Chinese
Daughter* and *The Joy Luck Club* is whether, while such texts may participate in contesting the processes of racialization in American culture in
local textual instances, they also succeed in harmonizing marginalized
experience with preexisting cultural narratives of liberalism and progressive development. This issue was raised in regard to Ronald Takaki's
Strangers from Different Shore, the textbook of pan-ethnic Asian American history, and his presentation of Asian American "voices" as historical
evidence. Fellow historian Sucheng Chan comments in regard to his
methodology, "[T]he ultimate effect of the oral history quotes is to affirm
the belief that, in America, even the downtrodden have a chance to demonstrate the triumphant tenacity of the human spirit" (Chan 1990, 97).
Evidence of collective oppression assumes an unavoidable totality when
placed within a specific framework; narrative assimilates individual
voices to a collective past, here, potentially based on the intellectual's
desire for semblance and identification with generations that have logi-
cally *produced* him.

Women's narratives have traditionally assumed the aura of oppositionality due to the feminist tenor in the 1980s of highlighting resistant
practices in texts by women, especially by women of color for whom the
undifferentiated category "triple oppression" is often invoked. Given the
link between academic popularity and political cast, there is necessarily a
concurrent feminist project that looks at the way in which narratives produce a version of "women's culture" easily harmonized with prevailing

attitudes. Both *Fifth Chinese Daughter* and *The Joy Luck* inscribe racial subjects in accord with uncritical notions of ethnic pluralism in part by affirming gendered universality, one through overt assurances about women's equality, the other through the romantic trope of feminine connection. In the context of these two texts, gendered narratives satisfy the simultaneous dictate of testifying to difference while rendering it knowable. In characterizing race/gender discursive overlap as a form of displacement, I am suggesting that such a conjoining is often hierarchically expressed, privileging the discourse most reconcilable to its dominant cultural context. This, I think, is the consequence of specific narrative structures rather than being symptomatic or representative of a "canon" of Asian American women's writing. There are certainly works that engage this structure with multiple and contradictory effects—*The Woman Warrior* comes to mind here—and feminist narratives that do not reflect an unequivocal notion of progressive history expressed through gender equality. And as I have shown, embedded within this narrative are local textual instances or elisions that disrupt the premises of liberalism to which their narrative structures conform.

As feminist narratives come to regulate representations of ethnicity, they enable a reconciliation of ethnic difference into the national landscape through gender, potentially locating in domestic feminism a project of validating women's likeness. In contrast, within a global context, Aihwa Ong notes that in Western feminist anthropology "much recent feminist study of Asian women already has had [the] function [of] producing epistemological and political gaps between us feminists and them 'oppressed' women" (Ong 1988, 81). Her comments imply that such a distinction is necessary to establishing the authority—and political urgency—of the Western feminist researcher's voice. But do feminist narratives fall along simple, dichotomous lines in the shift of focus from the national to the transnational, from Asian American to Asian women? My argument has heretofore emphasized a domestic context in addressing the issue of "internal minorities" vis-à-vis liberal multiculturalism. The question remains whether a similar function could be ascribed to gender representation in texts produced by Asian/American women writing about Asia from the United States. In the chapters that follow, I explore how gendered appeals function as interventions into Asian postcolonial politics, thereby implicitly commenting on the United States's role as global interventionist.

Four

Third World Testimony in the Era of Globalization

LE LY HAYSLIP'S BAD (GIRL) KARMA AND THE ART
OF NEUTRALITY[1]

> "Boo-sheeit! I ain't never gettin' hit in Vietnam."
> "Oh no? Okay, mothafucker, why not?"
> "'Cause," Mayhew said, "it don't exist."
> (*Michael Herr,* Dispatches)

> Tell all the Truth but tell it slant—
> (*Emily Dickinson*)

"[L]OOK INTO THE HEART of one you once called enemy," writes Vietnamese immigrant Le Ly Hayslip. "I have witnessed, firsthand, all that
you went through. I will try to tell you who your enemy was" (xiv). Hayslip's 1989 autobiography, *When Heaven and Earth Changed Places: A
Vietnamese Woman's Journey from War to Peace*, thus promises a
glimpse into what remained opaque and incomprehensible to both a tele-
vision viewing audience and the soldier in the field—the heart of "our
enemy." The autobiography marks yet another first-person contribution
to the discourse of a war that has been said to defy representation. The
incommunicability of the Vietnam experience has been a primary theme
within veterans' discourse, ironically in spite of the fact that it is dominated by experiential accounts that link notions of authenticity and authority to "being there." Michael Herr's portrayal of a soldier's belief in
his invincibility reflects two conventional perspectives on the war; first,
that Americans were only fighting themselves, and second, that the
trauma of the experience renders it essentially untransferable, hence un-
real. Le Ly Hayslip's autobiography stands out among these firsthand
accounts if only because it seems to offer an alternative view—that of a
Vietnamese peasant woman. And to some extent it does succeed in coun-
tering dominant American representations of the Vietnamese people as
mere backdrops to a hellish landscape. Vietnam and the Vietnamese, her
story testifies, *exist*.

Hayslip's story is a commodity in the glutted American media market
on the war only to the extent that her race, gender, national, and class

alterity would indicate that her account does not simply replay that of the journalist or solider in the field or the "multicultural" narratives of female nurses or African American GIs. But does it serve an alternative purpose either in the domestic sphere or in the context of global restructuring? The text does diverge from many of these accounts in the overtness of its intention. Hayslip's testimony performs a more specific function than reminding a forgetful American public that its so-called dirty war has continued to impact a nation. In its invocation of a firsthand experience of the war and its structure as a narrative of conversion, Hayslip's work reflects the activist potential of autobiography, where the life of the individual is intended as an allegorical commentary. The book's purpose is fairly straightforward—its goal is to "heal old wounds" by elucidating the effects of war and to call for the rebuilding of Vietnam through activism and humanitarian aid. The end of the text directs the reader to various agencies committed to this task, including Hayslip's own, the East Meets West Foundation. The 1993 sequel, *Child of War, Woman of Peace*, "America's story, written with a bamboo pen" (4), details not only the process of her acculturation to American society in the years following the war, but her efforts to establish the foundation's clinic. The message of healing and forgiveness embedded in both narratives and in Oliver Stone's subsequent film adaptation, *Heaven and Earth*, intervened at a strategic historical moment. In February 1994, President Clinton lifted the U.S. trade embargo in force against Vietnam since 1975.[2]

This shift in U.S. foreign policy coincides with the rhetoric of forgiveness reflected in present attitudes toward Vietnam to the extent that some vets can even overlook the irony of a former "draft dodger" "ending" the war: "it's time to stop rooting in that rag-and-bone shop of our hearts," notes veteran William Broyles Jr. "It's time for old soldiers, old enemies and old draft dodgers to make peace together" (cited in *Newsweek* 14 February 1994, 31–32). Even within the Vietnamese exile community in southern California, where political power remained in the hands of ardent anti-Communists, a *Los Angeles Times* poll revealed that a majority of Vietnamese Americans favored the establishment of full normal diplomatic relations with Vietnam, and approved Clinton's decision to lift a trade embargo that was once a litmus test of the nationalism of Vietnamese-in-exile.[3] But Hayslip's success in reaching an audience with her life story can only be partially attributed to the fact that its tenor is consistent with changing attitudes toward Vietnam. Her texts engage and circulate in a variety of discourses not only about the war but about the Asian immigrant experience in the context of multiculturalism, the increasingly global concerns of Asian American literature, Third World women's *tes-*

timonio, and, most significantly, the relationship between First and Third World nations within a modern world system. Her narratives of life in a war zone and afterward rely on conventions of realism that appeal particularly to her multiple and shifting positionalities as a gendered, class-specific, nationally marked subject. On the one hand, Hayslip's text performs the spectacle of collective Vietnamese suffering and provides American guilt a bodily form as part of its sentimental appeal to the war's civilian toll. On the other hand, the narrative's inscription of a self-reliant subject who refuses victimization is meant to produce an identification and likeness that furthers the text's didactic purpose, exhorting its American readers to move to a salutary and proactive acceptance of responsibility toward Vietnam similar to her own. Hayslip's position as an Asian female immigrant is intrinsic to the narrative's political message even though, as I discuss, the text is coauthored by a white American.

The text's representation of women's sexual trauma structures its persuasive appeal; *When Heaven and Earth Changed Places* foregrounds women's sexual circumscription as Le Ly[4] charts her way around not the literal minefields of war but a minefield of psychosexual choices. By the time she has been tortured by both the Republicans and the Viet Cong, sexually harassed and raped, abused by American "boyfriends," prostituted, and left an unwed mother, Le Ly realizes that her survival in Vietnam and hopes for a better life in the West are dependent on her emerging self-consciousness of her body's use value and her ability to control her sexual commodification. The text reveals that for women political allegiance is established through the body and, specifically for Le Ly, a matter of negotiating among the sexual demands of opposing sides represented by Viet Cong, Republican, and American officials, soldiers, and employers. Hayslip's work dramatizes the specific ways in which women's relationship to the state (or other institutions of governance) is established through determinations of sexual-as-political fidelity. But on another level the text's gendered discourse is intimately tied to its covert ideological agenda in which neutrality potentially justifies American interests. Usurping tactics of masculinist nationalism by linking femininity to a nationalist imaginary, *When Heaven and Earth Changed Places* attempts to invoke a maternal space that transcends national divisions; Hayslip's use of a gendered pacifism supports her implicit commentary on Vietnam's future direction within an international economy arguably dominated by its former adversary. Thus her text offers a caveat to generalizing the political function of Third World women's *testimonio*; in its portrayal of naturalized gender values that purport to be transnational, her text exemplifies the ways in which women's life stories potentially collude with what some might view as neocolonialism. At heart, the issue is not about

Hayslip's specific agenda, Vietnam War representation, or even about the status of the subject of autobiography but about rhetoric and the multiple political uses that experiential narratives authorized by claims of alterity can serve in their appeal to the real.

In "Third-World Literature in the Era of Multinational Capitalism," Fredric Jameson notes that the primary distinction between First and Third World literatures concerns their social investment. In regard to the Western realist and modernist novel, he notes that "political commitment is reconstructed and psychologized or subjectified by way of the public-private split" (Jameson 1986, 71). In contrast, in the literature of the Third World individual psychic and libidinal structures are always located within and determined in part by economic and political relationships. Thus, "the story of the private individual destiny is always an allegory of the embattled situation of the public third-world culture and society" (69). While Jameson's is an admittedly sweeping generalization, what is significant is not so much the distinction he draws between First and Third World literatures, but his emphasis on the social function of art as it is connected to the nationalist critique embedded in allegory.[5] Written by an American immigrant from Vietnam, a text such as Hayslip's clearly blurs the distinction between First and Third World literature but marks its function as committed art through its activist intent. Recounting the repatriation of a daughter in exile, *When Heaven and Earth Changed Places* is textual performance, a staging of the suffering undergone by a faceless and voiceless peasantry made human for an American audience. It succeeds in this most graphically by embodying women's sexual trauma in the figure of Le Ly. Following Western autobiographical convention, Hayslip's is a conversion narrative, an expiation of a "traitor's" guilt also intended to expiate the guilt of American agents of war. But however privatized and individual the origins of its form, as with ethnic autobiography in general the text is continually aware of its collective function. It self-consciously takes on the burden of representing a people through a singular life and the duty implied by Frantz Fanon's comment, "I was responsible at the same time for my body, for my race, for my ancestors" (Fanon 1991, 112). Hayslip's insistence on the activist role of autobiography would seem to reflect what Jameson notes as a general characteristic of Third World literature: its investment in a social, political world. Moreover, the narrative invites the reader to interpret its social critique through the allegorical relationship between the Vietnamese civil war and the conflicts in Le Ly's family.

Following American involvement in support of the Republican army, Hayslip reveals that the Viet Cong constructed this new American enemy,

like the Chinese, French, and Moroccans before them, as a threat to a
Vietnamese national family:

> Americans come to kill our people,
> Follow America, and kill your relatives!
> The smart bird flies before it's caught.
> The smart person comes home before Tet.
> Follow us, and you'll always have a family.
> Follow America, and you'll always be alone! (x)

"A nation cannot have *two* governments," the Viet Cong cadremen an-
nounce, "anymore [sic] than a family can have two fathers" (x). Yet Hayslip's narrative employs this same national-familial metaphor to support
its own underlying ideological purposes. As a child living in a central
village, Le Ly has loyalties to both the North and South by virtue of familial relationships to her brothers Bon Nghe, a member of the NVA, and
Sau Ban, who joins the Viet Cong to escape the Republican draft; and to
her sisters, who are aligned with the opposing side—Ba, married to a
Republican policeman, and Lan, a bargirl making her living off the
United State's military presence. The ease with which other village children switch roles in playing war games—the Viet Cong versus the Republicans—is complicated for Le Ly because whichever side she takes, the
enemy is still family. As sides are drawn over Le Ly's decision to marry an
American, the gulf between family members becomes metaphoric of a
national division:

> Although Vietnamese are raised to respect their ancestors and love their nation,
> they are not above civil war. In the triangle formed by our family's sad situa-
> tion—Lan's contest with me for our mother's affection, our struggle against the
> tide of a changing society, and our different feelings about Americans—I could
> almost see a fishpond version of the Viet Cong war itself. If I could not make
> peace with my family in such matters, how could the real fighters on both sides
> expect to resolve their differences? (349)

Yet what are the ideological implications of this national allegory?
While the danger in reading allegorically is the reduction of complex interactions to a system of simple equivalences, *When Heaven and Earth
Changed Places* suggests a more fluid set of relationships in which Le Ly
and her family alternately represent the political situation in Vietnam.
The gendered body operates within the context of two divisions: within
a family emblematic of a North/South split, and as the site where United
States/Hanoi differences are played out. In either instance, the text deploys feminine sexuality as the conduit through which the familial-as-
national conflicts are defined.

This relationship reflects the work of various international feminist scholars who note the ways in which representations of women and women's concerns become harnessed to the goals of nationalism.[6] As Cynthia Enloe points out, the connection between women and nationalism is often predicated on positioning women as needing protection from corrupting and exploitative outside influences rather than as "active creators of the nation's newly assertive politics" (Enloe 1990, 54). Her comment suggests that women's relationship to nation is most often expressed in ways that deny women's agency, indicating perhaps the activist limitations to nationalist appeals based on simple conceptions of feminine national embodiment. Hayslip's text exploits a somewhat different connection: as that which does not belong to women, feminine sexuality functions as a vehicle through which allegiance is read. Generally, it could be said that the feminine libidinal exists in a dialectical relationship to the public/private split: women's sexuality and desire have always been subject to the regulation of a phallocentric commodity structure. Gayle Rubin discusses this regulation through her concept of a sex/gender system that locates women's oppression within systems of kinship that define them as objects of exchange among men (Rubin 1975). Her description of this "traffic in women" that underlies the social fabric parallels Luce Irigaray's definition of the "specularization" of the feminine body—how it is transformed into a value-bearing object whose meaning exceeds its natural properties (Irigaray 1985, 180). For women, they suggest, desire is not a matter of individual agency, of an autonomous desiring subject. In *When Heaven and Earth Changed Places*, this "public" nature of feminine sexuality is manifested on several levels, particularly in regard to the way that the body becomes a determiner of national loyalty rather than an expression of individual desire. The political division in Le Ly's family is gendered; like Le Ly herself, her sisters are aligned with the South through their sexual liaisons in contrast to her brothers' allegiance to Hanoi signified by their military induction. Lan, a bargirl in Danang, supplements her job by "earn[ing] gifts" from American soldiers "just from lying on [her] back" (190). Yet Lan's "business" signifies more than a livelihood or even a repudiation of traditional values. Her involvement with American men is perceived to establish her loyalty to lover over father and as such represents a betrayal of fatherland:

> my sister . . . felt torn between honoring her father, as she had been raised to do and pleasing "her man," which was what the American expected. In the end, she told my father to wait and took her American into the bedroom—which was actually no more than a small area of the studio bounded by a curtain—and did what she had to do to please him. . . . There were too many differences,

she said, between the ways of the city and our father's to uphold the traditions. (170)

Lan's choice to "please her man" over her father becomes a means of locating her positioning as a counter to the traditional emphasis on filiation for which the Viet Cong purports to fight. The potential for being denounced as "she who sells herself to the American empire" (*Child* 123) signals a thematic thread woven throughout Hayslip's representation of her life experience: a Vietnamese woman's political loyalties in the war zone are to be determined through her sexuality rather than (or in spite of) an overt declaration of affiliation.

This equivalence between sexual and cultural allegiance carries significant costs; the price of a Third World woman's alliance with a foreigner is often estrangement from family and banishment from nation. Unlike her brothers, Le Ly lacks the opportunity to define her politics by joining the army of either side. Initially, as with the other children and adolescents in the village, her feats of minor thievery and stints at guard duty for the Viet Cong mark her affiliation as a matter of her own choice. But after her loyalty is made suspect and rape by two cadremen is her punishment, she begins to question not the merits of either position but the circumstances of war that draw boundaries and set criteria for loyalty. Yet her rape is also paradoxically figured as a reincorporation into and alliance with a powerless and manipulated peasantry:

> Both sides in this terrible, endless, *stupid* war had finally found the perfect enemy: a terrified peasant girl who would endlessly and stupidly consent to be their victim—as all Vietnam's peasants had consented to be victims, from creation to the end of time! From now on, I promised myself, I would only flow with the strongest current and drift with the steadiest wind—and not resist. To resist, you have to believe in something. (97)

The rape ruptures her sense of Vietnamese nationalism. No longer a virgin, she feels disqualified from fulfilling a traditional gender role that would define her alliance; like a soldier's, this is her blood sacrifice. The pacifism reflected in Le Ly's thoughts, the condemnation not of a people, an ideology, or a nation but of the structure of war, works to further the text's statement of neutrality on which Hayslip's appeal for humanitarian aid depends. Yet the passage contains a contradiction that belies this pledge of nonallegiance: victimization, she suggests, results from the people's consent, from their choosing sides. By relinquishing their agency, the Vietnamese break free from their exploitation. Yet Le Ly's refusal to choose, her decision to "flow with the strongest current" as a free agent, is itself a choice. The passage characterizes Hayslip's dual and contradictory portrayals of Le Ly as subject; she acknowledges the influence of uncontrollable external social forces that renders moot her own agency, her choices to ally herself with either the Republicans or the Viet Cong, but ultimately claims complete responsibility for her life. Such rhetorical moves simultaneously celebrate women's strength and self-direction at the same time that they refuse to assign accountability to history, nations, or the actions of individuals.

Le Ly's feeling of disqualification from a traditional gender role culminates in her decision to barter that which has already been taken from her, a decision that is ironically portrayed as a moment of embodied nationalism. The metaphors Hayslip employs to describe Le Ly's single act of prostitution draw a similar parallel between her body and Vietnam; like Vietnam, she "took seed from the invaders" in what was an American soldier's "final, nonlethal explosion" (260). Because her body's exploitation links her to her homeland, rather than an act of dishonor that services the desires of the invaders, Le Ly's prostitution is simultaneously constituted as a moment of national allegiance and the death of Le Ly's national identity. Prior to the act, she forces herself to "disregard everything I had learned from my family about honor, self-respect, VD, pregnancy, rape, [and] making love for love" (259). Just as her previous rape by the Viet Cong is described as a symbolic burial that links her to the earth, so too does her prostitution leave behind "the corpse" of her father's daughter. The act both binds her to and exiles her from Vietnam—her acceptance of the "American flags," or roll of twenty dollar bills, becomes a symbolic as well as literal exchange. Her sexual "choice" is portrayed as both a determiner of national identity representative of Vietnamese feminine strength and a betrayal of that identity.

Hayslip's representation thus counters what for others is a decisive indication of Le Ly's capitulation to the "capitalist running dogs" the war was meant to expel. Yet the exchange of her body for the safety American economic superiority can buy is constructed as the most logical way to assure her own survival. Her youth and apparent farm girl innocence become marketing advantages among the American men looking for "sweet, attractive, local girls" as companions. As attachments to American men are seen to be "an easy way out" (295), she risks her hopes on several "boyfriends" who end up abusing her: a navy medical technician pressures her to become a topless dancer, an Amerasian helicopter mechanic ends up trying to strangle her, and a Texan air force officer secretively ships out while living with her. Ironically, these men continue to represent her "ultimate goal of finding peace and safety" (326). After she accepts the "lifeboat of America" in the form of a marriage proposal from a civilian contractor from San Diego, Le Ly's guilt over what she experiences as her nationalist betrayal becomes externalized. As "Mrs. Ed Munro," she notes that

> I was no longer completely Vietnamese, but I was not quite American either. Apparently, I was something much worse. Even people I had expected to understand me, to be sympathetic to my dreams, looked down on me and called me names—not always to my back: *Di lay My! Theo de Quoc Ve My! Gai choi boi!* Bitch! Traitor! American whore! . . . No citizen of Danang was so poor or humble that he or she was not superior to Le Ly *Munro*—turncoat to her country. (353)

The narrative initially marks the space of "peace and safety" as American, yet Hayslip's pacifist message condemning not a specific side but war itself would only be convincing if tied to a position of neutrality. Hayslip reconciles this contradiction by refiguring "peace and safety" as a transnational space above the divisions created by war, thus positing her American marriage as the fulfillment of a Vietnamese daughter's duty.

The text achieves this shift through the strategic deployment of an essential feminine pacifism. The events of *When Heaven and Earth Changed Places* are ordered within a novelistic plot that provides conflict, denouement, and resolution. The challenge in Le Ly's return to Vietnam is to restore the position she has lost in the family through a marriage that represents an abandonment of family and country in crisis. Her uncertainty generates narrative suspense—how will her family and the Hanoi government receive the "American tourist," "capitalist stranger," and traitor to both her Phung Thi ancestors and Vietnam? The parallel between the national and the personal here is obvious: if her family has the capacity to forgive her repudiation of ancestral duty and her association with the enemy, then old political grudges and rifts can also be healed as the family, united by the "blood tie of birth" and "the blood bond of battle," recognize their shared past (*Child* 32).

The narrative achieves this reconciliation through the invocation of Le Ly's father as a sort of feminist patriarch and spiritual guide. Exhorting her to "choose life," a philosophy ironically belied by his own suicide, her father tells her, "Bay Ly, you were born to be a wife and mother, not a killer. That is your duty. . . . Go back to your little son. Raise him the best way you can. That is the battle you were born to fight. That is the victory you must win" (201). Throughout the narrative, her father's voice returns to remind her that, contrary to the ancestral myths about warrior women, her role is to nurture life. Thus even the writing of the book appears as the realization of the dictates of Vietnamese filiation:

> Your job is to stay alive—to keep an eye on things and keep the village safe. To find a husband and have babies and *tell the story of what you've seen to your*

children and anyone else who'll listen. Most of all, it is to live in peace and tend the shrine of our ancestors. Do these things well, Bay Ly, and you will be worth more than any soldier who ever took up a sword. (33, emphasis mine)

The role of nurturer is seen to bridge national divisions, recasting not only her unpatriotic and unfilial choices but justifying the "mission" of the book itself and later, that of the East Meets West Foundation. Le Ly's sexual infractions, those that she attributes to "bad karma" with men and those that result from her own agency, are thus portrayed as committed in the service of her ancestral duty. The jobs she takes that open her to sexual harassment, her act of prostitution, her involvement with a series of American lovers, and her eventual willingness to become "a good oriental wife" to an older man are all choices she makes justified by her need to provide a life for her son.

In the sequel, her father's spirit returns at strategic moments with increasingly specific advice ("Build a center, Bay Ly" [*Child* 261]). Hayslip's pacifist spirituality is also gendered female: "Such atrocities as I had witnessed in both countries could only be perpetrated by men with no awareness of the sacred origins of life. They considered children—even their own—as no more than weeds in a garden" (*Child* 174). Hayslip's appeal to an essential woman's knowledge located in the capacity to give birth grants her the authority to critique war as merely an "athletic field for showing patriotic prowess" and "a factory for building bad karma" (*Child* 266). Such an argument necessarily draws on women's relationship to the sentimental; in the context of the Vietnam War it also evokes potent connections between civilians and innocence: the horror of My Lai lies not in the actual death toll but in the massacre of women and children. Refashioning herself from sexual opportunist to maternally asexual nurturer, Hayslip posits her Americanization not as oppositional to her Vietnamese duty but paradoxically as its fulfillment. This rhetorical construction reveals the supposedly neutral maternal positioning to have a clear investment in international politics in addition to sustaining and reproducing naturalized conceptions of feminine difference.[7] Read allegorically, both autobiographies suggest that assuming a position of feminine nurturing transcendent of political affiliation indicates a true Vietnamese nationalism. The sequel takes this equation further by generalizing this caretaking duty as the rebuilding of Vietnam through humanitarian aid and economic investment and representing such a duty as a karma-building spiritual quest. In light of such a portrayal, it could be said that Hayslip's own karmic capital was substantially increased with the opening of a medical clinic in Vietnam called, appropriately, "Mother's Love."

The connection between this realization of the book's overt agenda, soliciting American financing of a clinic, and the text's ideological cast is thus fairly uncomplicated: "Mother's Love" is evidence of forgiveness. It is perhaps more difficult to speculate on the larger economic implications of this readjustment in the American collective perception of Vietnam. While it may be an overstatement to connect publicity over Hayslip's life story to the shift in U.S. foreign policy directly, it clearly contributes to and benefits from the rhetoric of healing that dominates current discourse on the war. And underlying the message of forgiveness in *When Heaven and Earth Changed Places* is a validation of Western technology and a call for increased intervention in a country that was subject to U.S. embargo and resistant to entering the capitalist fold.

This is clearly not a neutral position. And at the time of the text's writing, Hayslip was no longer the prodigal daughter returning to a country she seemed to have forsaken; rather, as an ambassador with a message of peace and reconciliation, her own position is decidedly maternal. As the American head of a nongovernmental organization, Hayslip no longer asks for Hanoi's forgiveness, she is in a position to bestow it. This shift is marked in the differences between *When Heaven and Earth Changed Places* and *Child of War, Woman of Peace*; in contrast to the former's emphasis on the personal and its depiction of her own tenuous reintegration into family as the return of the repressed, the sequel poses direct questions about who will step in as "savior" to Vietnam within the global family. Yet for the most part Hayslip's own political commentary remains on the level of extolling decent human interaction and the strength of family bonds as a means of forging alliances. Direct international political analysis is represented in the text as the dialogue between various government officials whose policies she will either approve or challenge. For example, assessment of the role of the World Bank in the economic recovery of Vietnam is conveyed through the commentary of a Soviet official, who tells her that the United States "not only refuses to help, it actively stands in the way of nations who want to try. It prevents the World Bank from making loans to the Vietnamese and discourages allied nations from trading with their old enemy." "Perhaps you can do something as an American citizen," he suggests, "to get your government to reconsider its policy" (*Child* 303). Because the appearance of impartiality is a necessary ingredient for trust in her humanitarian organization, these views are not expressed as her own; she merely validates their sincerity.[8]

Still, in addition to what in both texts are occasionally very clear signals of her belief in the superiority of the capitalist system ("How much would that old man and his teenage assistant give to trade places with me for even a day . . . to enjoy a taste of life in America?" 100), her "caught in the middle" stance is most directly belied by her thoughts upon viewing Ho Chi Minh's body preserved under glass in Hanoi. In what is the strongest passage indicating American bias in either text, she notes,

> Mothers like my own willingly sacrificed their sons to secure his vision of an independent Vietnam. It made little difference that his brand of "independence" brought a totalitarian system that could not feed and care for its own people. (*Child* 326)

Like her reflections upon seeing the Vietnam War Memorial in Washington, D.C., her thoughts on the unnecessary sacrifices of the dead lead her to invoke maternality as a means of authorizing her critique. Hayslip implicitly contrasts the sacrifice of Vietnamese mothers with "Uncle Ho's" failure to provide for his children. In doing so, her invocation of women as biological reproducers of nation mirrors a gender representation often exploited by nationalist causes (Yuval-Davis, 1997) but toward very different ends: her commentary is neither an anti-imperialist nor a neocolonialist indictment. Moreover, her denunciation of totalitarianism is consistent with her American-influenced rhetorical logic—the comment emphasizes the parents' responsibility to the children, a view inconsistent with Buddhist emphasis on ancestor worship.

Yet in spite of what I note as Hayslip's pro-American bias, the general reception of *When Heaven and Earth Changed Places* was divided in a way that fully substantiated one of its most salient themes, that she could please neither side. When the book was published, Hayslip's message of openness toward Vietnam was taken as a validation of its communist government; she was not only criticized by other Vietnamese exiles but received death threats from within the community, hate mail from veterans, and visits from the FBI. While one reviewer praised her "mature forgiving perspective," another found "the absence of judgment . . . in itself almost shocking."[9] While Hayslip's life story has dovetailed with and potentially influenced shifting American sentiment toward Vietnam, such a shift has not taken place without controversy. Thus throughout both texts Hayslip continually reiterates her neutral positioning. The East Meets West Foundation's publicity brochure presents its intentions straightforwardly: "The mission of East Meets West is to improve the general health, welfare, and socioeconomic condition of the people of Vietnam, and to provide a solid base for the self-sufficiency of our programs, as well as the individuals they serve. . . . Eventually, all the programs will be entirely run by Vietnamese."

Beyond this indication of the desirability of self-sufficiency and her belief in the potential of improving the lives of the Vietnamese people, Hayslip's work does not speculate on the implications of the increased involvement of a capitalist core nation like the United States on Vietnam's economic future or its post–Cold War commitment to a socialism purchased, as she herself shows, at such a cost. Economist Gary Gereffi reveals that Vietnam is already implicated in capitalist world system export networks particularly through the practice of "triangular manufacturing," the farming out of First World production orders from East Asian newly industrialized countries such as Hong Kong, Taiwan, South Korea, and Singapore to low-wage countries like Vietnam (Gereffi 1994, 114). Similarly, as Appelbaum, Smith, and Christerson note, "By the early 1990s manufacturers in the garment business in the United States, Hong Kong, and South Korea made clear that such far-flung sites as Vietnam, Guatemala, Burma, North Korea, and Mongolia were either targets of planned investment in export-oriented garment factories or had already gone on-line" (Appelbaum et al., 1994, 190). In 1997, two-year-old Nike factories in Vietnam were already being called into account for violations of workers' rights and refusal to pay a living wage.[10]

In addition to viewing the Vietnamese as a low-wage labor pool, American businesses are also looking upon them as potential consumers of U.S. goods: hours after the trade embargo was lifted, PepsiCo reportedly erected a giant inflatable soda can in the middle of Ho Chi Minh City and distributed forty thousand free bottles of Pepsi. "We wanted to make a statement," says Ken Ross, a PepsiCo vice president. "We wanted to tell Vietnam that we're open for business" (cited in Tom Post, "The War—To Cash In," *Newsweek*, 14 February 1994, 33). Such indications of American "forgiveness" on its own terms lend an eerie sense of prophecy to Hayslip's general comment, "Having outlasted a faltering America in an ungodly war of attrition, the Hanoi government found itself no match for America in peace" (*Child* 244). Given the effects of 1990s economic liberalization, the *New York Times* pronounced that in reverse of 1975 expectations, in fact, "Hanoi has become Saigon."[11]

Any evaluation of the significance of this "match" on different turf centers on the question, Who benefits? Will the lifting of the trade embargo, part of Hayslip's veiled agenda and the economic liberalization it augurs, result in a higher standard of living "for the common people"? Or, if Vietnam enters a world system dominated by core nations like the United States, will economic dependency come to undermine the very sovereignty for which the war was fought? *When Heaven and Earth Changed Places* does not skirt the issue of foreign imperialism—it questions U.S. military involvement in Vietnam and counters it with an appeal for forgiveness, emphasizing the United States's *human* responsibility to Vietnam now that the war is over. However, Hayslip's carefully strategic neutrality and use of the book as a charitable vehicle serve to mask another arena through which American imperial dominance is assured—not the overt control signaled by the presence of troops but the economic arena enabled by the opening of Vietnam to increased Western investment.

While Hayslip's message of forgiveness encourages U.S. involvement in Vietnam, it enacts similar ideological work within a domestic sphere. Consistent with the aims of ethnic American autobiography, her texts perform the experience of America's Other in order to contest, confirm, or otherwise define American national identity. Within the context of liberal multiculturalism, narratives detailing the Asian experience in the United States have served to challenge a narrow definition of America based on exclusion, while at the same time they may confirm its pluralist self-image. *When Heaven and Earth Changed Places* and *Child of War, Woman of Peace* engage this dual agenda while operating within the multiple discourses defined by Vietnam War representation, Third World women's *testimonio*, and Asian American autobiography. However, Hayslip's texts ultimately further a conservative multicultural agenda by reconciling Le Ly's racial, gender, and religious alterity with American liberalism.

John Carlos Rowe has pointed out that seemingly marginal accounts of the war produced by female nurses, black soldiers, and activist veterans have been incorporated into American popular consciousness in a way that co-opts their countercultural dissent. While "war at home" narratives can appear as "invariably liberal, leftist, or otherwise minority-oriented," he notes that their potential for radical commentary is contained by their recasting a "war of imperialist aggression into one of domestic conflict" (Rowe 1989, 208). As a point of evidence, Rowe cites the 1985 CBS documentary *The Vietnam War* in which no Vietnamese appear; they are replaced by exploited American soldiers of color. While Hayslip's work does not allow for this type of easy displacement, it problematizes Rowe's assumption that the presence of the Vietnamese subject is enough to ensure that a critique of American imperialism not be displaced. The ideological cast of *When Heaven and Earth Changed Places* and *Child of War, Woman of Peace* renders them more in concert with Asian American autobiographies of the previous generation than personal accounts of disenfranchised Vietnam veterans. In their representation of the individual overcoming adversity to settle in a place of refuge, both texts mirror and affirm mythic American values of opportunity, freedom, and class mobility. Le Ly is the prototypical immigrant heroine, fleeing her country to seek sanctuary and a second beginning in a new land. She not only survives but, as indicated by her "painted fingernails, and hygienist-cleaned teeth and four-bedroom home in California" (193), finds financial success; in *Child of War, Woman of Peace*, she discovers that her investments have made her a millionaire on paper. The implications of such a validation in the context of minority autobiography are obvious; what is less obvious is the way in which Hayslip is able to reconcile Le Ly's difference from the white, Christian, male norm with the precepts and beliefs of her adopted homeland.

Le Ly's Buddhism thus initially appears as a sharp contrast to the capitalist values she confronts upon her immigration. While her subsequent activism initially threatens the wealth she has earned, the dual missions of helping her homeland and investing her money are represented as parallel rather than oppositional aims: astrologers, gurus, and monks offer concurrent advice on her spiritual and financial well-being. Her comment on "fueling" her spiritual/activist desire forces Buddhism and American consumerism into odd harmony: "Souls are hungry. If the car is empty, you go for the gas" (cited in Karen Evans, "Epilogue: Le Ly Hayslip's American Life," *Los Angeles Times Magazine*, 5 February 1989, 9, 11, 15, 38–39). More significantly, Hayslip's rhetorical construction of her Buddhist-motivated activism ironically seems to adopt the terms of Christian prophecy. Le Ly's humanitarian mission takes the form of a jeremiad reflective of the rhetoric of Puritan America. Sacvan Bercovitch notes that this Puritan "political sermon" sustains and grants cohesion to a nationalism based in the belief of an American "errand in the wilderness."[12] She is chosen, a swami who looks like Jesus if "Jesus had been a surfer" tells her, to fulfill the mission of an ancient spiritual healer: "He says his connection to you goes back much further than your parents. And this is not the first time he has communicated with you. You have been visited by him in prior lives. He says that you will discover his identity only after you have accomplished your mission in life" (*Child* 218). Le Ly is thus portrayed as a prophet of another American "errand" extending back to Vietnam. Hers is a spiritual quest in which the individual struggles to influence the birthright of the collective: she is, the gurus of southern California inform her, "to lead a crowd in a long, hard climb. [She is] to practice the healing arts but not as a doctor, medicine man, or nun" (*Child* 219). Again, this is also a maternal jeremiad; like "a mother's hard labor," the writing of the book is characterized as a painful delivery sustained only by her conviction that she has "a million lost souls" behind her (*Child* 209).

If Hayslip's religious alterity can be portrayed as consistent with an American belief in an individual-as-collective destiny, her use of gender alterity authorizes this destiny. As I have suggested, gender provides the vantage point for her denunciation of the aggressive behaviors that support the military-industrial complex, a denunciation that would appear to be a clear counter to the masculinist war narratives that Susan Jeffords reveals justify domination on multiple levels: "war *is* the spectacle of the

masculine bond," she notes. "It is the optimal display of masculine collectivity in America" (Jeffords 1989, 25). Hayslip's work would seem to
prove an exception, an alternative to the hypermasculine accounts of the
war. Yet at one level her texts do not disprove Jeffords's general thesis;
while they may confound the pattern of masculine bonding that Jeffords
characterizes as endemic to Vietnam War representation, they merely reverse its terms, leaving patriarchal logic intact. If war is based on a masculine belief in things worth dying for, Hayslip counters with a peace
grounded in a feminine commitment to things worth living for.[13] Her text
dramatizes the way in which realism depends on an appeal to normative
conceptions of gender, specifically those that appear to be imbued with
moral value.[14]

Lynda Boose notes that Vietnam War counternarrative may be "feminized" when juxtaposed to a "masculinist" military policy located in the
"mythology of a national self born in and valorized by a history of conquest and dominance" (Boose 1993, 585). Hayslip's gendered pacifism
thus meshes with a genre of politically invested narrative already marked
as feminine. Yet such a pacifism loses its oppositional quality as imperialist critique if conjoined with a tone of absolution: Hayslip's texts refuse
to assign blame to the extent that the war appears to be perpetrated by
individuals who have little control over their own actions. Hence
throughout both texts she characterizes men, her rapists and john included, as "sad little boys." Rather than functioning as a radically oppositional discourse, Hayslip's deployment of feminine difference ends up
supporting American interests by refusing to hold either side accountable
for the war. Military aggression appears as a form of masculine childish-
ness; war and suffering occur, her texts seem to suggest, as a result of bad
karma.

Signaled early in the prologue's statement to GIs, "It was not your
fault," Hayslip's emphasis on American absolution is portrayed as the
logical outcome of a Buddhist-inflected personal philosophy derived from
a series of abusive relationships with men. After being abandoned by an
American for the third time, she reflects,

> I had risked my feelings on Paul—staked my happiness on his honesty. Now
> that it had fallen through, who had I to blame for my disappointment but
> myself? . . . If I could forgive Anh for abandoning me with a baby, Red for
> changing me around to suit his tastes, and Jim for almost killing me, how could
> I be less charitable to Paul, who had left me with nothing worse than pretty
> memories? . . . I decided I should draw the strength of compassion, not the
> weakness of bitterness, from this most important lesson—from the lessons I
> had learned from every American that fate or luck or god had sent to be my
> teacher. Even at their worst, each one had given me something which, to that

time, I had lacked in my life. I understood the choices I had made—and the things that resulted from them. What happened had been as much my doing as theirs. For a Vietnamese woman, realizing this was like emancipation to a slave. Hating people who had wronged me only kept me in their power. Forgiving them and thanking them for the lesson they had taught me, on the other hand, set me free to continue on my way. (325–26)

What is extraordinary about the evolution of her thinking is that it can both be lauded as praiseworthy—an indication, perhaps, of what *Playboy* saw as maturity—and dismissed as simple foolishness. Her evaluation that these sexually exploitative relationships produced positive results is based on the hindsight of her current activities: they put her on the path to the present moment. Empowerment, she suggests, lies in claiming women's agency, a recognition that is not incongruent with contemporary feminist thinking. The self-reliant attitude expressed here culminates in the narrative's final tone of triumphalism tempered by humbleness ("Do not feel sorry for me—I made it; I am okay" [366]). Nevertheless, what is most startling about this passage is not necessarily the capacity for compassion it expresses but, again, her unwillingness to assign accountability for male perfidy or abuse. While this refusal may well be rationalized as a purely individual and spiritual response, it also strategically authorizes the text's use of individual experience as a foundation for international diplomacy: nations, like individuals, must forgive in order to free themselves.

While feminists debate whether theories of feminine difference are necessary to feminist praxis or ultimately come at the expense of women, my concern is not to locate Hayslip's work within these debates but to note how her gendered (and, following passages such as this one, what some might characterize as antifeminist) rhetoric furthers a larger agenda.[15] However, I also want to point out that the events depicted in *When Heaven and Earth Changed Places* contribute to Third World feminism by problematizing any universal concept of feminist resistance. I have suggested that Gayle Rubin's and Luce Irigaray's Marxist-influenced theories are applicable to a text such as Hayslip's that describes women's circumscription within a sex/gender system. Yet both Rubin and Irigaray speak of feminist resistance in terms of women claiming their sexual pleasure and denying patriarchal systems such as marriage and heterosexuality that encode it. In contrast, Hayslip's work makes clear that Le Ly's resistance does not depend on the denial of these systems but on her ability to recognize and exploit them materially. As sex literally becomes a commodity bartered for survival, in controlling her sexual commodification Le Ly asserts the primacy of her own agency in her distribution. Trading on what she offers as a companion—youth, sexual service, and the allure of the Orient—is a self-conscious decision that is meant to signal her refusal to be victimized. Such an emphasis on Le Ly's agency marks a significant intervention in discourses that, in their portrayal of Asian women's bodies as simple sites of colonization, view them as nothing more than victims of Third and First World political economies or as national metaphors rather than agents of global intervention.

While Hayslip's work does not offer unequivocal evidence of feminist identity, it does indicate the necessity for developing a concept of complex agency in regard to Third World women, one that would, as Lata Mani notes, "simultaneously engage women's systematic subordination and the ways in which women negotiate oppressive, even determining social conditions" (Mani 1989, 21). This vigilance certainly applies in cases where the biases of Western feminists might intrude on an understanding of women's self-defined contributions to nation, particularly in the case of Hayslip, where these contributions are asserted through traditional associations between motherhood and national duty. As Cynthia Enloe writes, "Women in many communities trying to assert their sense of national identity find that coming into an emergent nationalist movement *through* the accepted feminine roles of bearer of the community's memory and children is empowering" (Enloe 1990, 55).[16] *When Heaven and Earth Changed Places* centers on Le Ly's ability to use her sexuality without feeling that she has compromised either her Vietnamese or feminine sense of self. By foregrounding the Asian female subject's intervention in constructing identity within the constraints imposed by nationalisms, gender, and partisan politics, the text reveals that in the process of cultural mediation Third World women are not simply co-opted by the gender role nor do they reveal a clear-cut repudiation of it.

When Heaven and Earth Changed Places suggests that there is something irreducible about rape, torture, and outcasting. Whatever claim one could make about the way the text functions ideologically, it succeeds in articulating the horrors of war from a peasant girl's point of view. This is why Oliver Stone's film, *Heaven and Earth*, can still be compelling as a positive contribution to a discourse that has ironically ignored Vietnamese presence in Vietnam; its initial focus on Le Ly as subject distances it from prior representations of the Vietnamese as voiceless, fleeing peasants, although it may also admittedly aestheticize and subordinate them to a lush, panoramic landscape. Such an embodiment as an appeal to realism is certainly efficacious in publicizing political causes: Rigoberta Menchú is a case in point. However, as Monique T. D. Tru'o'ng has noted, Hayslip's story has been reframed and reduced to fit an American revisionist view of the war in order to provide "the film equivalent of group therapy" (Tru'o'ng 1997, 237). More significant to my discussion of rhetoric here, Stone's interpretation of Hayslip's life jettisons the auto-biography's narrative structure, which centers on Le Ly's reconciliation of her supposed national betrayal in favor of both a simple chronology of events and the all too familiar American male savior/Asian female saved narrative of *Madame Butterfly* ("Steve, you Le Ly hero. You protect Le Ly"). In Stone's film, as likewise reflected in *The World of Suzie Wong*, *The Good Woman of Bangkok*, or *Miss Saigon*, what is being replayed—albeit with Japan substituted for Hong Kong, substituted for Thailand, substituted for Vietnam—is a durable narrative about the Orient that op-erates at the nexus of discourses on nationalism, colonialism, race, and gender. However much the film intervenes by recasting *Madame But-terfly*'s ending—the disintegration of the American vet contrasted to the triumphant Vietnamese woman's homecoming—it nonetheless reaffirms the dominant representation of Asian women in American film as noble whores finding salvation in white men who turn out to be the more angst-ridden, psychologically complex subjects. One can argue whether or not the film version of Hayslip's life refashions the fleshless allegorical figure of Madame Butterfly into an agent confronted with complex cultural choices or whether it works to confirm an Orientalist fantasy already embedded within an American popular consciousness.

The question of Stone's co-optation of Hayslip's life story raises the question of coauthorship: Is the white male American "veteran"[17] re-sponsible for the text's pro-American bias? Students of mine have posed the question another way, no less effectively: Who the hell is Jay Wurts? At the end of the text, Wurts is identified as a former Vietnam War Air Guard pilot but otherwise his participation as coauthor goes unre-marked. As Joseph Trimmer has noted, Wurts was responsible for much of the narrative crafting of what was initially a three-hundred-page man-uscript typed (and presumably partly edited and translated into English) by Hayslip's son, James (Trimmer 1994). By Trimmer's account, it was an active collaboration; Hayslip never relinquished control over the text or indulged Wurts's license as a storyteller.[18] Shirley Lim has raised the question of coauthorship compromising Asian American women's writ-ing (personal communication, December 1992); her doubts are similar to those raised historically in regard to other writers of color who have col-laborated with white editors and coauthors, most notably the abolitionist writings of former slaves suspected of being manipulated (if not actually solely authored) by white abolitionists. Lim's is a valid concern, particu-larly in regard to an autobiography such as *When Heaven and Earth Changed Places*, whose cultural capital is dependent on Hayslip's status as an authentic informant, in other words, on her embodying alterity. Nevertheless, this anxiety about collaboration arises from assuming a simple equivalence between subject positioning and ideological bias.

Overdetermining the mediation of a coauthor would seem to counter the
evolution of the text's philosophy and the fact that Hayslip consistently
takes pains to inscribe Le Ly as an active agent who refuses to give her life
over to the control of others; an overdetermination of Wurts's influence
positions Hayslip as merely an ethnographic dupe.

Understanding the nature of textual bias seems more crucial than an
attempt to ascertain the text's authentic or inauthentic parts based on
their source—the "real" Asian woman or white American vet. Without
definitively attributing the narrative structure to either Wurts or Hayslip,
I argue that the text's political bias is nonetheless intrinsically tied to this
structure; in chronicling her transformation from Viet Cong peasant girl
to American "tourist," the narrative moves to reconcile Le Ly's apparent
sexual transgressions by portraying them as a means of fulfilling expectations of women's nurturing. By characterizing a betrayal of country as the
fulfillment of her traditionally intended role, the narrative attempts to
reinscribe Americanization as that which paradoxically allows Le Ly's
adherence to her duty as a daughter of Vietnam. Wurts's influence has not
heretofore been a subject of great controversy, nor has Hayslip's veracity
been subject to the kind of scrutiny that Rigoberta Menchú's autobiography has undergone.[19] This might be attributed to the fact that while both
connect individual life stories to political change, Hayslip's narrative renders her ideological agenda much less overtly than Menchú's; her bias
may not be contested precisely because the narrative positions Le Ly
above politics. Hayslip's apparent openness and willingness to document
all no doubt contributes to this positioning: on one of her return trips to
Vietnam, she and her sons are accompanied by an American news crew
that asks her to show the exact spot where she was raped by Viet Cong
soldiers—and she does. It is as if in promoting the agenda of her foundation she acknowledges the need for hyper-realism (and the voyeurism on
which it depends) to validate her personal story.

To view Hayslip's work simply within the context of the bicultural
subject's identity formation in keeping with a singular focus on Asian
American immigrant literature would displace the impact of its circulation in a global context. The autobiographies do represent an intervention in a body of work dominated by second-generation Chinese and Japanese Americans; it is a Southeast Asian immigrant's reminder that
American intervention in the Third World is often the impetus for such
immigration. As Hayslip's life story testifies, "multiculturalism" is not
only concerned with internal dynamics of racial representation but with
the ways in which American beliefs and values can intersect with international interests. Analysis of this intersection provides a caution about the
ways in which alterity—in this case, that of a Buddhist Vietnamese
woman—can authorize American ideology while appearing to either

counter or remain neutral to it. The texts reinscribe one whose difference is literally marked—she is "our" enemy—into someone who is *like us*, compassionate, forgiving, and tired of war. The texts enact the work of liberal multiculturalism in their incorporation of racial and national differences into a harmonious, pluralist whole through the processes of differentiation and identification. The assertion of marginal identity is thus not a substitute for political affiliation, a point often assumed in early discussions of multiculturalism.

It may be unfair to ascribe to Hayslip's activism greater motives than she herself would claim. While I point out that her rhetoric may intersect with interests she may not have foreseen, I do not question the immediate contributions of the East Meets West Foundation to improving health care in Vietnam. The first edition of *When Heaven and Earth Changed Places* reveals that Hayslip was not a professional fund-raiser; the fact that the foundation's contact number printed at the end of the book was actually her home telephone number lends an oddly embodied immediacy to the relationship between author and reader. The humanitarian work that her books underwrite suggests a limit to the efficacy of any emphasis on discursivity. In other words, even in light of the implications I draw here, why *not* build a clinic? Hayslip represents a fairly clear-cut example of the committed artist, one among many Third World writers who, in the words of her fellow countrywoman Trinh T. Minh-ha, speak in the name of the masses by carrying "their weight into the weight of their communities, the weight of the world" (Trinh 1989, 11). Jameson's emphasis on reading Third World literature as national allegory highlights the commitment of writers like Hayslip who use art as a medium for social critique and a call to praxis. Her investment in the social would seem to realize both theorists' conditions for the artist engagé.

Yet on one level hers is not the call to praxis that either Jameson or Trinh T. Minh-ha may have envisioned. Beneath Jameson's valorization of Third World literature's narration of collective experience lies an implicit assumption that such a narration necessarily furthers a radical agenda. While her individual story intentionally reflects the "personal is political" dictate of identity politics, Hayslip is not the "cultural intellectual, who is also a political militant" that Jameson posits as the ideal native cultural worker (Jameson 1986, 75). Although emphatically critical of the way in which hegemony is assured through the use of force, Hayslip does not speculate on the consequences of Vietnam's reinscription in a world order hostile to its commitment to communism. As Viet Thanh Nguyen notes, "Hayslip's conclusion that 'what [the United States] wants more than anything, I think is to forgive you and be forgiven by you in return,' implies a symmetry of power that did not and does not exist" (Nguyen 1997, 626). An examination of Hayslip's text provides an understanding of the purposes that personal narrative may serve as it intersects and is invested in multiple discourses. Marita Sturken has noted that the Vietnam War Memorial "stands in a precarious space between . . . opposing discourses" of nationalist imperialism and the counternarratives that would challenge it (Sturken 1991, 138). As recounted in two autobiographies and a film, Hayslip's life story functions as another ambivalent memorial to the war; it ruptures the masculinist logic that justifies military domination only to replace it with persistent and open-ended questions about the other forms domination may take.

Five

The Gendered Subject of Human Rights

DOMESTIC INFIDELITY IN *IRRAWADDY TANGO*
AND *THE SCENT OF THE GODS*

> Sister Katherine said that just because something
> was imaginary did not mean it could not have
> consequences in the real. She told us to write that
> down, and that when we were older we would
> understand.
>
> (*Fiona Cheong*, The Scent of the Gods)

IN 1995, the *New York Times* pronounced the emergence of a new South
Africa, this time, in Asia.[1] Burma, now known as Myanmar, was reported
to be the target of an international divestment campaign on the basis of its
human rights and environmental abuses.[2] This shift from South Africa to
Burma as recipient of the dubious honor of greatest human rights abuser
arose from the events of 1988, in which the military fired on a crowd of
prodemocracy demonstrators, culminating in the detention of an esti-
mated three thousand political prisoners, including the house arrest of the
National League for Democracy (NLD) leader, Aung San Suu Kyi, in
1989.[3]

Although the events of the 8/8/88 democracy movement in Yangon
(Rangoon) were displaced in the American media by reports of the massacre in Tiananmen Square the following year, the Burmese democracy
movement gave the media one thing that the Chinese movement did not:
a living and breathing goddess of democracy in the form of Aung San Suu
Kyi, the Western-educated daughter of assassinated national independence leader Aung San. Like the papier-mâché goddess erected in Tiananmen Square, Aung San Suu Kyi quickly became the emblem of what
Burma lacked and a potent symbol of the collective desire of a people.
After casting about for an appropriate analogy for Aung San Suu Kyi
(Bhutto? Aquino?), the British press hit upon "Burma's Gandhi" in an
attempt to describe a platform familiar to the West: nonviolent protest,
democracy, human rights (Kreager 1991, 321).

These representations of Burma in the 1990s reinforce what has consistently been taken as Asia's difference from the West. Just as Rey Chow

has suggested in regard to Tiananmen Square (Chow 1991), coverage of the Burmese democracy movement was likewise a spectacle of Asian lack—of democracy, freedom of expression, the right of assembly—and an occasion in which Americans could indulge in reports of their national symbols reproduced for global consumption, whether of hastily constructed models of the Statue of Liberty on the streets of Beijing or of the Gettysburg Address recited word for word in English outside the American embassy in Yangon.[4] The construction of such differences, as Lisa Lowe has noted, serve specific American interests, not only justifying United States imperialism but producing the very idea of American national self-conception.[5] Most recently, reports of Asian lack of basic freedoms and civil liberties serve as a reminder of what the United States is proud to export along with its now triumphantly touted brand of capitalism. For example, a democracy such as Singapore, once lauded as a model of postcolonial modernization and now enjoying Asia's highest standard of living after Japan, has gained media attention in the United States for abrogating social freedoms. While Michael Fay's caning in Singapore in 1994 was not an event comparable in magnitude to the events in Burma, it was nonetheless heavily covered in the U.S. media; his punishment was the occasion for comparison to Asian philosophy and governance, in this case, as a means of evaluating the American domestic "crisis" over juvenile crime.[6] The American public was both entertained and shocked to hear about Singapore's "draconian justice" in which graphic descriptions of flogging supplemented reports of bans on chewing gum or smoking in public, and of fines for such offenses as littering ($625), failing to flush a public toilet ($94), and eating on the subway ($312) (Jay Branegan, "Is Singapore a Model for the West?" *Time*, 18 June 1993, 36).[7] The caning incident both assured Americans that they have what Asia wants—individual freedom—and reminded them of what they once had and lost—discipline.

In spite of the seeming contrast between such representations of Asia invoked by Aung San Suu Kyi's quiet courage while under house arrest, Harry Wu's cribbing notes in the margins of a dictionary in a Chinese prison, or an American bad boy unduly punished, an underlying similarity emerges: both representations depend on the figure of an individual who suffers the abuses of a regime in the name of abstract rights. Such images portray not just the violation of democratic rights, but the violation of democratic rights as *human* rights.

With the Cold War dead, the War on Drugs taking an uncomfortably domestic focus, and fears of Asian economic competition complicated by reports of Toyotas being manufactured in Kentucky and diminished by the Asian economic crisis, human rights has emerged as a dominant framework in which the United States places Asia. A testament to the strength of such a narrative, the emphasis on human rights succeeds in reconciling for an American public the economic and political situations of countries as various as Burma, Singapore, China, and Vietnam. For example, in spite of their shared history as former British colonies, Burma and Singapore have taken opposite courses. Under the leadership of a military junta since 1962, Burma was named a "least-developed country" by 1987. In contrast, held up as an economic success, Singapore is known as one of Asia's four "dragons," along with South Korea, Hong Kong, and Taiwan. Governed by single parties whose tenure has lasted more than three decades, both Burma and Singapore have been called to account for alleged violations, although obviously to different degrees.

At best, this concern over human rights abuses in Asia represents an increased awareness of the repressive methods of state control, a vigilance acknowledged to be the shared responsibility of global powers. At worst, it is merely a form of spectacle suitable for entertainment—one season's *The Year of Living Dangerously* starring Sigourney Weaver becomes next season's *Beyond Rangoon* starring Patricia Arquette. But as labor standards and political freedoms are increasingly linked to trade and international diplomacy, human rights issues become levied as strategic bargaining chips, as not-so-subtle forms of punishment and reward.[8] The selective sanctioning of nations on the grounds of human rights violations has been criticized as a form of Western hegemony as much as it has been hailed as an effective means of policing repressive regimes. "The Western community of nations presided over by the United States," Edward Said writes, "has given itself an internationalized and normative identity with authority and hegemony to adjudicate the relative value of human rights" (Said 1993, 197). Human rights is not merely a theory of universal citizenship based on equality, but, as critics of the Helms–Burton law have charged, a means through which the United States furthers its own interest.

Underlying the critique of human rights as a mask of cultural imperialism is a postmodern suspicion of universalist doctrine. Such cautions become especially urgent as the movement toward economic globalization provokes warnings about the erosion of state influence.[9] As Judith Butler has noted in regard to normative political philosophy, any position that "seeks to establish the metapolitical basis of a negotiation of power relations, is perhaps the most insidious ruse of power" (Butler 1994, 6). Such a recognition does not preclude the fact that metapolitical philosophy itself may be called on to interrogate insidious ruses of power. In asking its participants to speak on human rights, the Committee of the 1992 Oxford Amnesty Lectures noted the apparent contradiction between political commitment and postmodern philosophy. Its invitation to prospective lecturers posed the question, "Does the self as construed by the liberal tradition still exist? If not, whose human rights are we defending?" (Johnson 1993, 2). But philosophical suspicion of human rights' dependence on humanist ideals does not obviate the need for vigilance of violations such as state-sponsored torture, a violation that is, as Amnesty International notes, a "calculated assault on human dignity and for that reason alone is to be condemned absolutely" (Amnesty International 1984, 7). To paraphrase from Fiona Cheong's novel, *The Scent of the Gods*, just because the liberal subject is imaginary does not mean that it cannot have consequences in the real.

In affirming the universal rights of the individual, human rights discourse offers a specific ideologically invested rhetorical frame that can be deployed as a form of political persuasion "in the real." This is particularly evident in Asian American literature, which, like the media, is a site where representations of Asia are reproduced for American consumption. Thus, one could question literature's investment in this recent narrative on Asia, particularly in regard to countries that, like Burma and Singapore, have been in the public eye for human rights violations. Do such representations merely serve to reproduce, as Chow suggests, Asia's difference from the West?

Just as figures such as Aung San Suu Kyi become a means of accessing Asia in American culture, Asian American literature could be said to create analogous figures of political advocacy, but for potentially alternative purposes. Both Wendy Law-Yone's *Irrawaddy Tango* (1993) and Fiona Cheong's *The Scent of the Gods* (1991) deploy the rhetoric of human rights in order to critique methods of governmental repression justified by the construction of national crisis. In representing violations such as torture and detention without trial, the authors expose methods of state control as a means of commenting on the contemporary national politics of their "home" countries. *Irrawaddy Tango* suggests a fictive solution to an ongoing historical conflict in Burma by appealing to the individual's sovereignty as protected by the discourse of human rights. *The Scent of the Gods* draws an allegorical parallel between home and state in order to reveal how the mandate to modernize was positioned as antithetical to individual rights; the novel shows the loss of civil liberties to be foundational to the "fledgling nation." The emphasis is not so much, following Lowe's premise, that these fictional representations are constitutive of an Orientalized Asia that in turn create, sustain, or resist certain conceptions of Asian Americans (Lowe 1996). Rather, Asian American writers' placement in the United States enables them to produce critiques of postcolonial state politics that employ First World conceptions of individual rights. Moreover, as if in comparison to American strategies of ethnic homogenization, both novels connect postindependence promotion of internal ethnic disunity to securing the hegemony of single-party rule.

The overseas focus of both American novels appears to testify to both the "postnational" trend in American Studies and what Sau-ling Wong has called the denationalizing direction of Asian American Studies as it has shifted from domestic, immigrant models of minority group interaction with the dominant culture to emphasize global migrations and postcoloniality (Sau-ling Wong 1995). As I discuss in the introduction, marking a distinction between American minority and transnational modes of inquiry produces the perception of a paradigm shift in Asian American Studies. For example, while Susan Koshy acknowledges that "*transnational is not antithetical to the national*" in her critique of Wong's terminology, she nonetheless enforces such a distinction in a temporal argument that situates "old" sociological paradigms associated with early Asian immigration and dependent on linear models of acculturation against what she sees as the complex, nonstatic Asian migrations taking place in the era of transnational capital (Koshy 1996, 340). In suggesting that the discipline has failed to produce theories of literary canonicity that exceed an originary appeal to pluralist inclusion and pan-ethnic commonality, she argues that scholarship has failed to account for "the effects of transnational forces on Asian American ethnicity" as they appear in "newer" literary productions (331).

My goal here is not to reproduce the distinction between immigrant and diasporic, "new" and "old" paradigms, but to suggest one avenue through which literature reveals a mutual investment between American national and Asian postcolonial concerns; in this case, the works do not necessarily produce an account of Asian American ethnicity alternative to that located in the inaugural moment of the discipline, although they might well imply this. Rather, they suggest that what travels transnationally is not only labor and capital but rhetoric. What one witnesses in Law-Yone's and Cheong's depictions of Asia is the deployment of "universal" notions of individual rights in service of commentaries on current Asian national leadership. Significantly, such narratival configurations are not only nationally inscribed but gendered according to First World precepts about injury, women's rights, and individual redress. The force of both writers' commentaries depends on constructing a female subject of state reprisal—the repression of political dissent is depicted as the regulation of female sexuality. In keeping with the work of international feminist scholars who explore the role of gender representation in reproducing and securing nationalist imaginaries, Asian American women's literature reveals that gender difference is a means of signaling mechanisms by which affiliations are formed and consolidated, often against territorial, ethnic, or national allegiances. Interrogating the conflict between ethnic group interests and national unity via a gendered appeal, both works raise pressing questions about human rights' necessary subject.

The Discourse of Rights: State Torture and the Battered Woman

Officials tortured an ally of Aung San Suu Kyi to
death as part of a campaign of arrests, torture
and intimidation targeting opposition leaders, a
dissidents' group said Tuesday. Hla Than, 52,
died at a hospital Aug. 2 from internal injuries he
suffered during torture in prison, where he has
spent the past six years, the Washington-based
National Coalition Government of the Union of
Burma said, citing unidentified sources in Burma.
   (*Miami Herald*, 7 August 1996, A9)

[W]e don't like hurting other people. We refrain
from killing. We refrain from doing what you
might call unpleasant things.
   (Colonel Ye Htut, State Law and Order
   Restoration Council, Myanmar cited in *New
   York Times*, 17 September 1996, A8)

Under house arrest for a period of six years until July 1995, Aung San
Suu Kyi became a mobilizing force for a people living under a military-
controlled dictatorship since 1962, when General Ne Win came to power
in a coup d'état against the civilian government of Prime Minister U Nu.
The catalyst for international attention for her party, the National League
for Democracy (NLD), Aung San Suu Kyi is the embodiment of Burma's
prodemocracy platform, a single subject who voices collective desires,
suffers the abuses of the regime, and receives the accolades of activism as
well. Awarded the Nobel Peace Prize in 1991 while still incarcerated, she
continues to speak on behalf of the NLD platform, which advocates freedom of assembly and speech and condemns the junta's continuing measures against democracy supporters. In *Irrawaddy Tango* Burmese American Wendy Law-Yone gives us a more ambiguous national heroine than
Aung San Suu Kyi, one who solves the political ills of her country in a way
that her real-life counterpart cannot—she assassinates the military dictator, who is also her husband. As the embodiment of the abstract subject
of political torture, Tango bears a specifically gendered relationship to
the state; the novel's critique rests on configuring state power not as the
failure of benevolent paternalism but as conjugal abuse.
   In the course of creating "Daya" as a counterpart to Burma, Law-Yone
provides a utopian solution to what was in 1993 and continues to be a
political impasse: the National League for Democracy won the 1990 elec-

tion, but the military junta known as the State Law and Order Restoration Council (SLORC) refuses to relinquish the reins of power. As the daughter of the late Edward Law-Yone, a leading journalist imprisoned after General Ne Win's coup, Law-Yone has firsthand knowledge of methods of Burma's domestic repression. In representing the rise of a despotic and eccentric general whose xenophobia and strong-arm tactics give rise to increasing dissent near the end of his rule, her novel references specific elements of Burma's postcolonial history to suggest one avenue of political change. Rather than providing a forum for the student-led democracy movement, the novel addresses another form of organized dissent in its portrayal of ethnic insurgent armies along Burma's borders, the hill tribes who have sought autonomy in one form or another since Burmese independence in 1948. Yet, one aspect of the novel's representation of dissent in Daya and Western media attention to Burma remains constant: both center on the figure of a woman who becomes the singular subject of state reprisal, a body whose actions must be forcibly controlled for the continuance of the national status quo.

In the case of U.S. media representations of Aung San Suu Kyi, one could ask, what does it mean that a single subject comes to both incorporate and displace the more graphic image of the fired-upon masses? It is the same question one could pose about the image of the lone Chinese man standing down a row of tanks during Tiananmen Square, an image rapidly becoming iconographic. It is clear that the most generally accepted concept of human rights requires an individual for whom attention, concern, and then outrage can be channeled into activism. As the central figure for the NLD, Aung San Suu Kyi is the body through which political protest is made intelligible. Literary representation deploys similar strategies as a mode of rhetorical persuasion—the center of *Irrawaddy*'s not-so-thinly veiled critique of Burmese politics is its portrayal of the state-sponsored torture of its female protagonist, Tango. As in the media's emphasis on Aung San Suu Kyi, the novel's commentary is produced not through a direct appeal to a collective movement, whether prodemocracy or ethnic insurgency, but through an appeal to the figure of a woman. Although Aung San Suu Kyi's political legitimacy was first derived from her position as the daughter of Aung San, assassinated leader of the anti-imperialist coalition, the Anti-Fascist People's Freedom League and her activism might be marked as a form of filial inheritance, Burmese state politics have not perhaps relied on gendered images to secure the country's national self-image. As a case in point, Burmese officials would no doubt fail to see the irony in the fact that their delegate to the 1995 Fourth World Conference on Women in Beijing was a male army general. The gendered convergence in American media and literary representations of Burma thus speaks to the power of the women-as-nation allegory so often invoked in the service of postcolonial nationalism.

In its strategic use of gender, *Irrawaddy* dialogues with other Asian American women's writing in figuring women's political alliance as a matter of sexual betrayal. Despite one reviewer's characterization of the novel as an account of a woman's "sexual adventures," it is not merely a form of female picaresque but deploys sexuality to signal shifting collective allegiances (Jacqueline Trescott, "Tango of Emotions: In Wendy Law-Yone's Fiction, a Revelation of Dreams," *Washington Post*, 16 March 1994, C1). As critic C. Lok Chua notes, Tango is a cross between Eva Peron, Patty Hearst, and a black widow; her marriage to the dictator is clearly the Faustian bargain of an ambitious small-town girl with "potential," and her subsequent counterinsurgency only seems to come about via another sexual alliance as mistress of the leader of an oppressed hill tribe. But, as important, the novel's emphasis on the single, tortured female body reveals the gendered structure of the novel's political appeal as it resonates with contemporary discourse on human rights—it exposes the dictator's irrational despotism as it is waged not against a national body or ethnic group but against his wife. In the novel, the military's unfitness to rule appears as abusive dominance in the home, hence as a violation of women's rights.

This domestic-as-national parallel seems to rely on the discourse on domestic abuse popularized after the women's movement in the United States, linking the novel's First World placement to its international advocacy. For example, as if to suggest "Battered Woman's Syndrome" as a form of popular psychology, the novel portrays the dictator's crisis of mastery as a series of possessive behaviors and physically enforced demands for obedience followed by extravagant promises of contrition and future reform.[10] The fictional general's beatings of his wife initiated by charges of infidelity are significantly couched in terms of national representation as Tango's desirability comes to represent a form of international recognition:

> I saw the way that American son of a bitch had his big hand on your flesh, there where the back of your waist was bare. Did it feel good? Tell me how it felt and don't lie. Did it make you itch? Did you feel that nerve running down the center of your crotch swelling and twitching? Were you thinking what it would be like to have a huge American prick up you for a change? . . . I'd give him the low-down he wanted. I'd describe step by step, from foreplay to climax, the imagined infidelity. (104–5)

The accusation of infidelity initiates a false confession of betrayal, the purpose of which is not to provide information but to provoke his desire through the process of narration, a function only fulfilled as long as the narrative remains avowedly fictive. As an act, Tango's confession is without content—like rape, it has not to do with substance but with transmission: rape, we are told, is not about sex, but about (his) power. The "confessions" prefigure the scenes of political torture by unmasking the idea that the need for information during interrogation is the motive for cruelty; as Elaine Scarry writes about the structure of torture, the content of the prisoner's answer may be inconsequential, but "the fact of his answering is always crucial."[11] The episodes end in a reminder that power is ultimately the ability to control meaning: he jerks her head back by the hair to pose the question, "Love me?"—an inquiry that, given its context, has but a single answer.

The use of this discourse on wife battery as gendered political appeal allows Law-Yone to reflect on complex notions of victimization and resistance, shifting from the battered woman as a single agent to a national or ethnic minority population undergoing despotic and irrational mistreatment. The novel depicts domestic violence throughout the trajectory of Supremo's violent rise to power as it is linked to suppressing ethnic insurgency; Tango's belated recognition, "My God, I'd married a maniac," might also be the national sentiment.[12] The dual meanings of the word "domestic" conjoin: just as the police are often reluctant to interfere in domestic disputes, roughing up groups within one's national borders is not a global, but an internal, affair. Just as Burma's policy of isolationism places its treatment of ethnic insurgency beyond the realm of international intervention, the parallel suggests, batterers' enforcement of social isolation secures their partners' dependency and prevents interference in the relationship. Tango's mixture of quiescence, calculation, disgust, and accommodation provides a partial answer to why there seems to be no more than token resistance to political despotism: one can only hope that certain accommodations will prevent the escalation of mistreatment.

It is thus that the novel sets up a suggestive link between what in the discourse of battery has been called the "learned helplessness" of women's social conditioning and the inability to resist despotism. Law-Yone's conjugal-national parallel resonates through explanations of why battered women do not leave based on a conditioned acceptance of naturalized masculine authority; the power of the despot is likewise always already legitimated by the fact that he occupies the position of authority.[13] Of course, to ascribe lack of resistance to the pathology of a people, as the narrator does, is akin to blaming the victim for her own abuse. Political rule, after all, is a condition of military backing, not merely a failure to act decisively, or the "learned helplessness" of a diverse people. The analogy ends as the answer to why there has been almost a half century of authoritarian rule in Burma can be conveyed through a simple explanation about the use of force. The novel makes these tactics of power clear in reporting the apparent lack of resistance to Supremo's rise to power in a "quiet" coup—Tango's assessment that "nobody resisted" is ironized by her subsequent acknowledgment that all members of the cultural elite have been "detained." Law-Yone's fictional representation of the coup resonates with General Ne Win's takeover in 1962, an event reported by her father, Edward Law-Yone, editor and founder of the *Nation* prior to his own five-year "detention" as a political prisoner.[14]

It is perhaps not such a great leap to suggest that the methods of submission employed by the state easily mesh with forms of conjugal violence: feminist work on domestic abuse in the late 1980s in fact engaged studies of state-sponsored torture to describe the psychological and physical tactics used by domestic batterers.[15] Both discourses rely on sedimented First World conceptions of individual sovereignty, injury, and pop psychology; Law-Yone's novel plays on these conceptions in its graphic representation of sexualized state violence. In employing such a discourse, the novel potentially reinforces both humanist constructions of self and traditional parallels between women and nation even as it engages a gendered form of advocacy. The accusation of treason after Tango's capture as "rebel queen" marks her political betrayal as indistinguishable from adultery; her torture comes at the hands of agents of a husband whose authority is that of the state. What is treason, the novel seems to imply, but infidelity on a larger scale?

If, as Deniz Kandiyoti suggests, women are controlled "in the interests of demarcating and preserving the identities of national/ethnic collectives," the female body is the site of policing transgressions of affiliation and loyalty (Kandiyoti 1994, 382). Thus, the instrument of Tango's political punishment is fittingly represented as a reflection of her "crime" of infidelity: she is raped with the barrel of a gun in a version of Russian roulette. Reflecting the Maoist axiom that political power grows out of the barrel of a gun, the novel's use of a substitute penis to represent the instrument of state power associates masculinity with a naturalized but arbitrary hierarchy of rule. In this case, Tango's sexual violation with a weapon carries further national resonance: if the word for Daya also signifies "wound," an injury in which the skin or other external surface is pierced or broken, her penetration evokes the nature of the crime, the penetration of the national body by ethnic insurgents along its border. The punishment for abetting the violation of national sovereignty is thus the violation of the boundaries of the individual subject, but with specifically gendered resonance. Amnesty International defines torture as an act intended to destroy one's humanity; the intention behind torture is the dissolution of the subject through the infliction of pain (Amnesty International 1973, 30). A means of embodying the authority of the state, rape is a specific form of torture that reduces the female subject to her defining bodily orifice, confirming the subject position that woman inhabits as the negation of man. In substituting a symbol of state power for the phallus, rape as torture confirms Scarry's point that "pain is a pure physical experience of negation" (Scarry 1985, 52).

In writing about torture, Scarry begins with the premise that physical pain not only transcends signification through its incapability of being shared, but actively destroys it, "bringing about an immediate reversion to a state anterior to language, to the sounds and cries a human being makes before language is learned" (Scarry 1985, 4). This deconstructive process represents "the loss of the world" as pain obliterates meaning. The novel's depiction of Tango's torture reveals that political power is the ability to control meaning, not just in the sense that official propaganda can be exposed as a form of doublespeak, but that absolute power is the power to subvert meanings assigned to signifiers. "We're shaving you so you won't worry about getting hurt," Tango is told in prison. "We don't hurt nuns; good Buddhists never hurt nuns, see?" (173). Such an assurance is rendered meaningless prior to her rape, as she is told both "Didn't we tell you we don't fuck nuns?" and "Especially we don't fuck whores!" (177). The distinction between nun and whore, purity and defilement, no longer matters; the torturer's power is not just the ability to reassign meanings within systems of classification, but to render such classification superfluous.

Similarly, when common household objects are used as weapons, as instruments of pain, they become divorced from their referents, demonstrating the ease with which the mundane can be rendered diabolical. When Tango becomes the assassin and makes use of such innocent items as duct tape and an electric fan to kill, the token of her power is not only the violence of her act but the fact that, like the torturer, she transforms the banal into an agent of pain. The novel configures narration as a form of political power, revealing that torture indicates not merely the state's power to induce pain, but, as Scarry notes, to unmake the world. While incarcerated, part of her punishment is to anticipate varieties of torture from a fellow prisoner apparently driven mad by torture, a narratival form of punishment meant to induce extreme dread. The woman's story of involuntary orgasm during genital torture with electric shock implies that the torturer has the power to undo meaning, to transform pain into pleasure, erasing agency: "you can't avoid what happens, Little Sister. You have—how to say it? A climax. A low moment for a woman. But what can a woman do? Nothing" (177).[16]

The novel's portrayal of torture elicits horror and sympathy for the abused female body, thereby appealing to human dignity as a fundamental right. Significantly, it reflects the translation of global human rights violations into terms familiar to an American audience. If the effectiveness of agencies such as Amnesty International depends, as Scarry notes, on their "ability to communicate the reality of physical pain to those who are not themselves in pain,"[17] this familiarity in part explains how the discourse of wife battering can work to expose foreign political repression. Simply, the appeal is effective if offenses against female political prisoners are defined as somehow *more* heinous than those against men. Given that women are perceived to be more embodied, they may be more easily imagined as threatened *in* their bodies by playing on traditional conceptions of sentimentality and women's vulnerability. Moreover, women's association with the domestic, "nonpolitical" realm signals the state's violation more acutely. But there are more complex resonances: the novel's collapsing of distinctions between treason and adultery, political torture and domestic abuse, allows Law-Yone to engage the concept of individual and collective rights simultaneously. The belief that "women and children have an absolute right to live free from bodily harm" (Jones 1994, 5), for example, is one way the concept of *group* rights has entered an American lexicon. *Irrawaddy* appeals not just to the abstract human subject of human rights, but to an individual who is also part of a collective group—a woman.

Tango is apparently tortured for advocating the sovereignty rights of an ethnic minority. In making her a spokesperson on behalf of "the Jesu," Law-Yone has chosen to model her fictional hill tribe on the Karen, a Christian ethnic group on Burma's eastern border with Thailand who have been involved in a secessionist war with the central government since 1948. Although the Shan have also been involved in an armed struggle for sovereignty, like the Kachin, their human rights cause in the West may be compromised by their alleged involvement in drug trafficking.[18] By modeling the Jesu on the Karen, Law-Yone focuses on an ethnic group whose secessionist claim can be represented most forcefully as the right to religious freedom.[19] This choice of ethnic group among the many represented in the hill regions thus does not muddle the question of who should have "rights"—the Karen can be represented as freedom fighters rather than drug smugglers. The emergence of human rights as a concern in Southeast Asia might have given the long-standing armed insurrection new urgency had it not been supplanted by mass demonstrations for democratic reform, an event the novel vaguely refers to as a "spectacle of protest and massacre" (247). The Karen's armed struggle against the central government has garnered little attention in the West aside from some media coverage of the threat of their forced repatriation from refugee camps in Thailand. Ironically, one way the Karen came into Western perception was through their conscription of children into the army, a circumstance implicitly portrayed as a violation of human rights—a form of child abuse.[20] Such a portrayal only highlights the ease with which appeals to moral universals can be deployed in support or criticism of specific political causes. My point is not to draw one-to-one correspondences between historical events and literary depictions, but to highlight the similarity between fictional and media representations of, in Scarry's terms, the lives of those "whose name[s] can barely be pronounced" (Scarry 1985, 9) as a means of accessing an Asian "over there" in terms that are very much "over here."[21]

By invoking the body in pain to highlight both the ethnic right to self-rule and the more general stance against despotism, the novel affirms the individual necessary to the concept of human rights as it is currently understood and that each human subject has intrinsic worth because of his or her uniqueness. In contrast, the idea of sovereignty and self-rule as human rights cannot be reconciled to liberal ideals, a point debated by delegates to the United Nations charged with ratifying a Universal Declaration of Human Rights in 1948.[22] That the novel ultimately makes its appeal to the Karen-as-Jesu sovereignty movement through Tango may suggest that gender is a form of group identity perhaps more easily reconcilable to the concept of individuality than racial or ethnic group affiliation.

This reconciliation is echoed in Hillary Rodham Clinton's anxiously anticipated comment at the 1995 Fourth World Conference on Women in Beijing: "If there is one message that echoes forth from this conference, let it be that human rights are women's rights and women's rights are human rights, once and for all."[23] Virginia Woolf's famous dictum on women's ambivalent allegiance to patriarchal nationalism—"[A]s a woman, I have no country. As a woman I want no country. As a woman my country is the whole world" (Woolf 1938, 197)—signals a similar belief in woman as global citizen whose naturalized humanitarian concerns transcend borders. Intended as a statement against the recent record of human rights abuses of the conference's Chinese hosts, the First Lady's direct condemnation was internationally applauded, indicating that issues referenced in the speech such as bride-burning, the rape of POWs, female infanticide, domestic violence, genital mutilation, and coerced abortion or sterilization somehow obviated previously contentious debates on cultural practices versus the rights of women-as-individuals transcendent of context. That such issues maintain the appearance of universals suggests that liberalism can encompass women's rights as a form of group rights more easily than ethnic or racial rights, except perhaps in cases of genocide. "Woman" can appear as a collective entity unvexed by issues of territorialization, allowing for a subject who is not wholly individualized.[24]

Yet, the novel's portrayal of human rights as a method of soliciting international attention is both self-conscious and cynical, a cynicism that extends to the efficacy of coalitional identity politics in the United States. What brings Dayans, "that most minor of minority groups," into the American spotlight is not the spectacle of protest but "another disaster, far more newsworthy than anything the internal affairs of our country could have generated: the disappearance of an American rock star in the wilderness of our northern jungles" (247). Law-Yone comments on the fact that political concern is based partly on self-interest, and that recognition of the collective must be concretized through individuation—or better, celebrity. In this ironic aside on the hapless rock star—not the massacre—as the reason for Daya's return to international visibility, one cannot help but think of media focus on Aung San Suu Kyi, indicating perhaps that the politics of caring keeps a cause in public memory better than disembodied issues. But this is, in effect, a strategy the novel deploys as well; the sovereignty issues of the Jesu—"self-rule, religious freedom, human rights" (128)—are conveyed to the reader and the fictional world through a single female spokesperson. Tango resists this role as collective representative in a direct repudiation of the very appeal in which the novel engages:

> I didn't want to be an activist or a born-again crusader for human rights and other civil liberties or to go on the torture circuit. . . . Even for a good cause, I wanted no part of it. Even if the point was to educate the humanitarian American public on inhuman practices in other parts of the world. Even if the public could then get involved by writing to their congressman or calling an 800 number to pledge support. (248)

While this resistance to public confession might be read as an individual's logical response to trauma, it is more significantly a rejection of democratic politics as it appears to be practiced in the United States as a form of identity politics, a rejection of, as Lauren Berlant has noted, the moment in which "private life" becomes indistinguishable from notions of citizenship and civic responsibility (Berlant 1997). In repudiating the salutary and politicizing effects ascribed to consciousness-raising through public confession, Tango refuses, as Wendy Brown puts it, "the steady slide of political into therapeutic discourse" (Brown 1995, 75). In its resistance to using experience to mobilize for change, the novel foregrounds the ineffectiveness of coalitional democratic representation for influencing diplomatic policies in the "Turd World." The novel portrays coalitional politics as mindless caterwauling: from within the United States, Dayan exiles are "neutralized" as one of many special interest groups naively lobbying Washington for attention and aid in the manner of Berlant's infantile citizen who optimistically believes in the utopian promises of the system (Berlant 1997).

While Tango's outsidedness upon immigration to the United States echoes Asian American portrayals of expatriate alienation, it is also part of the novel's refusal to locate the United States as a model political system and an expression of impatience with its perhaps undeserved reputation as global interventionist.[25] In spite of—or perhaps because of—the National League for Democracy's support within and outside of Burma, the novel refuses to portray the democracy movement as an effective form of resisting a military regime. References to such a movement are noticeably absent, aside from Tango's belittling comments to the effect that "nonviolent protest" is deemed an "idiot phrase," and the cry "What do we want? Democracy! When do we want it? Now!" a "mindless chant." Moreover, the acronym for the novel's "Foundation for Asian Democracies" is "FAD." In keeping with Lowe's situating Asian American literature as a site where the contradictions of American national promise are uncovered (Lowe 1996), the novel exposes the contradiction between American democratic rights as the fantasy of each citizen's equal influence on state policy and the United States as arbiter of human rights in the international realm.

Given that *Irrawaddy Tango*'s critique of the military junta is not identical to an appeal to general democratic rights, does the novel's solution, as Barbara Harlow would claim for resistance literature, "insist on the collective historical consequences of individual experience" (Harlow 1987, 119)? The novel raises the question of whether Tango's act of violence represents a collective, political action or is simply an act of revenge. At one level, the novel seems to ask the reader to understand Tango's behavior as a psychological response to trauma; she murders not as a show of solidarity with the Jesu rebels or the Dayan people; rather, either her return to the site of trauma is a step in healing—a point she consciously rejects—or the assassination is a form of payback. One might easily inscribe Tango's actions in the familiar terms of the talk-show confessional she abhors—"women who kill: victims who turn the tables on their abusers." Her question as she awaits the judgment of the rioting masses outside, "But I'd killed the beast out of revenge—nothing but revenge. Had I really serviced a nation?" (286), references the personal-as-political link invoked by the epigraph, "either I'm nobody, or I'm a nation." Yet, the epigraph asks that the novel be read allegorically whereas its protagonist resists collective association. While its emphasis on a lone heroine may be dictated by narrative convention, one consequence is that the novel can individualize tyranny as well.[26] It is as if Law-Yone is aware of Berlant's caution about the uses of sentimentality in the service of activist causes. Berlant notes, "when sentimentality meets politics, it uses personal stories to tell of structural effects, but in doing so it risks thwarting its very attempt to perform rhetorically a scene of pain that must be soothed politically" (Berlant 1998, 641).

Unlike Jessica Hagedorn's critique of the Marcos regime in *Dogeaters*, which condemns the tripartite collusion of big business, elected officials, and the military in the country's governance, however, Law-Yone's attention to character may present Daya's problems as too simply located in the actions of a single power-hungry individual, rather than in the systematic intertwining of civil and state methods of control. The open-endedness of the novel rests not on interpreting the collective implications of the individual's act of transgression, but in translating this act in terms of political systems. Ironically, Tango's act of individual aggression inscribes her within an American national ethos and her final thoughts are of Washington, D.C., where she has previously marked her alienation from American national symbols. Still, *Irrawaddy* stands out as a model of postcolonial commentary that resists advocating what the Third World is always presumed to lack; interestingly, it questions the current democracy movement precisely at a moment in which "democracy has . . . replaced development as the 'buzzword' of the 1990's" (Qadir, Clapham, and Gills 1993, 415).

Law-Yone's *Irrawaddy Tango* is clearly a commentary on the past despotism of General Ne Win and the ongoing abuses of a military-controlled state. The work might indicate that Law-Yone is no fan of the democracy movement; elsewhere she has suggested that what is lacking in Burma is not active resistance but a common agenda and unity among the many opposition groups—NLD leaders, fugitive students, and ethnic insurgents. As she rightly predicted in 1989, the NLD's call for multiparty elections did not assure a transfer of power (Law-Yone 1989). Rather than invoking the revered figure of Aung San Suu Kyi, known in Burma simply as "The Lady," the novel offers a morally ambiguous heroine who, in knowing both how to fuck and how to kill, is no lady. In the end, it is not so much the nature of the solution envisioned that marks the novel's political commentary. Its message—"assassinate the dictator, free the people"—is not the most original vision of change; dispatching a fictive hitwoman to resolve a historical dilemma is not a blueprint for Burma's remaking. In transforming the national body into the body of the oppressed individual, the single body in pain who bears the brunt of state-sanctioned violence, the novel may ironize the work of human rights relief agencies, but ultimately it does not dispute their ability to focus public attention. *Irrawaddy Tango*'s invocation of the discourse on battered women to expose methods of political repression inverts the relationship established by feminist studies that draw on reports of the treatment of political prisoners as an analogy to domestic abuse. The image that remains from the novel is not the shot-upon crowd, nor, in the end, the embattled ethnic insurgents. Rather, a wife is being beaten.

Such an argument is not meant to deflate the effectiveness of the appeal or to suggest the trivialization of a national call to action; rather, it highlights the ways in which Asian American literary expression utilizes the tactics of postcolonial nationalism linking gender and nation, but to subversive effect. International feminists have suggested some of these tactics in critiquing the ways in which, for example, images of emancipated women are made to signify postindependence modernization (Kandiyoti 1994), feminine sexuality is used to promote national industry (Heng 1997), or political parties use women's issues to broaden their appeal (West 1992). In this case, however, what I would foreground is the novel's First World investment, its use of what have become normative values in the United States concerning women's rights in the service of its Asian postcolonial commentary. Law-Yone's work thus exemplifies the gendered politicism of Asian American women's writing as it interrogates the juxtaposition of competing collectivities: women, ethnicity, nation. This interrogation reflects V. Spike Peterson's point that although women have been situated as ancillary to international relations theory through their association with the private sphere, this association places them as primary to the production of group loyalties, affiliations, and identificatory processes central to nationalist projects (Peterson 1995). Peterson's taxonomy of the relationship between women and nation suggests, following Kandiyoti, that women are often invoked to signify other group differences, "to delineate the boundaries of group identity" (Kandiyoti 1994, 132).

Such is the relationship explored in Fiona Cheong's *The Scent of the Gods*, which exploits women's association with domesticity to reveal the state's intrusion into the private sphere as it legislates new group loyalties upon Singapore's independence. The narrator's innocent rumination on the wooden fence separating "the family's property from the rest of the country" (122), that "a wind was coming soon which was going to blow on the fence just hard enough to topple the fence over" (135), metaphorizes the novel's concern with the erosion of the border between public and private. Just as Homi Bhabha has noted that the "recesses of the domestic space become sites for history's most intricate invasions" (Bhabha 1994, 9), the novel exposes the methods by which state-mandated affiliations are created and upheld by drawing allegorical resonance between civic duty and gendered associations with submission and self-preservation.

The Age of Consent: State Regulation in *The Scent of the Gods*

He who is subjected to a field of visibility, and
who knows it, assumes responsibility for the
constraints of power.
  (Michel Foucault, *Discipline and Punish*)

It was May 1969. . . . The government had begun
to take care of everything. . . . We had peace now.
We had progress. . . . There was to be no more
poverty in Singapore, no more slums.
  (Fiona Cheong, *The Scent of the Gods*)

If *The Scent of the Gods* suggests a national allegory in its treatment of
domestic space, it is the continual violation of the realm of the "private"
that provides the force of Cheong's commentary on postindependence
Singapore, violations that signify an encroachment on the freedoms of the
individual. The divisions in Cheong's fictional family mirror the potentially volatile divisions of the state as ethnic loyalty competes with national duty at the moment that kinship and family begin to cede their
functions of socialization to the public sphere. Yet, the family is not simply a microcosm of the state, nor is *Scent*'s bildungsroman an allegory of
Singapore's rapid modernization and development. From 1965 to 1990,
Singapore went from being a small island with no natural resources to a
metropolitan city-state with the highest gross national product in Asia
after Japan. Dubbed the "Orient with plumbing," Singapore has been
taken as model society whose rise is largely attributed to the postindependence policies of the ruling People's Action Party (PAP) led by Prime Minister Lee Kuan Yew from 1959 to 1990. Given its success, Singapore was
held up as a model for economic development not only in the Third
World, but in the West as well. Although the protagonist of Cheong's
novel remarks in hindsight, "In a few years Prime Minister Lee would
prove himself" (107), the work is not a celebration of Lee Kuan Yew's
policies, nor is it entirely a condemnation of his three-decade tenure.
Rather, in depicting the year of Singapore's expulsion from the Federation of Malaysia in 1963, the first anniversary of the republic in 1966,
and the subsequent leadership of 1969, the novel reflects a 1990s concern
with the erosion of civil liberties. Like *Irrawaddy Tango*, *Scent*'s postcolonial commentary depends on a parallel between the repression of individual rights and the containment of feminine sexuality.
  The Scent of the Gods reveals how the longevity of the PAP was secured both through legislated means of civil control and through the rhet-

oric of impending crisis, which secured voluntary compliance with the official mandates of modernization and "multiracialism" in the years following Singapore's "forced" independence from Malaysia. Instilling allegiance through the rhetoric of crisis legitimates authority and consolidates power, a point the novel mirrors in both the domestic and the national spheres. From the grandmother's point of view, "divine protection" provided by ancestors in the face of unspecified malevolence justifies traditional ethnically based filiation. Just as Grandma portrays the family as besieged by willful gods whose intentions remain cryptic, Singapore cultivated the image of a besieged Chinese isle within a hostile Malay region and of a democratic isle threatened by communist expansion. The novel reflects the PAP's potentially contradictory task in 1965: to invoke fear of the *overseas* Chinese influence among Singaporeans and to promote the progress-oriented interests of its English-educated Chinese population without seeming to encourage "Chineseness" as the cornerstone to Singaporean identity. Hence, the official discouragement of ethnic tribalism through the promotion of "multiracialism" served the purpose of differentiating two types of Chinese—red and loyal.

Like other Asian American texts, the novel exposes the general dynamic in which the production of an ethnic margin constitutes the legitimacy of the center. Paralleling yet distinct from Lowe's discussion of Asian American racial formation as it serves the purposes of American national self-definition (Lowe 1996), in this case the concept of difference exploited by the state could not simply fall along racial or ethnic lines, but according to loyalties to political and economic systems. As the novel reveals, the success of such ethnic management against the construction of an external enemy contributed to the longevity of the PAP and a highly stable polity that some now characterize as soft authoritarianism. Following both academic and mainstream media critiques of the loss of democratic rights in the wake of rapid modernization and three decades of single-party rule, the novel questions the methods of securing, as Esha, the narrator, notes, "peace and progress." Although concerns over state influence on the dissemination of information and the general impression of lack of journalistic freedom, for example, may be a far cry from the methods of state control now employed in Burma, as Singapore's publicized use of corporal punishment reveals, the state has developed a significant civil apparatus for dealing with both dissenters and lawbreakers. The PAP has been particularly successful in using the legal tools of democracy as instruments of control: the deregistration of radical unions, the withdrawal of newspaper licenses, the threat of defamation suits, and selective prosecution for tax law violation.[27] While representations of prohibitions and penalties do not suggest that they are violations of human rights, other criticisms of Singapore law focus on the Internal

Security Act, an "emergency" measure allowing for detention without trial that originated out of fear of communist subversion.

In portraying the disappearance of Esha's Uncle Tien, who goes into hiding and presumed exile rather than face arrest when suspected of involvement with the Barisan Socialis, or Socialist Front, the novel highlights the use of the Internal Security Act in quashing internal dissent, a measure that meant, as Li Shin explains to Esha, "If the government suspected someone of being a Communist, that person could be arrested and sent to jail" (50). Originally the only party with the potential support to challenge the PAP, the Barisan Socialis had broken from the more moderate PAP in 1961 in order to campaign against a federation with Malaysia that had outlawed communism. Through the Internal Security Act in 1963, one hundred Barisan leaders and supporters were arrested and held without trial in what was dubbed "Operation Cold Store." This sweep and the Barisan's boycott of the 1968 election effectively eliminated the development of a viable two-party system in Singapore, allowing for a PAP ascendancy that continues. At the time of the novel's publication, "detainees" from Operation Cold Store were still being held.[28] As Geraldine Heng has shown, this authoritarianism has extended to women; the measure was deployed against the women's movement in the 1987 detention of two founding members of the feminist organization AWARE (Heng 1997).

In recalling the PAP's most blatant violation of human rights in the figure of Tien, the novel reveals the accusation of subversion to be a blanket charge to suppress dissent, an irony heightened by the implication that Tien merely supports the academic and personal freedoms associated with liberal democracy. In foregrounding the loss of civil liberties that occurs in the name of guaranteeing democracy, *The Scent of the Gods* links postcolonial history to a contemporary concern with human rights in global politics. Its portrayal reveals these losses to be not aberrant but foundational to the formation of the state. Yet, *Scent*'s commentary is not simply to be deduced from a straightforward representation of historical events. Rather, its historical content is understated, filtered through the limited consciousness of a child moving toward adolescence. A form of bildungsroman, the novel is not overtly analytic; Esha's beliefs are still unformed and much of her thought is focused on moments in which she comes to some awareness of sexuality. History may appear at times as a backdrop to these flashes of recognition, but because Esha's maturation is always portrayed in conjunction with events that highlight reaction to governmental policy, it is clear that Cheong's specifically gendered genre serves to articulate her political commentary. In contrast to Shelley Sunn Wong's reading of the bildungsroman as a narrative of progressive incorporation into and identification with majority culture and thus an ideologically suspect genre for Asian American women writers, the bildungs-roman is the vehicle for Cheong's critique of the connection between maturity and the acceptance of the postcolonial state's disciplining authority (Shelley Wong 1994).

Female maturation is characterized by constraint; Esha is subject to a new set of prohibitions that are meant as both safeguards and messages to others about oneself: she must keep her knees together, keep her shirt on, and learn to walk like a girl. In witnessing the public humiliation of a schoolmate forced to stand in front of the class without her panties in punishment for displaying mildly pornographic images of "naked British people chasing one another around" (140), she learns that sex is not just secret but is, like masturbation, a punishable offense. Such warnings about self-discipline and proper behavior are meant to convey one message: to overstep the boundaries of decorum is to invite violation. Esha's interior reflection and the political terrain converge in the representation of Auntie Daisy's rape and subsequent pregnancy. Esha witnesses Daisy's virtual incarceration in the house when bars are placed over her window, bars she is told that "*Auntie Daisy herself* had asked for" (161, emphasis mine). The identity of the rapist remains unknown and the blame falls on her aunt for her previously "free" behavior. Esha's recognizes that the grown-ups need to blame Auntie Daisy for the rape because they cannot deal with a "horror without a source"; it may also be implied, however, that a horror without a source has potential uses: an undefined evil makes all the more urgent the necessity to discipline one's own behavior and to submit to protection for one's own good. Whereas the judicial response to rape often hinges on the issue of consent, within the framework of Cheong's gendered political allegory the question of consent bears relevance to Singapore's current state of affairs: Does Daisy consent to the curtailment of her freedoms? Are the bars designed to keep others out also meant to keep her in?

The fact that neither the woman nor the girl becoming a woman can object to measures taken in the name of her own defense resonates with sociologist Chua Beng-Huat's statement concerning the government's characterization of repressive measures as forms of civic responsibility: "Politically, the conflation [of government and society] rationalises and justifies all state interventions as preemptive actions which 'ensure' collective well-being and, as such, are measures of good government rather than abuses of individual rights" (663). Just as Daisy and Esha suffer the restriction of their movements based on a "caring" paternalism, so the populace appears to consent to a restriction of freedoms based on the assurance of the benevolent caretaking abilities of the state. The family's justification of Esha's seclusion in a convent after she gets her period is echoed without overt judgment by Esha herself: "In Great-Grandfather's house the family had to be protected. That was the law. It had always been. It would always be" (247). Her innocent commentary on gender role conformity implies that what now appears as sacrifice—a request to modify individual behavior—is justified by the payoff of future security: "Men were going to treat me according to how I behaved. One day when I was older, [Grandma] said, I would understand what she meant, and I would be grateful that she had taught me the proper graces" (9). As Grandma and the government both recognize, such feelings of gratitude can only be produced by transforming the representation of restriction from punitive to merely regulatory. The gendered contrast between Li Shin's desire to be a soldier and Esha's lessons in feminine behavior reveals the roles to be directed toward an identical purpose, that of instilling self-discipline. The roles are complementary and reciprocal—a duty to protect implies those who need to be protected. The idea of consensual behavior modification (the family's request of Esha) may be distinct from the threat of detention (the government's threat to Tien), but they operate under the same logic; an appeal to national citizenship and collective survival justifies the suspension of individual freedom.

If Esha is to stand in some measure as a reflection of Singapore's postindependence population, Cheong represents her as neither eager to acquiesce nor entirely passive or duped by authority. This balance is enacted through her portrayal of Esha's growing consciousness of sexuality: although she does not rebel against it, Esha reads beyond the adults' representation of sex-as-threat enough to understand that she is only receiving the authorized narrative. Thus, in seeing her cousin's penis, his "almost grown-up birdie," for the first time, she is astonished at its soft helplessness. Its presence ruptures its prior characterization—what previously she cannot look at or discuss is revealed to be nothing fearful at all. Unlike *Irrawaddy Tango*, in which the penis-form becomes an instrument of state power, the analogy here is that like the unseen but potentially threatening Communists, the penis serves as the sign through which the appeal for modifications in behavior is elicited, a sign whose effectiveness is only assured by its nebulousness. As she matures, Esha is implicitly and explicitly warned about the dangers of sexual contact and the need for self-discipline just as the "grown-ups" are warned to submit to government curfews purported to protect them. Yet, in spite of attempts to convince her that sex is dangerous, Esha becomes emotionally aware of not just the beauty and deep intimacy of the sexual act, but of the power it wields over others. Cheong's gendered commentary thus plays on the very beliefs in women's vulnerability that international feminists have noted serve postcolonial national cohesion; as Cynthia Enloe notes, nationalist men often represented women as a resource in need of protection from outside influences, particularly from "progressive" Western exports such as feminism (Enloe 1990). Here, however, the nuanced connection between gender and nationalism relies on the analogy between communism and sex as they signal both illicit temptation and physical violation.

But it is not merely through grafting political resonance on to Esha's observations that Cheong's critique is derived; Esha's ability to comprehend the motivations of the adult world is limited, her knowledge is partial. Depicting a period where "meaningful answers were not spoken" (3), Cheong renders poetic the divide between feeling and perception as a commentary both on coming of age and on the climate of a specific postcolonial moment: "[T]here were things you knew," Esha thinks. "There were things you did not know, too, but some things you knew" (38). The narrative is retrospective but rarely allows for retrospective awareness—the clarity of an adult perspective based on historical hindsight—to intrude on the partial consciousness of the child's narration. For Esha, meaning is always elusive and deferred until an unspecified moment in the future, a moment the adults assure her will come, if only as the rationale for keeping her now in ignorance: "[Grandma] was telling me something I was not expected to understand yet. . . . Someday all that I had kept of hers, all that she had passed to me, would be taken out, unraveled, and given away, and it would become useful. How this was to happen, I did not know" (100). One reviewer's comments reflect discomfort with the novel's insistence on maintaining the tension between knowing and not knowing, between historical "fact" and the consciousness of an eleven-year-old, seeing Esha's lack of "strong perceptive reasoning" as a failure of character development (Jonetta Rose Baras, "Writer Debuts in Tan Tradition," *Washington Times*, 3 November 1991: B7). Yet, this evaluation fails to see that partialness is the point—and not only because Cheong's choice of narrative voice can be seen as a commentary on the way perception is conditioned and delimited by those in authority. Her use of the faux naïf is not like Hisaye Yamamoto's or Sandra Cisneros' coming-of-age fiction in which the reader is invited to read beyond what slips past the child-woman's awareness. Rather, Cheong's choice of point of view—Esha's lack of "perceptive reasoning"—carries specific historical resonance.

The narrator's (and ultimately the reader's) incomplete information on the deaths of her parents and Li Shin, the rape of Auntie Daisy, and the disappearance of Uncle Tien produces a climate of anxiety and confirms her subordinate place in the household. Her lack of access to the complete story parallels the situation of a populace whose acquiescence is assured by a state of uncertainty, neither knowing if Communists might infiltrate the island nor, conversely, if the home will be infiltrated by the state. This connection between national and domestic space is likewise reinforced by Li Yuen's and Esha's growing suspicion of adults, which results in alliance between them, a circumstance reflecting the reconfiguration of alliances and loyalties along ethnic lines in the early stages of independence. The children's perpetual state of unenlightenment breeds paranoia about whom to trust: "We were only two of us, now. Anyone else could be an enemy, and we did not know what the grown-ups might do" (233). Although taught to obey the authority of adults, Esha and Li Yuen begin to draw a clear division between spheres, just as the adults themselves draw tighter ranks around the household against multiple, vaguely specified threats—the Malays, would-be rapists, Chinese Communists, vengeful gods, and visits from government men. In language pregnant with hints of conspiracy, Li Yuen warns, "Grandma hears everything" (189), as a caution about monitored behavior and the potentially punitive forces of the lawgiver; for the adults, it is becoming increasingly clear that "[n]o one escaped the government's eye" (81). Although the absence of definitive information in the faux naïf certainly reflects a postmodern concern with the bias of knowledge production, in portraying the effect of siege mentality in parallel spheres, Cheong's use of limited consciousness as the narrative's point of view carries additional political meaning by reproducing the climate of the times.

As Sister Katherine confirms in a lesson about the equator, the imaginary does have consequences in the real; in *Scent*, several "imaginaries" are instrumental in securing the hegemony of the current regime, most notably that of a Singaporean citizen where there were once only Chinese, Malays, and Indians, and of the ever-elusive communist presence that unified through the threat of siege. In exploring the effect of government policy on one Chinese family, *Scent* reveals the ways in which national identity as "imaginary community" is often secured through the projection of both external and internal threats that define common affiliation; the novel's original title, *Soldiers*, underscored this point but was rejected as unmarketable by the publisher (personal communication, 13 May 1998). In signaling the politically invested interests in which identifications are formed and consolidated, the novel engages the theoretical dynamics noted by numerous scholars concerned with difference as a constitutive element in national cohesion, a dynamic reflecting Stuart Hall's assertion that Englishness, for example, "was always negotiated against difference . . . in order to present itself as a homogenous entity" (Hall 1991, 22).[29] Thus, in discussing the novel as a form of historiography, I am less concerned with whether the threats of communist infiltration and ethnic disunity were actually imminent than with the uses to which such claims of crisis were put. What becomes clear in the hindsight of the novel's writing is that the "Red scare" served both as a source of common interest for a populace divided by generation, ethnicity, and class and as the PAP's initial justification for the abrogation of civil liberties and the implementation of social controls in the civic realm.

The Scent of the Gods exposes the ways in which the "Red scare" served the purpose of nationalism, but it does so without condemning the abuse of power as clearly as does *Irrawaddy Tango*; its nostalgic tone reflects an ambivalence about what sacrifices are necessary for progress. In regard to her family's deliberate forgetting of her ambiguously murdered cousin, Esha reflects: "I understood why the names had to disappear, put out like flames of unwatched candles that might burn down a house. It was not punishment for the dead. It was protection for the living. But Li Shin I had loved" (226). The family's manipulation of history is not overtly questioned; Esha "understood why" future security requires a willful disregard of the past. Nonetheless, even as the novel portrays the state itself as more threatening than the increasingly nebulous enemy, her comment seems to support strategic "forgetting" in the political realm, where individuals are sacrificed for the collective good. Love is the surplus of such forgetting, a sentimental excess of the drive toward futurity. Intimacy is an attachment that has no place unless redirected toward the affiliations produced and regulated by the state.

Although the government claims that policies enacted in the years following independence such as multiracialism, bilingualism, integrated government housing, and modernization are responsible for producing "social harmony," one can as easily say that they have succeeded in turning Singapore into the embodiment of the Panopticon in which discipline is enforced, if not by constant surveillance, then by the internalization of surveillance. The enforcement of social control in Singapore does not appear as absolute tyranny because, as Foucault writes in regard to the Panopticon, its end is not power itself but the strengthening of social forces "to increase production, to develop the economy, spread education, raise the level of public morality; to increase and multiply" (Foucault 1979, 208). If acceptance of the loss of democratic rights in the name of the public good and social evolution becomes internalized, it is because technologies of power are not merely repressive but productive and the loss comes to represent a fair exchange for a higher standard of living. And, given the thirty-four years of single-party rule in Singapore, as David Brown notes, "Once government equates the maintenance of social and political stability with its own dominance and legitimacy, then the concept of democracy becomes redefined so that it begins to refer, in effect, merely to the degree of public acquiescence of government and its policies" (D. Brown 1985, 1008). It remains to be seen whether the affluent middle class will initiate the call for more freedoms, or whether its own dependence on the state will preempt a move for greater democratic participation. In light of this contemporary context, *Scent* lays out for critique the suspension of individual rights in the name of the collective; its depiction of Singapore's history highlights transgressions ironically justified by the need to guarantee a political system meant to ensure those rights.[30]

As the means of their advocacy, both *The Scent of the Gods* and *Irrawaddy Tango* represent the years following independence as the source of contemporary political conflicts linking 1960s postcolonial nationalism to a 1990s concern with human rights as it had become part of an American cultural idiom. In highlighting tactics that secured the rule of specific regimes, the works represent postindependence history as continuous with the policies of the present, past repressions with contemporary abuses of power. Both novels focus on human rights abuses as if to highlight Weber's definition of the state as the agent of a set of institutions specifically concerned with the enforcement of order, and as such, the holder of a monopoly of legitimate violence. The works point to complementary methods of social control; what Foucault would call the "traditional, ritual, costly, violent forms of power" employed by SLORC have been superseded in Singapore by a "subtle, calculated technology of subjection" based on corporatist population management (Foucault 1979, 220). An appeal to human rights gestures toward one agency of potential policing not bounded by the state, and one effective for soliciting international attention.

But, just as standardized measures of time and space can be said to represent a move toward globalization, the philosophy of universalism underlying human rights is itself subject to questions of influence.[31] The Oxford Amnesty Lecture Committee's question, "Whose human rights are we defending?" is itself a response to philosophical suspicion of a subject transcendent of history. But as Judith Butler notes,

> To take the construction of the subject as a political problematic is not the same as doing away with the subject; to deconstruct the subject is not to negate or throw away the concept; on the contrary, deconstruction implies only that we suspend all commitments to that to which the term, "the subject," refers and that we consider the linguistic functions it serves in the consolidation of and concealment of authority. (Butler 1994, 14)[32]

The invocation of human rights and its necessary subject implies not a suspension of commitment but a call to intervention, one overtly intended to oppose oppressive authority. If the idea of human rights is recognized as a necessary fiction, a "contingent foundation" on which activism is mobilized, the question becomes not "What is the status of the subject of human rights within postmodernity?" but "How can this individual subject be deployed as part of a collective appeal?" Moreover, Richard Rorty invites us to reconceive "universal" notions of justice as matters of loyalty, asking, "Should we describe such ... moral dilemmas as conflicts between loyalty and justice, or rather, as I have suggested we might, as conflicts between loyalties to smaller groups and loyalties to larger groups?" (Rorty 1997, 47). Hence, human rights would no longer assume the aura of transnational morality, but be recognized as an expression of loyalty to Western conceptions of justice.

Irrawaddy Tango reflects this consideration of competing loyalties by questioning whether an appeal to activism based on a woman's torture is equivalent to an appeal to ethnic sovereignty rights or national reform; its portrayal mirrors American coverage of Burma's ongoing state of affairs, which depends on a female subject positioned in opposition to a military-controlled state, an appeal meant to extend beyond the single body. The fact that Burma's national self-image may not be particularly gender-invested only reveals the extent to which specific configurations of gender difference can be mobilized within the United States in service of critiques of Asian leadership. For example, like the novel, Hollywood's 1995 portrayal of the democracy movement in *Beyond Rangoon* engages a female point of view to depict its protagonist's political involvement in Burma as a response to gendered trauma—the loss of a child, attempted rape, and murder. The protagonist's psychic healing culminates in a commitment to humanitarian, non-national activism as she joins a doctors-without-borders-type outpost in the jungle.[33] In contrast, as Geraldine Heng has shown, Singapore's ruling party harnessed gender representation to postindependence mandates for national unity, from its conditional support of the women's movement to its utilization of eroticized sexual allure in the form of the "Singapore girl" to sell its national airline (Heng 1997).

As international feminist scholars have cautioned, yoking gender to the promotion of nationalist imaginaries does not always reflect the best interests of Third World women, particularly as such representations often fall into traditional appeals to women's reproductive duty or women as "nationalist wombs."[34] Women are also called on simply to symbolize the nation's relationship to modernization to signal degrees of either progressiveness or precolonial authenticity. As Aiwah Ong has pointed out, even feminist studies of women in development fall into a reductive binarism by evaluating gender inequality along this single opposition among modernization and tradition. The only distinction, she writes, is that "feminists mainly differ over whether modernization of the capitalist or socialist kind will emancipate or reinforce systems of gender inequality found in the Third World" (Ong 1988, 82). Moreover, as Kandiyoti notes, women's symbolic use as boundary markers among national, ethnic, or religious collectives may jeopardize their emergence as full-fledged citizens (Kandiyoti 1994, 382). Thus, it is important to emphasize that the gendered advocacy of these two Asian American novels does not reflect a feminist commitment to Asian women as much as an understanding of how the gender tropes that saturate American culture can be put to use. One could argue that Law-Yone's appeal to the injured female body plays on traditional ideas of women's victimization by reinforcing limited concepts of empowerment from injury.[35] Similarly, Cheong's coming-of-age narrative relies on gender-differentiated models of agency and passivity to parallel the state's methods of soliciting loyal citizenry: feminine submission to protective custody becomes the analog to masculine conscription.

These literary representations linking women and political advocacy speak to the potency of gendered metaphors in American national consciousness and their potential efficacy in eliciting sympathetic awareness of what inevitably is shown to be the patriarchal heavy-handedness of Asian governance. While this certainly reverses colonialist portrayals of a feminized Orient, both novels may reinforce the notion of Asia's absolute difference from the West—Law-Yone through representations of barbarous and inept Asian military rule and Cheong through implicit comparisons between Asian "guided" and Western "free" democracies. In reproducing Asia through differentiation, as Lowe suggests, these portrayals may sustain the narrow characterization of the always alien Asian American subject. Significantly, however, both works' emphasis is not on the contestation of Asian inclusion or exclusion in the United States. Rather, in keeping with Lowe's and other Americanists' general thesis on American nationalism discussed in chapter 1, the works reveal the processes of ethnic management to be endemic to the nationalist enterprise—here, under postcolonialism. Moreover, Cheong reverses presumptions about the West's construction of the East to show how Singaporean nationalism itself relied on distinctions between East and West to secure its sense of Asian ethnic cohesion. Gender difference becomes the vehicle for exposing how postindependence regimes constructed ethnically differentiated internal and external "enemies" as predicates of national unity and the legitimacy of their own rule.

As gender is positioned as a sign that secures group cohesion, it mediates the formation of collective identifications in the state's re-formation of affiliations and roles and becomes a means of defining group loyalties. As I have suggested, the rhetorical connection between women's sexual transgression and national betrayal is one bridge across the presumed divide between ethnic American and transnational perspectives in Asian American Studies. Just as Third World nationalists may position feminism as an imported Western corruption of indigenous tradition or female figures as betraying national collectives, so too have ethnic cultural nationalists represented gender concerns as a betrayal of ethnic American solidarity and continuance. Here, gendered discourses familiar to an American readership (spousal abuse, women's rights as civil rights) work to intervene in postcolonial Asian politics. This is certainly in keeping with Lowe's view of literature as one site where "the individual invents lived relationship with the national collective" as he or she becomes "immersed in the repertoire of American memories, events, and narratives" (Lowe 1996, 5).

But rather than wholly realizing the oppositional nature of Asian American cultural productions that Lowe envisions, this immersion can also produce a strategic replaying of American national narratives, as I suggest in chapter 4, a staging of values normative to the First World. Thus, an emphasis on the uses of gendered appeal is one means of displacing the distinction between exilic and immigrant sensibilities in Asian American art, given that it focuses instead on an interrogation of how U.S. investments influence representations of "home" or vice versa.[36] This is not to imply Asian American cultural enfranchisement as much as a familiarity with, for example, gendered rights as a tool for advocacy; there is, of course, a certain irony to my point given the tradition of valuable scholarship showing that civil rights have not historically extended to, or do not currently extend to, populations within the United States marked by class, race, or sexuality. Asian American positioning suggests an immersion in—and an ability to manipulate—First World ideologies and discourses, an ability particularly significant for writers who continue to have stakes in reenvisioning the governance of their countries of origin.

Highlighting literature's investment in the national thus speaks to Sauling Wong's compelling caution about the shift in focus from domestic to diasporic perspectives in Asian American Studies, a movement that potentially elides the class and coalitional history of Asian Americans that motiviated the formation of the discipline. Certainly, as Koshy notes, new Asian American literary production cannot be conceptualized simply within national boundaries; however, rather than a strategic forgetting of, in her terms, "outmoded identity politics," it is important to recognize how literature advances political advocacy in terms reflective of the rhetoric of rights intrinsic to the inception of the field (Koshy 1996). Of consequence is not so much that the texts I discuss here inscribe modes of Asian American subjectivity, although they may well do this, but that their narratives are partly authorized by, in Sau-ling Wong's words, their authors' "land of residence" (Sau-ling Wong 1995a). Conversely, if Asian American literature is singularly situated as American minority literature, it can be erroneously positioned in opposition to postcolonial literature as interventionist political allegory. This opposition is implicit in reviews that found *Scent*'s historical contextualization an awkward intrusion; one concluded that Cheong was "not as brilliant as Tan or Kingston." Such an assessment suggests that an association with the canon of "minority" literature, at least in mainstream perception, leads to a misreading and would relegate the history of social upheaval in such texts to a backdrop for narratives of identity quest. This association would position *Scent*'s bildungsroman not as the vehicle for commenting on political developments, but as a genre merely concerned with maturation and the "intensity of a young girl growing up in a lush and beautiful land," as one review noted, or the cultural conflict between tradition and modern values.[37] Although less an issue for *Irrawaddy*, emphasis on the novel's use of the picaresque ("a woman's sexual adventures") can displace a reading based on Tango's relationship to the state as a shifting collective alliance motivated by sexual activity.

Rather, in both novels "identity quest" becomes the vehicle for revealing the role of the state in conditioning the bounded expressions of identity and structures the authors' national commentaries. Both reconcile hard-and-fast distinctions between "minority" American literature and postcolonial literature by revealing that the gendered configurations of ethnicity, family, and nationality that figure into expressions of hyphenated identity are also vehicles for postcolonial critique. Both means of situating Asian American literature converge in a specifically gendered rhetoric that comes to structure political advocacy.

Wong's call for historicizing the push to globalize Asian American cultural criticism can be seconded by a need to historicize literature's simultaneous investment in global activism and domestic values. With this assertion of investment comes a necessary caution: although my discussion of the "universal" concept of human rights highlights literature's appeal to a transnational means of governance predicated on the rights of the Enlightenment subject, such appeals may carry implicit Western ideological agendas even as they advance ideals that seemingly transcend American national interests. Far from rendering Asian American literature postnational, an emphasis on a national rhetoric of gendered rights reveals the literature to be imbued with potentially hegemonic First World values.

Scarry has noted that Amnesty International's effectiveness depends on its "ability to communicate the reality of physical pain to those who are not themselves in pain" (Scarry 1985, 9). While the novels engage situations of differing urgency, both narrate the body's pain and the trauma of loss as a reminder that the "collective task of diminishing pain" does not end with independence from colonial domination. In Burma, the status quo is uneasily maintained as SLORC (now self-designated the State Peace and Development Council) continues to isolate Aung San Suu Kyi and disrupt assembly outside her home. Ironically, the ethnic secessionist struggle for Kawthoolei, a Karen homeland, now lives on in fiction after suffering a historical setback: Radio Myanmar reported the fall of the Karen National Union central headquarters in Manerplaw, forcing thirty thousand Karens across the border into refugee camps in Thailand in early 1995.[38] *Scent*'s portrayal of the PAP's implementation of "emergency" measures such as curfews or the Internal Security Act in the years following independence reveals the crisis surrounding communist subversion to be the initial justification for the suppression of internal dissent, which continues into the present. The tactic of invoking national crisis to elicit consent for state mandates continued into the early 1980s: as Geraldine Heng and Janadas Devan note, in 1983 Prime Minister Lee Kuan Yew charged educated (ethnic Chinese) women with a failure to regenerate the population in proportions equivalent to the moment of the nation's founding; theirs was a dereliction of the patriotic duty to reproduce a genetically superior workforce to secure Singapore's future (Heng and Devan 1992).[39] Both novels' representation of postcolonial Asian politics invokes the increasingly influential discourse of human rights as a reminder that the past is only rendered accessible in the terms of the present; and in doing so, they situate Asian American literary production as a medium of timely global commentary. As the treatment of political dissidents increasingly narrates the individual's relationship to the state, the more urgent the need to understand the ways in which "universal" concepts such as human rights transcend neither history nor context, but are deployed in the interest of specific political agendas.

Multiplying Loyalties

THE ACCUSATION OF BETRAYAL introduces a rupture into collective association; in doing so, it suggests the inadequacy of identity categories to
represent subjects. The texts I have engaged here use sexuality to interrogate political alliance and expose the socially constructed and politically
invested nature of affiliation. In proposing that identifications (and thus
identities themselves) emerge through contestation, my inquiry inherently
questions identity as a stable foundation for truth claims. This questioning is perhaps disappointing to those who, having noted the constituency
my subtitle invokes, have turned to this book as a source of empirical data
about Asian American women.

While writing this book, I was reminded of how this desire for hard
facts underlies a traditional sense of liberal education, bringing to light
the seemingly antithetical intentions of teaching and criticism. In a commentary column of the student paper, a freshman biology major in my
class on Asian American literature urged fellow students to take humanities courses like mine as a corrective to what had been left out of their
educations. Emphasizing the importance of knowing a repressed history,
she wrote, "[This class] is about reading an eclectic collection of stories,
plays, poems and essays and becoming a more informed and cultured
person. . . . In my opinion, everyone should take at least one humanities
class here at college. After all, it is the best deal you could get. Where else
are you going to find an English, history, anthropology, sociology and
psychology class in one?" (Parul Khator, "Humanities Classes Reveal
Unknown History." *Miami Hurricane*, 30 April 1999).

I was gratified by her validation; I want my students to be those informed and cultured persons that my teaching might help them to be. But
I also want them to think critically about how history is represented, to be
aware of what has been selectively disseminated for the record and how
rhetorical arguments inform that record. Her comments invited me to
think about my goals in teaching and writing about a literature with a
clear investment in the material world.

The texts analyzed in this book have one thing in common beyond
their various treatments of the shifting and at times treacherous nature of
loyalty and allegiance; they all engage realist strategies for storytelling.
This may not be surprising given that the marketplace for ethnic literature

was initially governed by a desire for ethnographic reportage, making autobiography a standard genre in the field. Many of the works I have addressed also share an activist intent, whether as an insider's account of history or as critical commentaries on continuing sociopolitical conflict. This emphasis on political intervention creates a specific challenge for interpretation. Because realism has the appearance of being documentary, its methods of persuasion can often remain invisible as the details and drama of events drive the narrative forward. Invocations of a world in crisis can subordinate rhetoric, rendering communication seemingly transparent and unmediated. When a text converges with history, accuracy and authenticity are more often at stake than the ways narrative structure creates a text's persuasive appeal.

Suggesting that rhetorical analysis is not always vigorously applied to the evidence that documents oppression and resistance, Wendy Hesford and Wendy Kozol call for an interrogation of the "realist strategies that continue to secure legitimacy for certain truth claims" (Hesford and Kozol, 5). In the opening essays of *Feminists Theorize the Political* (1992), Joan Scott and Judith Butler attempt to reconcile the activist premises of, for example, Women's Studies, against postmodern recognition of the discursive nature of experiential evidence. Put another way, is a loyalty to realism necessarily a betrayal of postmodern skepticism? In mediating between the discursive and material, *Betrayal and Other Acts of Subversion* is concerned with literary portrayals of women's experience, but more specifically with the gendered nature of women's political appeal. This book attempts to locate the social intervention of Asian American women's literature within its methods of rhetorical persuasion. My emphasis on how the scaffolding of narrative structure itself produces meaning has been intrinsic to my strategy of reading.

Yet my own critical endeavor might be said to deauthorize subjects in an ironic parallel to the way in which the accusation of betrayal itself undermines the subject's authenticity. As Butler notes on claiming "queer" as a political identity, "[T]he terms to which we do, nevertheless, lay claim, the terms through which we insist on politicizing identity and desire, often demand a turn *against* . . . constitutive historicity. . . . As much as identity terms must be used, . . . these same notions must become subject to a critique of the exclusionary operations of their own production" (Butler 1993, 227). As Butler implies, the challenge is to articulate theoretical positions that question the emergence of the subject and relieve it of foundationalist weight while at the same time presuming a subject who acts. This book has thus sought a method of reading that acknowledges literature's commitment to the material world—and the real women who people it—while being sensitive to the contingencies of its own production and reception. I hope this work has established an argument for the term "Asian American women" even as postmodern skepticism marks the use of identity categories as a necessary capitulation. I have thus insisted on highlighting texts by women as a way of marking their activist commitment and as a reminder that the stakes for generating gendered discourses are higher for women. However, the broadest suggestiveness of my readings cannot circumvent the historical specificity of each ethnic context, nor would I want to effect bland pronouncements on Asian American women as a constituency. Emphasizing rhetorical convergences across Asian ethnic texts is not meant to sidestep issues surrounding the inevitable insupportability of invoking this broad pan-ethnic category. Rather, I hope to inscribe Asian American women's agency, for one, as an authorial practice of textual manipulation not in order to privilege intentionality, but to situate Asian American writers as agents of ultimately political acts, acts that in turn exhibit awareness of how women have too often been positioned as mere objects of history.

I also want to mark a feminist reading practice that refuses to locate discourses of gender alterity on the side of unequivocal resistance even as it acknowledges the risks that speaking from the margins entails. I hope this practice of reading signals a wariness about situating gender (as well as racial) alterity as always challenging to dominant narratives. Pointing to the ways that sexuality works to resolve a crisis of citizenship provoked by racism, for example, may itself constitute a betrayal of the activist aims of Ethnic Studies and Women's Studies. Yet exposing the pervasiveness of ideology by naming the way in which hegemony functions is as equally a crucial and politicized endeavor as naming the ways it can be countered. Chandra Talpade Mohanty writes,

> I do challenge the notion "I am therefore I resist!" That is, I challenge the idea that simply being a woman, or being poor or black or Latino, is sufficient ground to assume a politicized oppositional identity. In other words, while questions of identity are crucially important, they can never be reduced to automatic self-referential, individualist ideas of the political (or feminist) subject. (Mohanty 1991, 33)

The same caution applies to narratives wherein discourses of race, class, and gender are presumed to work in concert rather than competition, and is particularly applicable given the association between women's literature and affect. On the equivocal nature of sentimentality, Lauren Berlant writes, "in order to benefit from the therapeutic promises of sentimental discourse you must imagine yourself with someone else's stress, pain, or humiliated identity. The possibility that through the identification with alterity you will never be the same remains the radical threat and the great promise of this affective aesthetic" (Berlant 1998, 648). *Betrayal and*

Other Acts of Subversion attempts to delineate the contours of that promise, particularly as sentimentality is deployed as a means of international intervention. It is also a meditation on the way in which this identification becomes a means of eliciting domestic consent and how speech from the margins must be legitimized by cultural norms in order to obtain a forum. Nevertheless, a question opened by these chapters as a parallel inquiry might be, can a more radical feminist vision emerge in Asian American literature given the terms I have engaged here?

I have argued, for example, that the posture of hyperfemininity is positioned as a requirement of (qualified) national citizenship and public being. In contrast, can masquerade and identification initiate a collectivity beyond the national? Literature does inscribe an alternative possibility for masquerade in portrayals of a seemingly transhistorical bond between women that enables them to claim ethnic solidarity beyond a First and Third World division. Instances that depict Asian American women's "going native" express both a desire for women's connection based on diasporic peoplehood and test the authenticity of that connection. Mimicry in this sense is a form of national passing that entails the deliberate erasure of sexuality as a sign of First World association. A means of trying on identities, masquerade is not a strategy of integration or asserting civic presence as in chapter 2, but a means of establishing ethnic-, gender-, and class-based alliances.

Andrea Louie's depiction of a Chinese American woman's spiritual quest in China in *Moon Cakes*, for example, raises the question of whether ethnicity trumps nationality. Attempting to pass as one of the masses, Maya strategically chooses cheap, ill-fitting Chinese-made clothing and ventures out into the hotel lobby:

> I stare at myself in the mirror, my body clad in these poorly made and slightly scratchy clothes. Do I look Chinese? It's the same me. I wish I were paler, thinner. . . . I feel the bellhops looking at me. What must they be thinking? . . . Do I look the part? Do I look like I belong here? (Louie 1995, 221)

Her masquerade expresses a desire for racial connection that surpasses national citizenship; Maya "goes native" as a test of her Chinese authenticity. Performing Chineseness necessitates class passing; her intent is to signal material deprivation ("poorly made" clothes, appearing underfed). The childlike uniform attempts to subsume her sexuality: she wipes off her lipstick and chooses a conservatively feminine blouse with a Peter Pan collar. Like Julia Kristeva's moment of self-reflection before a group of Chinese women, "Who is speaking, then, before the stare of the peasants at Huxian?" in *About Chinese Women*, and like Mukherjee's anticipation of how her adolescent, sari-clad self appears to a local underclass,

Maya attempts to project her image from the bellhops' point of view as the site of authentic witnessing. Paralleling Spivak's point that Kristeva's reflection is evidence of obsessive Western self-centeredness in the face of its Asian "Other" (Spivak 1988, 137), this instance can likewise be read as a Westerner's negotiation of subjectivity in the face of a foreigner's impenetrable gaze. Yet her passing intends to confirm her sameness to them, to confirm a racial bond. This desire for native likeness, to apprehend the self not through negation but through affirmation, is also a desire for a sense of self beyond nationality and beyond the artifice of (Western) femininity. Nevertheless, while this masquerade is in part a demonstration of sexlessness, her question, "What must they be thinking?" both affirms the power of the (Asian) male gaze to approve her new status at the same time that it fixes them as fundamentally alien to herself.

This instance of masquerade is not, as I have argued, a path to American integration but appears later as a means of testing women's alliance. A trivial exchange with a stranger who bumps her accidentally offers a sign of the success of Maya's "disguise": "*Duibuchi, jie jie*," she says to me. Excuse me, older sister, she is saying. "*Meiguanshi*," I whisper. "Don't worry about it, I reply in Mandarin" (222). Appearing unremarkable to a Chinese woman is the proof of her accomplishment; the address reassuringly interpellates her into China's gender and generational hierarchy. In contrast to Houston's and Mukherjee's portrayals, Maya's act suggests alternative possibilities for transnational connection in its evocation of diasporic ethnic belonging; interestingly, it suggests that ethnic incorporation necessitates deforming markers of culturally coded femininity, here, transforming the sexual into the familial.

Depictions of passing also expose the limits of global solidarities based on race and mediated through gender performance: as Amy Tan's Chinese American heroine embarking on a personal quest to China remarks, "Even without makeup, I could never pass for true Chinese" (Tan 1989, 312). The comment raises the question of whether or not the "traits" of First World femininity can ever be adequately masked even as they appear to be products of self-conscious art. Marie Hara's short story, "Old Kimono," establishes Japanese women's bonds across divisions of history and territory at the same time that it implies that connection's contingency. The story depicts a Japanese American, Hawaiian local who finds a used kimono at a rummage sale and intends, to the disapproval of the elderly women who sell it to her, to use its fabric in one of her own fashion creations. Her intent to create a culturally hybrid entity would involve, in part, the destruction of the kimono. Despite her resistance to tradition ("I don't wanna wear dis kine old-fashion stuff"), upon trying on the kimono in front of the mirror, she undergoes a momentary transformation—she experiences herself as a traditional Japanese woman and takes on her mannerisms, posture, and philosophy: "The line of her back now had some starch to it, and her face grew masklike as if dreaming deeply. Erasing her individual expression, she had traded it for something more adequately female" (Hara 1994, 43). The protagonist is momentarily seduced by her own now ultrafeminine image, by a sense of likeness and connection (if not also eroticized self-love) created in mimicry. Unlike Proust's madeline, the kimono does not return her to a prior memory but evokes a presumably latent diasporic connection to Japanese women. This link to heritage is not portrayed as in *The Joy Luck Club* as dormant "in the blood" but is instigated by the outward trappings of femininity, the external attributes—clothing, posture, movement, attitude—that visually invest one with a gendered social identity.

In the story, this epiphany is fleeting: her mother comes in and efficiently informs her that she has the kimono on backwards: "Anybody who know anyt'ing—all da people who see dat—dey gonna laugh at you" (45). The story speaks to, in Lisa Lowe's terms, the infidelity of translation, to the impossibility of refashioning what is locally Hawaiian and Japanese American into what is authentically Eastern (Lowe 1994). The protagonist's moment of kinship is ephemeral because, like the vase of red anthuriums (tellingly described as "boy flawahs") on her bureau that look so crudely robust and thus *natural*, she is too unapologetically local to be wrested into another feminine context. The story ends ambivalently, at once celebrating the protagonist's connection to Japanese women across the expanse of time and questioning whether this transnational identification can be sustained or is, in fact, desirable. The story suggests a potentially empowering view of femininity as cultural performance at the same time that it may situate this performance as particular to Japanese culture, its heightened sense of aesthetic feminine perfection. However, by exposing femininity's outward artifice, the story implies that what can be put on can also be, like the kimono at the end of the story, taken off and discarded. Masquerade here initiates women's connection while revealing it to be inextricably valenced by history and context.

In neither of these vignettes does identification with the "native" Asian woman necessarily express a desire for class solidarity. From scenes of diasporic longing, then, I turn now to the domestic realm in which class divisions form a barrier to women's unity in spite of shared gender oppression. While I have suggested in chapter 2 that identifying with the phallic woman promises access to the national imaginary, Nellie Wong's poem, "Woman in Print," hints that women's identification with one another may produce a different result, the politicization of consciousness.

Evoking uncertainty, denial, and empathy about kinship based on class
and gender, the poem finds its speaker poised at a moment of breakthrough to a collective identification initiated by the halting recognition
of likeness. The poem centers around the image of an aging prostitute
who becomes the catalyst for the speaker's own reflections about herself
and her social position.

Woman in Print

In the coffee shop I see a woman in a print dress.
It is 38 degrees outside, but she wears no coat.
She merely sits quietly,
alone
smoking a cigarette,
her gray hair combed back.

I have seen this woman, always coatless,
walking by a construction site.
I have watched construction men watching her
and I assume
she descends their darkened stairs.

She is as naked as any woman I have ever seen
or do my eyes deceive me
in this downpour?

I am a woman.
I wear a coat.
    (N. Wong 1977, 28).

The recurring sight of the older woman in a thin cotton dress in winter
causes the speaker to assume that she is forced to prostitute herself as a
means of survival. The final two lines of the poem indicate the doubleness
of the speaker's relationship; as a woman she is subject to the same gender
"construction" yet her class background shields her from the necessity of
bartering her own sexuality so literally—she wears a coat because she can
afford one. The tension between the literal and the figurative reflects the
duality of the speaker's feelings: she identifies as a woman but speculates
on the difference between them. The woman is in a print dress, yet committed to print by the speaker's words; the woman is both nakedly or
easily read and she is naked because she wears no coat. The men work a
construction site, yet also construct through their sight—the male gaze
forces the feminine body to submit to a gendered specularization that
erases her individuality and replaces it with the mark of sexual difference.
Placing the woman "in print" and thereby forcing her to conform to the
speaker's speculation sets up a complicity between the "construction"

men and the writer, a complicity that disrupts the gendered likeness of the two women.

The form complements the duality of the meaning—the final two lines are separate but form a sort of couplet. The absent conjunction between the lines signals the disjunction between the subject and the speaker: the speaker is a woman, *but* she wears a coat. The tonal flatness and decisiveness of the two declarative sentences counter the very undecidability the lines initiate. Likewise, the concrete simplicity of the images—"gray hair combed back," "38 degrees"—is undercut by the speaker's uncertainty, which renders even the representation of the image speculative: "do my eyes deceive me / in this downpour?" The overall movement of the poem is one of connection and distance; the speaker identifies with the woman's condition ("I am a woman") at the same time that she is aware that their class positions distance them ("I wear a coat"). The end of the poem finds the speaker both poised at a moment of collective recognition and aware of the differences between women that inhibit collectivity.[1]

For the speaker in Wong's poem, the question is not so much "Who is the woman in print?" but "Who am I (not) before this woman?" The process of speculation implicates the self in multiple categories of identity, power, and authority in ways that deny easy oppositions. The poem locates in gender likeness the seeds of a more radical, although still ambivalent solidarity not based in national community but in the shared experience of women. Like Hara's story, which portrays a moment of identification enabled by masquerade, the poem depicts witnessing women's constructed femininity as the means through which women imagine alternative identifications, multiple loyalties. Engaging the same dynamics of performativity and witnessing discussed in chapter 2, but to different effect, these portrayals highlight the ways in which a seemingly transhistorical femininity enables women to claim other forms of community beyond the national.

These vignettes thus offer one means of bridging the divide between domestic and transnational literature that, as I discuss in the introduction, has attained the status of a paradigm shift in Asian American Studies. In affirming collectivities not based on relations between nations, they multiply sites of potential connection and allegiance to situate this divide as merely one arena of concern within Asian American literature. However, this book contributes to the debate on the "postnationality" of the literature not through an attempt to confirm or refute whether Asian American groups maintain ties to Asia and successfully shuttle between loyalties as a testament to cultural hybridity. Rather, one focus of this work is the mutual investment between the United States and Asia as the First World precepts embedded within Americanized gender norms are deployed in literature. I emphasize not so much a commonality of women's experience that binds them across ethnicities and cultures, but a commonality of the authors' modes of persuasion that I suggest are readily influenced by their awareness of these cultural norms. I have deliberately chosen to balance texts associated with the early formation of the discipline with lesser known texts to demonstrate not only rhetorical convergences across ethnicities but also across time periods. On one level, these norms can become graphed onto—or willingly appropriated by—the Asian Others as a means of reconciling or "domesticating" racial difference. On another level, like Wong's and Hayslip's goodwill messages, Asian American women's literature can unintentionally serve the interests of American diplomacy and capital abroad. In Cheong's and Law-Yone's novels, the discourse of human rights marks a particularly contemporary American means of representing Asia. In drawing a direct connection between domestic discourse and postcolonial politics, this project reorients discussions on the globalization of culture, on whether transnational cultural exchange is a reciprocal process or dictated by U.S. global hegemony, what Pico Iyer has called the "Coca-colanizing forces" of American culture (Iyer 1988). Literature bears a direct if muted role in this exchange if what travels across national boundaries is not only labor or commodities but rhetoric itself, which conveys American values and precepts as readily as popular culture. However, I am not making an argument about the impact of Asian American literature overseas as much as about the ways it potentially contributes to American understanding of Asia in terms that are readily accessible to American audiences.

In examining literary advocacy, I have argued that gender discourse is one means of accessing First World ideas of fairness, equality, pacifism, and justice without self-consciously marking a First World investment. My emphasis invites other avenues of literary inquiry that might likewise blur the distinction between Asian American literature as a domestic or a transnational body of work. Does the rhetoric of infidelity appear in literary treatments of postcolonial sites that I have not addressed, for example, appeals to Korean unification or critiques of American military presence in the Philippines? Does what I have noted as a gendered universalist discourse structure other calls for American intervention into purported human rights abuses in Asia?

Such questions move beyond literature, pushing us to think about the use of women as boundary markers in a world where national borders are seen to be eroding. I began this study with two postwar examples of ethnic Japanese women who embody the site of rupture between two competing affiliations and whose notoriety is a result of their troubling homosocial compacts. What their examples reveal is that the processes of imaginary identification are most perceptible when the bonds that these identifications forge are traumatically severed. Like that of Japanese American internment, Tokyo Rose's case demonstrates how effectively the state can mobilize its resources to unify against a common "enemy." As the state pinpoints the traitor within to legitimize a political program or justify increased internal surveillance, those marked by racial difference become vulnerable; this is particularly true in the case of Wen Ho Lee, who has been accused of spying. To consolidate or refigure alliances defined by region, religion, or ethnicity, or as consortiums between nations, invoking disloyalty is a strategy that exceeds the confines of the state. It can also be deployed against the state's interests, whether by the internal ethnic groups who petition it, workers who labor within or outside its boundaries, insurgent armies who wage war against it, or nongovernmental organizations that claim a politics transcendent of territorial interests. As I hope to have shown, such tactics bear specifically gendered resonance as concepts of fidelity, patriotism, peace, or ethics become harnessed to the figure of the traumatized or treacherous woman. Asian American women's writing challenges us to recognize how women solidify alliance in the service of both local and larger loyalties. As the rhetoric of allegiance comes to govern the dynamics among individuals, ethnicities, and nations with increasingly violent consequences, the more necessary it becomes to understand how gender regulates group belonging.

My first-year student's testimony as to how reading Asian American literature contributes to her education reminds me, then, both of what I am glad that she takes away from my classroom but also of what I need to impart more forcefully. I want not merely to replace what was previously unknown with empirical knowledge, but to question the very ways in which language produces meaning and how positionality and context are intrinsic to that production. My goal as a teacher and a reader of texts is to expose literature's political investment, and in doing so, give students the tools to do the same. My student's comments remind me of the dual goals of interpretation and also push me to define what I hope the reader takes away from this book. I have chosen to highlight Asian American women's putative betrayals in order to analyze how lines of affiliation are drawn and, indeed, policed. To be outcast from any collective is to come face to face with its terms of inclusion, to confront the internal dynamics that render it coherent and stable to its members. Asian American women's literature eloquently attests to the stakes behind the maintenance of these lines, particularly for those who transgress them. In doing so, it reveals that the question of identity is also invariably one of loyalty. As literature produced by Asian women in the United States engages assumptions about the First and Third Worlds and confronts competing conceptions of the gender role, it betrays an American ideology infused with global concerns, wedding the national and the transnational. Urging us toward an understanding of the processes by which identifications and thus identities emerge through contestation, Asian American women's writing offers us utopian possibilities in an imperfect world as well as calling that world into account.

Notes

Author's Note: All book reviews, interviews, personal communications, newspaper and magazine articles, and miscellaneous popular media sources have been cited in the text or discursive endnotes.

Chapter One

1. Fluxus originated as an avant-gardist art movement in the 1960s, a loose affiliation of international musicians, visual artists, and poets who were known for staging "Events" or performance art pieces involving audience participation or task-oriented activities. Ono's association with the Fluxus movement began in 1960 and included a concert of performance events at Carnegie Recital Hall in 1961.

2. This is not to say that hostility against her no longer exists; see, for example, the oddly anachronistic website, "Me Against Yoko Ono," inviting surfers to logon if they agree that Ono broke up the Beatles. The site is subtitled, "Yoko Ono: She's everywhere you don't want her to be." http://www toptown.com/ DORMS/SGT.PEPPE/yoko.htm

3. Ono cited in Barbara Haskell and John G. Hanhardt, *Yoko Ono: Arias and Objects* (Salt Lake City: Peregrine Smith, 1991), 5. Lennon cited in Jonathan Cott and Christine Doudna et. al., *The Ballad of John and Yoko* (Garden City, N.Y.: Doubleday, 1982), 115.

4. See Jon Wiener's "John Lennon Versus the FBI." Jon Wiener, *Professors, Politics and Pop* (London: Verso, 1991). The INS concentrated its efforts on deporting John Lennon in the summer of 1972 out of fear that he would hold a political rally to disrupt the Republican National Convention where Nixon was to be renominated. Wiener notes that Lennon's application for permanent residency would be approved in 1975, after it was conceded that such targeting was part of the Nixon administration's obsession with New Left activism. See also Jerry Hopkins, *Yoko Ono* (New York: Macmillan, 1986).

5. Other comments were more direct, as in Paul's, George's, and Ringo's purported jokes about Ono being the "Jap Flavor of the Month" and having a slanted vagina (Hopkins 1986, 80).

6. For the history behind the arrest of Tokyo Rose, see Harry T. Brundidge, "Okinawa Deal Led War Correspondents to 'Tokyo Rose' Find: Brundidge, Lee Reach Jap Capital Before Occupation; Quiz Radio Siren," *Nashville Tennessean*, 9 May 1948, 1. Cited in Nathaniel Weyl, *Treason: The Story of Disloyalty and Betrayal in American History* (Washington, D.C.: Public Affairs Press, 1950), 387. Cited in Russell Warren Howe, *The Hunt for 'Tokyo Rose'* (Lanham: Madison Books, 1989), xvii. See Masayo Duus, *Tokyo Rose, Orphan of the Pacific*, trans. Peter Duus (New York: Harper and Row, 1979), 12, and Stanley I. Kutler, "Forging a Legend: The Treason of 'Tokyo Rose,'" Reprinted in *Asian Ameri-*

cans and the Law: Historical and Contemporary Perspectives, vol. 3, ed. Charles McClain (New York: Garland, 1980), 434.

7. Cited in Clark Lee, *One Last Look Around* (New York: Duell, Sloan, & Pearce, 1947), 85, and Harry T. Brundidge, "Arrest of 'Tokyo Rose' Nears," *Nashville Tennessean*, 2 May 1948, A14.

8. For example, while awaiting charges in a military prison during the American occupation, she discovered that a contingent of visiting congressmen was granted permission to ogle her while she bathed (Duus 1979, 98).

9. The story does not leave this difference between them unchallenged. The woman on the train disconcerts the narrator by the sensuality of her next act: she loosens her hair in what to the narrator is an act of seduction that psychically reconnects her to the erotic, nostalgic pull of the women of her youth. The narrator's smugness in interpreting the woman's class, caste, and conjugal status is confounded by the fact that the woman can, by this simple action, subvert the narrator's assessment.

10. Rich's essay, "Disloyal to Civilization: Feminism, Racism, Gynephobia," attributes the phrase to antilynching activist Lillian Smith (*On Lies, Secrets, and Silence: Selected Prose 1966–1979* [New York: W.W. Norton, 1979], 284).

11. As Sau-ling Wong astutely comments in a footnote, "Paradoxically, another cultural consequence may be . . . the rise of various forms of fundamentalism worldwide, with their insistence on purity, absoluteness, and inviolable borders" (Sau-ling Wong 1995, 21).

12. For example, see Masao Miyoshi on the loss of national sovereignty to multinationals in "A Borderless World? From Colonialism to Transnationalism and the Decline of the Nation-State," 1993.

13. Or, as Robert Wade simply states, "Populations are much less mobile across borders than are goods, finance, or ideas" (Wade 1996, 61). On the erosion of state power, see also Linda Weiss, "Globalization and the Myth of the Powerless State," 1997.

14. See Deniz Kandiyoti for a discussion of these stakes. As long as Third World women are used as symbols for the preservation of national, ethnic, or religious collectives, she writes, "their emergence as full-fledged citizens will be jeopardised, and whatever rights they may have achieved during one state of nation-building may be sacrificed on the altar of identity politics during another" (Kandiyoti 1994, 382).

15. In contrast to Lowe's thesis, it is interesting to note that Smith-Rosenberg excludes Asian Americans from her list of influential racial Others in exploring the transformation of Europeans into Americans, an exclusion based on the *early* historical presence of other groups: "[H]ow," she asks, "did white Americans imagine themselves the true Americans, and imagine all other Americans—American Indians, African Americans, and Hispanic Americans (all of whom resided in America far longer than most white Americans, who are, for the most part, descendants of nineteenth and twentieth-century European immigrants)—as peculiar, marginal types of Americans?" (177). Carroll Smith-Rosenberg, "Captured Subjects/Savage Others: Violently Engendering the New American," *Gender & History* 5:2 (Summer 1993): 177–95. Arguments on the centrality of domestic

racial subjects parallel claims in feminist scholarship on the role of gender in American construction as well; reflecting Nancy Armstrong's point that the domestic woman was the first modern subject, Gillian Brown's *Domestic Individualism* argues that nineteenth-century American conceptions of individualism were created through a domestic ideology marked as feminine and interior, apart from the masculine public sphere. Gillian Brown, *Domestic Individualism: Imagining Self in Nineteenth-Century America* (Berkeley: University of California Press, 1990).

16. For example, Rosemary Hennessy characterizes the tension thusly: "In some instances, questioning feminism's claim to speak for all women has led to fears that dismantling the identity 'woman' may well lead to the dissolution of feminism itself. At the same time, the myriad forms of violence against women, the persistent worldwide devaluation of femininity and women's work, and the intensified controls over women's sexuality and reproductive capacities are daily reminders of the need for a strong and persistent feminist movement" (Hennessy 1993, xi).

17. As Kumari Jayawardena notes, "those who want to continue to keep the women of our [Asian] countries in a position of subordination find it convenient to dismiss feminism as a foreign ideology" (Jayawardena 1986, ix).

18. See, for example, Kandiyoti 1994; Enloe 1990; Peterson 1995; and Lois West, ed., *Feminist Nationalism* (New York: Routledge, 1997). These scholars note the ways in which gender issues further the cause of nationalism whether through, if not feminism per se, traditional gender representations of women as "nationalist wombs" (Enloe), of the emancipated woman as a symbol of progress (Kandiyoti), or more generally the ways in which women have been situated in regard to national processes (Peterson).

19. Lois West's typology connecting ethnic cultural nationalism and nationalism bears significance for this link. In her suggestion that feminism and nationalism coincide under three types of social movements, as internal identity rights movements, as national liberation movements, and as movements against neocolonialism, West ties the consolidation of group identification to gendered state politics (West 1992).

20. See my article, " 'For Every Gesture of Loyalty, There Doesn't Have to Be a Betrayal': Asian American Criticism and the Politics of Locality" in *Who Can Speak?: Authority and Critical Identity*, ed. Judith Roof and Robyn Wiegman (Urbana: University of Illinois Press, 1995), 30–49.

21. Angela Gilliam, for example, has noted that the "analysis of sexuality as it relates to national liberation is different from the questions that U.S. women are accustomed to formulating, i.e., in this [Third World] context sexuality is understood within the context of economics and politics, rather than simply male domination" (Gilliam 1991, 230).

22. Tan's comment comes in reference to her objection to having Asian American literary works reviewed together because they may have "nothing in common except for the fact that they are written by Asian Americans"(7). Amy Tan, "Required Reading and Other Dangerous Subjects," *Three Penny Review* (Fall 1996): 5–9.

23. The phrase is Eric Sundquist's, used to express the relationship of African American literature to the European American canon (Sundquist 1993, 22).

Chapter Two

1. Antiprostitution movements fueled anti-Chinese sentiment. Using Census reports, Lucie Cheng Hirata estimates that 85 percent of Chinese women in San Francisco in 1860 were prostitutes. "Free, Indentured, Enslaved: Chinese Prostitutes in Nineteenth-Century America," *Signs* 5:11 (Autumn 1979): 3–29.

2. See, for example, Gatens 1997 and Iris Marion Young, "Polity and Group Difference: A Critique of the Ideal of Universal Citizenship," in *The Citizenship Debates*, ed. Gershon Shafir (Minneapolis: University of Minnesota Press, 1998), 263–91.

3. Nira Yuval-Davis writes, "Ursula Vogel (1989) has shown that women were not simply latecomers to citizenship rights, as in Marshall's evolutionary model. Their exclusion was part and parcel of the construction of the entitlement of men to democratic participation which conferred citizen status not upon individuals as such but upon men" (Yuval-Davis 1991, 63).

4. This equation is emphasized in the film version. While the biographical novel embeds the man/nation association, the film focuses on Polly's romance with future husband Charlie Bemis as a contrast to her relationships with the Chinese men who end up abusing, controlling, or deserting her. Near the end of the film, Polly rides out with the rest of the Chinese being driven out of the territory by anti-Chinese hysteria but in a dramatic moment she turns back to Warrens and presumably to Charlie. The decision is represented not only as the fulfillment of romantic love, but as the determiner of her national identity. The only woman in a group of displaced Chinese men, she is the only one allowed the luxury of return.

5. My emphasis on narrative is not to invalidate the fact that, as studies on the internment trauma have shown, internment produced lasting psychological effects. See, for example, Nagata and Takeshita 1998, and Donna K. Nagata, "The Japanese American Internment: Exploring the Transgenerational Consequences of Traumatic Stress," *Journal of Traumatic Stress* 3:1 (1990): 47–70.

6. After internees protested, question 28 was rephrased, "Will you swear to abide by the laws of the United States and to take no action which would in any way interfere with the war effort of the United States?" As a result, 98 percent of issei responded, "Yes" (Weglyn 1976).

7. Among the War Relocation Authority (WRA) photographs documenting internment, Wendy Kozol has noted a startling set of images depicting Japanese American children in blackface performing a slave auction. Identified only as a play for a "Harvest Festival Talent Show" performed at Gila River Relocation Center in Arizona in 1942, the photographs raise questions about what it means for one racially stigmatized group to put on a masquerade that is so historically loaded. As Kozol notes, the possible resonances can be contradictory: while blackface may enact a form of resistance by invoking slavery as a critique of Japanese American incarceration, it may also merely make a bid for national

acceptance by participating in the subordination of African Americans (Kozol, forthcoming).

8. Jeannie's flair for public performance can be read as a tribute to and challenge of the masculine role-playing of her father, a talented mimic, and brother, Woody, whose postwar profession is touring the country with "Mr. Moto," a Japanese wrestler, portraying "his sinister assistant Suki" (18). While the self-consciously artificial venue of professional wrestling may signal parodic intent, it is ironic that Woody willingly plays up the very racial fantasy that led to the internment.

9. I am approaching masquerade here in a way distinct from Traise Yamamoto's discussion of masking in the same text. For Yamamoto, masking refers to a specific reticence or tonal flatness in Japanese American autobiography that she argues is a means through which Japanese American women reclaim agency (Yamamoto 1999).

10. Prefiguring Judith Butler's concept of gender performativity, Riviere makes no distinction between "genuine womanliness and the 'masquerade'" (Riviere 1986, 38). Butler nonetheless questions where Riviere's concept of masquerade leaves lesbian women if desire is presumed to originate in masculine heterosexuality and does not allow a female object of sexual desire (Butler 1990).

11. Jeannie's circulation is also a sign of her father's economic-as-sexual impotence specifically in relation to her mother's history. Houston tells us that "Mama was worth a lot" (38) on the Japanese marriage market in the United States, a worth that the text reveals is largely squandered in her love match with Jeannie's father. If the phallic daughter cannot possess her mother, she must attempt to redress her degraded position through her own sexual commodification.

12. Elsewhere Mura implies that his addiction to pornography is the result of sexual abuse. See David Mura, *A Male Grief: Notes on Pornography and Addiction* (Minneapolis: Milkweed Editions, 1987).

13. I am indebted to Daniel Kim for this reference.

14. Or more succinctly in the publisher's note that accompanies Irigaray's text, mimicry is an "interim strategy for dealing with the realm of discourse (where the speaking subject is posited as masculine), in which the woman deliberately assumes the feminine style and posture assigned to her within this discourse in order to uncover the mechanisms by which it exploits her" (Irigaray 1985, 220).

15. As Bhabha notes concerning the racial stereotype, "the black is both savage (cannibal) and yet the most obedient and dignified of servants" (Bhabha 1994, 82).

16. The redress movement initiated by the Japanese American Citizen's League (JACL) in 1978 resulted in lump sum payments of $20,000 each to adult survivors as well as an official apology in 1990. See Roger Daniels, "Redress Achieved, 1983–1990," in *Asian Americans and the Law*, ed. Charles McClain, vol. 3 (New York: Garland, 1994), 389–93; and John Tateishi, "The Japanese American Citizens League and the Struggle for Redress," in *Japanese Americans: From Relocation to Redress*, ed. Roger Daniels, Sandra C. Taylor, and Harry H. L. Kitano (Salt Lake City: University of Utah Press, 1986), 191–95.

Chapter Three

1. For example, Shirley Lim's *Among the White Moon Faces* locates immigration to the United States as a move from alienated rootlessness toward communal belonging, in effect, a movement opposite to the one I am naming here.

2. While Rio's account suggests the gendered narrative I am tracing, the postmodern ending implied by Pucha's competing version of events throws into question the authenticity of Rio's narration. In answer to my own question, the novel offers multiple and competing models of complicity and resistance: in Joey's narrative, "America" functions as a means of enforcing passivity through utopian promises. Daisy Avila's narrative provides an alternative model to Rio's immigrant conclusion. Nevertheless, Hagedorn herself has noted, "Perhaps what I value most in Western culture has been this profound sense of 'freedom' as a woman—a freedom of movement and choice that is essential to any human being, and certainly essential for any writer" (Hagedorn 1994, 175).

3. Robyn Wiegman's *American Anatomies: Theorizing Race and Gender* is a notable exception. In exploring the analogy between "blacks and women" to reveal both their differential and complementary uses, she asks, "What does it mean that in discourses of civic inclusion and political rights, the social marks of gender have often provided the rhetorical means for constructing as well as depriving the slave's common humanity?" (Wiegman 1995, 62). The "analogic wedding of 'blacks and women,'" she notes, has been historically asymmetrical, emerging in both politically resistant and complicit contexts in the nineteenth century.

4. Elaine Kim reads Wong's "desire for personal success through aquiescence" as understandable, but ultimately accommodationist (Kim 1984, 72). Writer Frank Chin dismisses her "propaganda-as-autobiography" as a "snow job" (Chin 1974, xviii).

5. Chow is, in this case, discussing the native, who "in the absence of that original witness of the native's destruction, and in the untranslatability of the native's discourse into imperialist discourse," is always already wrested away from her "authentic" precolonial context. The critical desire in contemporary cultural studies to (re)place the native in her historical, "original," context is therefore suspect (Chow 1993). My analogy to a Chinese American "native" is thus inexact: there is no originary home for Wong. The narrative's attempt to register difference as per the dictates of Wong's self-conscious intention is mediated by the necessity of rendering likeness.

6. I make a distinction between the author, Wong, and her representation of Jade Snow, the character who plays out Wong's dramatization.

7. Critical desire to seek a more oppositional voice for Wong underlies interest in, as mentioned in *Aiiieeee!*, the two-thirds of the original manuscript excised by her editors. It may be easy to romanticize what is missing as the source of a more critical vision of American culture.

8. Milkman suggests that the impact of World War II on gender equity is somewhat overstated: it resulted in increased female labor force participation but not greater opportunity in male-dominated fields or wage equity. She attributes women's reincorporation into low-wage, low-status, gender-segregated jobs to

postwar management hiring policies rather than either unsatisfactory job performance or the union-enforced seniority system (Milkman 1987).

9. She has not deviated from these beliefs fifty years later: according to Karen Su, Wong said in a convocation speech at Mills College in 1993, "Your work is going to be your intellectual satisfaction, but it will be your marriage and children who will fulfill you as a woman" (Su 1994, 15).

10. The repeal of these laws by President Roosevelt in 1943 occurred after an alliance with China and was proffered as "additional proof that we regard China not only as a partner in waging war but that we shall regard her as a partner in days of peace" (37). See *The China White Paper*, August 1949, vol. 1, n.p. Originally issued as "United States Relations with China: With Special Reference to the Period 1944–1949." By 1950, however, the U.S. Navy was deployed in the straits of Taiwan.

11. Wong herself did not want to relinquish her belief in transhistorical collective traits and understandably so: her value as informant was based on her ability to interpret timeless cultural distinctions between Chinese and Americans. During her trip to the People's Republic in the early 1970s, her generalizations were met with incredulity. Speaking Chinese according to the conventions learned from her father, she is corrected: "As we left, the Chinese equivalent words for 'Thanks'— 'I am not worthy of this service'—came automatically to my lips. They replied indignantly, 'What kind of language is that? We do not know it'" (J.S. Wong 1975, 213).

12. Jane Marcus has pointed out her own need as a feminist critic to construct Gilbert and Gubar and Showalter as "daughters of anger" as an analogy to Virgina Woolf's invocation of Charlotte Bronte and Judith Shakespeare (Marcus 1988).

13. I experienced the deflation of the ideal recuperative feminist enterprise upon meeting her in 1987. Although she agreed to speak with me, she stated flatly, "I'll give you ten minutes. You young people think you can just ask for an interview and I'm supposed to drop everything. I'm making a living here." She was, however, interested in how I had come to my reading and while neither validating nor denying it assured me that she "wrote the truth—'Daddy's wife'" (personal communication, 10 December 1987).

14. I am indebted to Daniel Kim for this reference.

15. See Denise Chong, "Emotional Journeys through East and West," *Quill and Quire* 55: 5 (May 1989): 23. Ironically, Chong's own family memoir, *The Concubine's Children: The Story of a Chinese Family Living on Two Sides of the Globe* (1994), avoids the sentimentality of *The Joy Luck Club*. The fairy-tale quality of some of the *Joy Luck* mothers' stories stands in contrast to the realism of the economic struggle of Chong's Chinese Canadian workers trying to provide for extended families on two continents. While the focus is thematically similar to *The Joy Luck Club*—the degraded second wife, "lost babies," and sibling reconciliation—*The Concubine's Children* details the ways in which changes in political landscape, labor opportunities, and immigration laws influence generational conflict and connection.

16. In pointing to multiple contexts in which Tan refuses this binarism, Malini Scheuller makes an opposing point. However, I would argue that maintaining the

distinction America-choices, China-no choices in the *mothers'* stories works in conjunction with what must eventually be acknowledged as gender oppression's commonality in the daughters' stories by the end of the text.

17. According to Chodorow, the consequence of a feminine ego based on connection and relation in contrast to the individuated male ego is boundary confusion with others: if "mature dependence" characterized by a strong sense of self is not developed, "immature" dependence characterized by the need to look to others for self-affirmation and self-esteem follows (Chodorow 1974). Tan's mothers reflect this type of connectedness with their daughters, and all four daughters struggle with their ambivalence toward it. Significantly, however, the daughters' ethnic negotiation is posed in terms of their connection with and need to separate from their mothers.

18. See Bharati Mukherjee's essay, "An Invisible Woman," for the ways in which Canada's policy of multiculturalism impacts segregation (Mukherjee 1981).

19. Sky Lee notes that Western concepts of lesbianism depend on a sexual definition: "On the issues of bisexuals being lesbian or not, I just can't imagine half of the world not loving another half of the world because, I don't know, because they're lesbian or het. I just can't imagine that world, and I don't want to believe in it. But in an Eastern sense, a woman's community is very interesting. Women love women in my sense of the Asian community, which has, as its source, the village where my mother came from. . . . But interestingly enough, in the Asian sense, women are allowed to be women, left to play or work together, probably because the relationships between men and women are often more taboo—more rules about how you relate to your uncle than how you relate to another woman, because that's the kind of patriarchal control of women's bodies which is important. Still, in my mother's community, of course women love women. So what is lesbian?" (S. Lee 1990, 122).

20. Tan eventually published the story, her first, in *Seventeen*, where it caught the eye of agent Sandra Dijkstra. With Dijkstra's encouragement, Tan wrote two more chapters, "Waiting Between the Trees" and "Scar," and an outline of the others (one of which merely stated, "A woman goes to China to meet her sisters with expectations and discovers something else"), just before embarking on a trip to China with her mother to meet her half sisters (26). Upon returning to the United States, Tan found that she had offers on the yet unfinished book; she completed *The Joy Luck Club* within four months after the bid. Although she still thought of the work as a collection of stories "connected by theme or emotion or community," she compromised with her publisher, who labeled it a "first work of fiction" (Barbara Somogyi and Dan Stanton, "Amy Tan: An Interview," *Poets and Writers Magazine*, September/October 1991, 24–32).

Chapter Four

1. An earlier version of this chapter appeared in *Prose Studies: History, Theory, Criticism* 17:1 (April 1994): 141–60 and is reprinted in *Haunting Violations: Feminist Criticism and the Crisis of the "Real,"* ed. Wendy S. Hesford and Wendy Kozol, forthcoming, University of Illinois Press.

2. In 1994, the secretary of state, Warren Christopher, met with the Vietnamese foreign minister in an effort to normalize Vietnamese-American relations, the first meeting between the foreign policy chiefs of Vietnam and the United States since 1975 (*New York Times*, 10 July 1994). Since 1995, the United States and Vietnam have established diplomatic ties but have yet to achieve full economic and trade normalization. An agreement pending in July 2000 is not expected to receive opposition once it goes to Congress.

3. The poll was conducted in March and April 1994 in Orange County, California, which has the largest concentration of Vietnamese outside Vietnam. Sixty-eight percent of Vietnamese American voters there were registered Republicans, "many believing it takes a harsher view of Communism" than the Democratic Party (*Los Angeles Times*, 13 June 1994, A24). Fifty-four percent approved lifting the embargo, and 53 percent favored full diplomatic relations with Vietnam (*Los Angeles Times*, 12 June 1994, A32).

4. Throughout this essay I make a distinction between Hayslip, the author who constructs the narrative, and Le Ly, the representation of herself as the character who plays out the action of that narrative. The fact that these entities are often presumed to be identical testifies to the strength of realism as a genre and the illusion of unmediated access to the subject of first-person narrative.

5. Although Jameson's comments are in regard to the novel, the generic distinction between fiction and autobiography is not relevant to my argument here. While it is true that as a genre autobiography more specifically reflects, in the words of Michael M. J. Fischer, a "commitment to the actual" than the novel, I am interested in the rhetorical structures that render autobiography novelistically. It is certainly the case, however, that Hayslip's narrative would not have received attention had it not been perceived as factual, especially in a genre such as Vietnam War narrative, where authority is so clearly aligned with a first-person experience of the war.

6. See, for example, Jayawardena 1986; Kandiyoti 1994; Peterson 1995; Heng 1997; Lois West, ed., *Feminist Nationalism* New York: Routledge, 1997); Yuval-Davis 1997; and Nira Yuval-Davis and Floya Anthias, eds., *Woman-Nation-State* (New York: St. Martin's Press, 1989).

7. In regard to other Asian American women's texts, this construction is most notably reflected in Helie Lee's *Still Life with Rice: A Young American Woman Discovers the Life and Legacy of Her Korean Grandmother*. While less overtly interventionist than Hayslip's autobiography, this as-told-to *testimonio* recounting a woman's life during the Korean Civil War draws on concepts of maternal bonding in its plea for Korean reunification. The text ends, "I wait, hoping, aching, for the political gate that separates my son from me to fling open. And when it does, I will run in laughing and crying and singing out his name. How do I know? I am Korean, and we Koreans have this unshakable faith, for we are a strongwilled people. History proves it to be so. For more than a millennium we have lived as one people and I am certain we will be united again. Unification is possible! I say this as a woman who has survived over eighty years of living; also, I say it as a woman who has given life" (H. Lee 1996, 320).

8. Reuters reports that since returning to the international financial fold in 1993, Vietnam has received $8.5 billion in development assistance (Adrian

Edwards, "Rights Group Appeals to Donors over Vietnam Unrest," Reuters, 10 December 1997). World Bank donors pledged $2.4 billion in aid for 1998, anticipating that Vietnam would not be significantly affected by the 1997 financial crisis in Asia, as it did not allow free securities trading and did not have a stock market (Edwina Gibbs, "Donors Pledge $2.4 Billion in Aid for Vietnam," Reuters, 12 December 1997). However, the foreign investment pledges reaching $8 billion in 1996 plunged to $2 billion in 1999. Economic reform has been slow, frustrating even the most resilient multinationals, including Nike, Caterpillar, and Cargill, the major U.S. investors in Vietnam. Vietnam viewed trade liberalization warily even as an agreement to normalize trade between Vietnam and the United States was pending in July 2000 (Joseph Kahn, "U.S. and Vietnam are Said to Agree on Normal Trade: Little Resistance Seen in Congress After Four Years of Talks," New York Times 13 July 2000, A1).

9. It may not be surprising that the former comment praising her forgiving perspective on the war—and by extension the sexual violence perpetrated by the men who waged it—was published in Playboy. Digby Diehl, "Books," Playboy, July 1989, 26. Eva Hoffman, "A Child of Vietnam Grows Up to Write of the Horror," New York Times, 17 May 1989.

10. For a discussion of Nike's labor abuses in Vietnam and elsewhere, see the website for Global Exchange at http://www.globalexchange.org.

11. Craig R. Whitney, "Hanoi Now, Meet Saigon, Then," New York Times, 28 1997, 6. Of course, such comments in the American media may merely reflect a rescripting of the Vietnam War in which the United States, like Rambo, wins in the end.

12. Echoing the rhetoric of this "national covenant," Hayslip's Child of War, Woman of Peace could easily be the focus of Bercovitch's assessment of Thoreau's Walden, which he sees as "a conversion narrative that fuses the laws of nature, reason, and economics with the spirit of America" (Bercovitch 1978, 185).

13. A reading of When Heaven and Earth Changed Places does, however, challenge Jeffords's privileging of gender over racial difference in her analysis of Asian women, a privileging she makes self-conscious in her statement, "it could be just as important to understand [Vietnamese women's] construction as 'enemy' in terms of their race" (Jeffords 1989, 178). Her analysis of Vietnamese women focuses on the way in which the "sexual difference between men and woman is used to defer racial differences," rendering them mere vehicles for signifying power relations among white, black, Native American, Latino, and Asian men in a war zone (Jeffords 1989, 178). The centrality of Le Ly's point of view in When Heaven and Earth Changed Places does not allow a reading in which gender trumps race; the text reveals that both are integral to her self-conception as a Vietnamese woman and influence her representation of that positioning.

14. Viet Thanh Nguyen makes a similar argument in his discussion of how Hayslip's work serves the purposes of global capitalism through its appeal to a naturalized feminine body located in the "nostalgic fiction of Viet Nam as agrarian, precapitalist, and fundamentally stable and 'natural' in its social organization" (608). His work goes further to suggest how Hayslip's self-representation might also reconcile her to a Vietnamese audience through its convergence with classical literature. He notes that Hayslip's story resonates strongly with Nguyen

Du's "The Tale of Kieu," in which "ideal duty must be compromised in the face of contingency" (Nguyen 1997, 633) as the protagonist sacrifices bodily chastity in order to fulfill her filial duty; what redeems her as a nationalist heroine is her ability to retain a sense of spiritual chastity in the face of loss. My thanks to Sau-ling Wong for bringing this article to my attention.

15. Elizabeth Grosz's question characterizes this distinction: "Is the concept of sexual difference a breakthrough term in contesting patriarchal conceptions of women and femininity? Or is it a reassertion of the patriarchal containment of women? Is the concept essentialist, or is it an upheaval of patriarchal knowledges?" (Grosz 1989, 87).

16. Lois West also makes this point in noting the convergence of male and feminist nationalists on the centrality of the family and pro-natalist (antiabortion) stances to nationalist social movements: "Feminist nationalist criticisms of Western cultural values underlie their perception that Western feminists downplay or even undermine the importance of family and kinship relations" (West 1992, 574).

17. Trimmer notes that in fact Wurts merely elected to fly transport missions and never saw combat, landing in Vietnam once on a secured airstrip (Trimmer 1994, 34). Ironically, one can see how such a personal history would undermine Wurts's authenticity in a discourse where authority is assigned on the basis of action seen.

18. Trimmer notes, "Eventually Wurts and Hayslip agreed on a plot, conceiving the book as two journeys—a young girl's escape from Vietnam and a mature woman's return to her homeland. But to develop this plot, Wurts needed a new strategy for gathering information. He began compiling pages of written questions, asking Hayslip to remember the specific scenes and conversations he needed to complete the story of her two journeys" (Trimmer 1994, 34). Certainly Wurts's influence on the text can be surmised by the use of idiomatic English, for example, "She nudged my arm and I hopped to it" (*When Heaven* 12). But this influence may also be attributed to James Hayslip; *Child of War, Woman of Peace* recounts that the first book was originally written in longhand in Vietnamese so that Dennis Hayslip, who disapproved of the book project, would think his wife was merely writing letters.

19. Following the controversy that David Stoll's *Rigoberta Menchú and the Story of All Poor Guatemalans* generated, Menchú herself was initially willing to attribute any inconsistencies in her text to the influence of her collaborator, Elisabeth Burgos-Debray, whom she deemed "officially the author of the book." The controversy surrounding the facticity of her autobiography only reveals the extent to which discourses of the real rely on individual embodiment as an authenticating precondition. See *New York Times*, 15 December 1998, A10.

Chapter Five

1. *New York Times Magazine*, 2 April 1995. See also Joye Mercer, "Morality in Investing," *Chronicle of Higher Education*, 29 March 1996, A49–A51. I would like to thank Wendy Law-Yone and Fiona Cheong for speaking with me about their work.

2. In electing to retain the use of "Burma" rather than "Myanmar," the name chosen in 1989 by the military junta, the State Law and Order Restoration Council (SLORC), I follow the lead of the author whose text I am discussing. My decision is also based both on readers' familiarity and on political considerations in spite of the fact that the name change has been widely adopted by the media. Maureen Aung-Thwin and Thant Myint-U note that "Burma" is "merely another way of saying Burma in Burmese" (Aung-Thwin and Thant Myint-U 1992, 75). Journalist Michael Fredholm marks his choice to retain "Burma" more politically, stating that "Myanmar" means "strong" in Burmese, the language of the Burman ethnic majority, and therefore the name change is not accepted by all ethnic groups (Fredholm 1993, 7). However, original citations using "Myanmar" have not been changed.

3. The number of political prisoners is an estimate; SLORC has acknowledged the detention of 1,200 people between 18 September 1988 and 18 August 1989, according to Amnesty International (1989).

4. As *The New Yorker* noted, "Some demonstrators carried the American flag, and at one point, a group of students came to the front door of the Embassy and recited the Gettysburg Address word for word in English" (Sesser 1989, 80–81). It is unclear whether the use of English, knowledge of American history, or the feat of memorization was more astounding to the American journalist.

5. In suggesting that the American citizen has been defined in opposition to the Asian immigrant, Lisa Lowe's *Immigrant Acts* uncovers the ways in which Asian immigrants "have been fundamental to the construction of the nation as a simulacrum of inclusiveness" (Lowe 1996, 5). As Asian subjects in the United States are constructed partly as a response to U.S. economic and military interests in Asia, she writes, legal definitions of belonging are likewise constituted by various projections of Asian difference.

6. Detractors of Fay's punishment ranged from President Clinton, who called the sentence "extreme," to those who saw flogging as a form of torture. Still others seemed far more outraged at the *lack* of outrage expressed by a complacent citizenry: as one journalist put it, "[Michael Fay is] going to be thrashed and bloodied in a foreign land, and America doesn't seem to care" (19) (Michael Elliott, "Crime and Punishment: The Caning Debate," *Newsweek*, 18 April 1994, 18–22).

7. In addition to corporal punishment, there is a mandatory death penalty for murder, and trafficking in 15 grams of heroin or more brings the death penalty as does dealing in illegal firearms. There are regulations on hair length for men as well as prohibitions against fruit or flower picking on public land, noise after 10 P.M., and sidewalk or street dancing. Failure to report a change of address within two weeks could incur a fine of $5,000, five years' imprisonment, or both (915). (W. Timothy Austin, "Crime and Control," in *The Management of Success: The Moulding of Modern Singapore*, ed. K. S. Sandhu and P. Wheatley [Singapore: Institute of Southeast Asian Studies, 1989], 913–27).

8. During the 1996 conference on trade and economics involving twenty-five leaders of Asia and Europe, for example, members of the Association of Southeast Asian Nations (ASEAN) and China, Japan, and South Korea lamented that Europeans "only want to preach to them about human rights" rather than talk business (*New York Times*, 1 March 1996).

9. See, for example, Masao Miyoshi's "A Borderless World? From Colonialism to Transnationalism and the Decline of the Nation-State," which views transnational corporatism as a form of neocolonialism (Miyoshi 1993). In contrast, economists have noted that fears of the death of the state in global restructuring are overstated. See Hirst and Thompson 1995, Wade 1996, and Weiss 1997.

10. The term comes from Lenore E. Walker's influential study, *The Battered Woman* (1979).

11. Scarry notes that what the torturer desires in compelling confession is not information but confirmation that "intense pain is world-destroying" (Scarry 1985, 29).

12. Given the excesses of Burma's General Ne Win during his twenty-six-year term as leader of the military-dominated Burma Socialist Programme Party until his resignation in the face of mounting protests in 1988, Law-Yone's depiction of "Supremo," head of the "People's Party Council," required potentially little embellishment to convince readers of this irrationality. For example, in keeping with his belief in numerology, Ne Win wreaked havoc on Burma's economy by changing the denomination of larger bills to reflect his lucky number, 9, rendering the previous bills worthless. He once canceled an official state visit to France after interpreting an accident in his welcoming motorcade as an inauspicious omen (Fredholm 1993, 243–44).

Like other colonial independence movements, Burma's independence was furthered through an uneasy anti-imperialist coalition among diverse ethnic and political groups who experienced different treatment under British rule. The territories of the Karen and the Shan, for example, were administered as separate from the interior; both tribes' resistance to the new state arose from the feeling that they experienced greater autonomy under British control (Silverstein 1980). Perceiving that the newly independent state privileged the Burman ethnic majority under its state policy of "burmanisation," and unable to reconcile themselves to the administration of the centralized state after independence, both the Karen and the Shan continue to wage active warfare, now against SLORC. But, despite this longstanding history of opposition, these groups have mounted a relatively ineffectual challenge to the sovereignty of the state or the rule of the military regime (Law-Yone 1989).

It is this history of increasingly token resistance that elicits condemnation from *Irrawaddy*'s narrator, Tango: "Help was not forthcoming from any quarter as far as this eye could see—not from outside, not from inside the borders. Not from the only other men with the guns—those eternally bickering separatist groups . . . who couldn't set aside their petty quarrels long enough to gang up on [the general] for the ultimate kick in the head" (261). Her comment recasts insurgent armies with a long history of political causes—"self-rule, religious freedom, human rights" (128)—as squabbling siblings who, in addition to their failure to join forces to oust a despotic ruler, seem more significantly to lack a self-help movement, a point later resonant with Tango's disparagement of experientially based coalition politics in the United States.

13. Walker's *The Battered Woman* is one source of the phrase, "learned helplessness." An obvious problem with this concept is that it marks the battered woman as tangentially complicit in her victimhood via a conditioned passivity.

This complicity also makes problematic translating the idea of "learned helplessness" into political analogy; along the same lines, links have been drawn between Burmese Buddhism and the longevity of Ne Win's rule. It has been said that the Burmese believe that the power of a ruler is a function of the merit he is born with; hence Ne Win's authority could be seen to be derived from the merit he had accumulated from a previous existence (Sesser 1989, 76). Of course, such an assessment may reveal as much about the West's fascination with Buddhism as about the existence of culturally conditioned passivity.

14. The substance of this 1962 report was the cause for a heated exchange between Law-Yone's sister, Marjolaine Tin Nyo, and Sao Ying Sita, "Princess of Yawnghwe," in the 1988 editorial pages of the *New York Times*. Sao Ying Sita contested the representation of the takeover as "bloodless," a description she felt was belied by the murder of her brother at the hands of General Ne Win's forces during the coup. Her letter charged Edward Law-Yone with cronyism, a point rebutted by Marjolaine Tin Nyo, who attributed the use of the phrase to *The Guardian*, another English-language daily (*New York Times*, 12 September 1988, A:20, and 13 August 1988, 1:26).

15. Reports parallel methods of eliciting compliance, including beatings, burning with cigarettes, sleep deprivation, social isolation, and withholding medical care; these converge most forcefully in methods of sexual torture—the insertion of objects into vagina or rectum, coerced sex acts, and rape. Mary Romero draws a direct comparison between tactics used on American POWs in Korea and battered women in "A Comparison between Strategies Used on Prisoners of War and Battered Wives" (Romero 1985). Diana Russell cites A. D. Biederman's schematic, "debilitation, dread, and dependency" to draw an analogy between tactics used to break down the resistance of prisoners of war and those used by batterers (Russell 1982). See also Boulette and Anderson's discussion of the "Stockholm syndrome" (Teresa Boulette and Susan Anderson, "Mind Control and the Battering of Women," *Community Mental Health Journal* 21 [1985]: 109–18) and Tifft's use of Elaine Scarry's discussion of torture (Tifft 1993).

16. This is an imperfect example of what Scarry might see as torture's deconstructive ability; after all, the inverse of pain is not pleasure, but the cessation of pain.

17. Scarry writes, "When, for example, one receives a letter from Amnesty in the mail, the words of that letter must somehow convey to the reader the aversiveness being experienced inside the body of someone whose country may be far away, *whose name can barely be pronounced*, and whose ordinary life is unknown except that it is known that ordinary life has ceased to exist" (Scarry 1985, 9, emphasis mine). Her comment unwittingly reveals that international agencies such as Amnesty International locate the West as an implicit center for human rights activism.

18. The U.S. Drug Enforcement Agency (DEA) has viewed Khun Sa, former leader of the Shan United Army, as an opium drug lord. Khun Sa claimed to be fighting for an independent Shan state, but the DEA alleged that he had raised a personal army to protect his heroin business (Reuters World Service, 15 May 1995). In contrast, the Karen apparently fund their activities by taxing goods smuggled into Thailand (Sesser 1989, 74). Based on SLORC's record of human

rights abuses, the United States is now reluctant to lift its arms embargo on Burma, even to fight the "War on Drugs" in the region between Burma, Laos, and Thailand known as the Golden Triangle and cut drug enforcement aid after the events of 1988 (see Mathea Falco, "Don't Make a Deal," *New York Times*, 17 July 1994; and Peter Reuter, "Myanmar's Drug Habit," *New York Times*, 3 April 1995). Ethnic groups claim that the government was using antiopium herbicides on insurgent armies' food supply (Law-Yone 1989; Sesser 1989).

19. The novel could not foresee the factionalization of the Karen movement two years later. The Karen National Union was divided by a progovernment Buddhist group, the Democratic Karen Buddhist Army, who forced some refugees to repatriate from camps in Thailand (*New York Times*, 23 February 1996).

20. For example, this from *Time*: "Gentle in gesture and speech, the Karens do not seem capable of nurturing hatred. Nor do the guerrillas seem capable of dispatching their children to the front lines to fight, and die, alongside the men. But they do" (Alessandra Stanley, "Burma: Junior Rambos," *Time*, 18 June 1990, 41). The *New York Times* has been consistently fascinated by a radical offshoot of the Karen cause, God's Army, which staged a suicide raid on a Thai hospital, taking eight hundred hostages. More noteworthy to the *Times*, however, is the fact that God's Army is led by gun-toting, cheroot smoking, twelve-year-old twins, Luther and Johnny Htoo, believed by their followers to be the reincarnation of ancient Karen heroes and imbued with supernatural powers. The Western journalist who visited their camp devoted as much space to their actual cause as he did to the fact that the boys do not know how to play (Seth Mydans, "Burmese Boy Rebels Languish in Jungle," *New York Times* 19 July 2000 A12).

21. Eliza Noh's work analyzing the rhetoric of the international campaign, End Child Prostitution in Asian Tourism (ECPAT), offers an interesting contrast to my analysis of Law-Yone's "transnational" method of appeal. Noh reveals that ECPAT's Christian ecumenical representation of Asian sex workers enforces Asian difference from the West in the course of its activism, an approach that she suggests functions as a recolonizing gesture (Noh 1997). I see this method of representing Asian "otherness" as very much in force in U.S. media coverage of Asia, a point I make in the chapter's introduction. In contrast, however, one thing I am suggesting is that Law-Yone's treatment of gender (and later, Fiona Cheong's) appeals to likeness over difference through its evocation of domestic abuse. I am suggesting that this appeal may take on universalist overtones while being rooted in specific post-women's movement American context.

22. Members of the Soviet bloc of nations objected to a liberal construction of freedom that ignored group rights—the right to speak one's own language, ensure the protection of one's national culture, or guarantee the rights of national minorities. The Soviet Union put before the delegates a draft amendment reflecting group rights that was subsequently rejected (*Yearbook of the United Nations 1948–49* (Lake Success, New York: United Nations/Department of Public Information], 535).

23. The statement is also reflected in Article 14 of the Beijing Declaration and Platform for Action disseminated by the United Nations, 15 September 1995. The conference's keynote address was delivered by Aung San Suu Kyi via a smuggled-in videotape (*New York Times*, 6 September 1995, A4).

24. Of course, one would only have to look at specific instances to show how this distinction cannot be sustained. Jenny Bourne points out as much in her discussion of how Jewish feminist identity politics in Britain fails to take a stand on Zionism (Bourne 1987).

25. Ironically, the push toward democratization, the First World cure-all to Third World turbulence, is a trope that appears in contexts other than that of international diplomacy. In a curious convergence, feminist studies of domestic abuse also speak of solutions to battery in terms of political systems. For example, Romero compares the tactics of domination used by wife batterers to those employed by the Chinese captors of American POWs in Korea in order to suggest that "deprogramming" victims "ought to include the resocialization to feminist values within a supportive and *democratic* environment" (Romero 1985, 545, emphasis mine). If, like the political despot, the male batterer inappropriately uses violence to maintain inequities in power, studies suggest that among other strategies, stopping domestic violence lies in equalizing the gender hierarchy that legitimates masculine entitlement in order to remedy the lack of consensual decision making found in more "democratic" relationships. See Tifft 1993. One of the problems evident in the analogy is that researchers of domestic abuse tend either implicitly or explicitly to place their comments within a comparative moral framework. For example, Russell notes, "Americans were recently outraged by the treatment of the hostages in Iran, even though . . . they suffered no 'systematic' or 'sadistic' beatings. *Much worse* treatment is going on every day and every night in many American homes" (Russell 1982, 273, emphasis mine).

In contrast, Romero's work explains the apparent disparity between academic attention to POWs and battered women in terms of ideological systems: "Strategies used on POWs were studied in detail because the possibility that United States soldiers could be converted to Communism was threatening to America, whereas wife battering may serve to support aspects of social control (e.g., the traditional family, male dominance, and other aspects of the American way of life)" (Romero 1985, 545). My intention in placing the discourses of political coercion and domestic abuse side by side is not to replicate such a hierarchy, but to note that they are mutually sustaining in their reliance on a conception of individual rights.

26. Law-Yone notes, "If you grow up in a society like the one I was trying to describe, the whole notion of introspection is different. Especially in a Buddhist society, the idea of self, the individual as the ego, is just not prevalent. . . . On the other hand it takes a certain kind of introspection to be an interesting character. Especially in the Western tradition, the whole direction has been toward telling secrets. . . . In Asia it is your job as an artist not to challenge, not to subvert, but to reproduce reality and make it palatable. The self is not important, it is the community that is important" (cited in Trescott 1994, C1). Law-Yone makes clear that she locates herself against this nonpolitical, nonconfrontational character of writing in Asia, thus situating her writing within a tradition of advocacy marked as Western (personal communication, 28 December 1996).

27. See Chua Beng-Huat 1994. This fear of libel suits may or may not extend to fictional representations of the regime. For example, *The Scent of the Gods* was available and reviewed in Singapore at the time of its publication; Cheong recalls

her trepidation in anticipating official response but was not officially "scolded" for her portrayal in government-owned newspapers. She attributed this lack of response both to the literariness of the representation and to the relative newness of fiction about Singapore produced in the West (personal communication, 12 June 1998). As Shirley Lim notes, creative political critiques may be unlikely if only because, as part of the English-educated elite working in government-controlled institutions, Singapore writers have interests "inextricably bound with governmental, bureaucratic aims" (Lim 1989, 541).

28. Chia Thye Poh, arrested in 1966 for allegedly advocating armed struggle against the PAP government while a member of Parliament representing Barisan Socialis, was released in November 1998 after being held in a form of internal exile on the island of Sentosa.

29. Reflecting Homi Bhabha's recognition that "the production of discriminatory identities . . . secure[s] the 'pure' and original identity of [colonial] authority," this structure of argument appears in numerous writings on the relationship between nationalism and alterity (Bhabha 1994, 112).

30. In commenting on the irony produced by defying democratic principles to ensure democracy, the novel reveals that the PAP dealt with this contradiction by drawing a distinction between Western "free" democracy and Asian "guided" democracy. Li Shin repeats the PAP line: "We were not like America. America was a free democracy, he said, because American people did not like being guided." "How come we don't want a free democracy?" I asked. "Because we're Asians," he said. "We don't always believe the same things as Americans" (50).

31. For example, Immanuel Wallerstein notes the dual use of ideologies of universalism underlying not only human rights as a form of international law, but science communities and principles of citizenship within sovereign states as well: "[I]t is precisely because there is in reality a hierarchy of states within the interstate system and a hierarchy of citizens within each sovereign state that the ideology of universalism matters. It serves on the one hand as a palliative and a deception and on the other as a political counterweight which the weak can use and do use against the strong" (Wallerstein 1991, 171).

32. Rey Chow also notes that human freedoms are themselves contingent. Freedom of the press, she writes in regard to American coverage of Tiananmen Square, is not "a basic existential condition to which all are entitled (though this is the claim that is made) but a network of demands, negotiations, and coercions that are themselves bound by historical determinants constructed on slaughter and bloodshed" (Chow 1991, 85).

33. The film reinforces the representation of the individual-as-collective in its depiction of the moment a beatific Aung San Suu Kyi single-handedly stands down a line of government soldiers during a mass demonstration.

34. The phrase is Enloe's (1990). See also Heng and Devan 1992; Peterson 1995; and West 1992.

35. See, for example, Wendy Brown's exploration of the limitations of Catharine MacKinnon's theory of sexuality as the eroticization of gender inequality. MacKinnon's concept of gender, she suggests, forecloses prospects for radical social change if there is no agency for subjects seemingly wholly constituted by dominant power (W. Brown 1995). Brown's comments are suggestive for Asian

American coalitional democratic participation, but such an inquiry is beyond the scope of this essay.

36. See, for example, Campomanes 1992. His positioning of Filipino American literature as exilic literature may blur an important distinction between the political statuses of the exile and the émigré. As Edward Said notes, immigration suggests the possibility of choice rather than banishment (Said 1984). Said, however, does not go on to stress political exile as a condition of banishment as a punishment enforced by the threat of violence where return is rendered impossible. For example, Wendy Law-Yone's stakes in representing false charges of conspiracy against the state are linked to her condition of exile. In addition to witnessing her father's detention and his subsequent participation in former Prime Minister U Nu's government in exile, she herself was held at secret police headquarters in Rangoon in the late 1960s after trying to leave the country illegally to meet her American husband, an act she recognized as "defiance amounting to treason" (Law-Yone 1994, 41). Moreover, Campomanes's distinction may also unwittingly imply that immigrant literature is characterized by an uncomplicated relationship to national culture.

37. Few reviews discuss Singapore's political climate. Although Howard Coale's review opens by acknowledging governmental repression, calling Singapore "a Stepford country" and an "Asian version of 1984," he validates the fact that the novel "manages to avoid being overtly political" (Howard Coale, "Porcelain Dreams," New York Times, 24 November 1991, sec. 7, 22). See also Baras 1991, and Christine Bell, "In Times of Trouble, A Search for Identity," Los Angeles Times, 28 January 1992, E6.

38. The New York Times estimates the number at fifteen thousand. Many Karen remained in Thailand, fearing harsh treatment upon repatriation, but their welcome has been strained as Thailand seeks business opportunities with Myanmar (BBC Summary of World Broadcasts, 8 May 1995 and 13 May 1995). Despite fears that the Thai government would reverse its twenty-year policy of granting haven to Karen refugees, Thailand agreed not to force repatriation of 2,300 unarmed Karen. See Seth Mydans, "In Thai Camps, Fear of Burmese Troops Grows," New York Times, 3 March 1997, and "Thailand Says Refugees Can Stay," New York Times, 4 March 1997.

39. Heng and Devan write, "Cabinet ministers began to exhort graduate women to marry and bear children *as a patriotic duty*. Obediently taking their cue from the government, two (nonfeminist) women's organizations accordingly proposed, in a disturbing collusion with state patriarchy, that women be *required* to bear children as a form of National Service—the equivalent, in feminine, biological terms, of the two-and-a-half-year military service compulsorily performed by men for the maintenance of national defense" (Heng and Devan 1992, 348).

Afterword

1. My students invariably give an alternative interpretation of the poem. They read the speaker as envious of the woman's sexual freedom, her bravado in displaying her body.

Works Cited

Abel, Elizabeth. 1993. "Black Writing, White Reading: Race and the Politics of Feminist Interpretation." *Critical Inquiry* 19 (Spring): 470–98.

Amnesty International. 1989. *Myanmar (Burma) Prisoners of Conscience: A Chronicle of Developments Since September 1988.* New York: Amnesty International

——. 1973. *Report on Torture.* London: Duckworth with Amnesty International Publications.

——. 1984. *Torture in the Eighties.* London: Amnesty International Publications.

Anderson, Benedict. 1990. *Imagined Communities: Reflections on the Origin and Spread of Nationalism.* London: Verso.

Anzaldúa, Gloria. 1987. *Borderlands/La Frontera: The New Mestiza.* San Francisco: Spinsters/Aunt Lute.

——. 1983. "La Prieta." In *This Bridge Called My Back: Writings by Radical Women of Color,* ed. Cherríe Moraga and Gloria Anzaldúa, 198–209. Latham, N.Y.: Kitchen Table: Women of Color Press.

Appadurai, Arjun. 1994. "Disjunction and Difference in the Global Cultural Economy." In *Colonial Discourse and Post-Colonial Theory,* ed. Patrick Williams and Laura Chrisman, 324–39. New York: Columbia University Press [1990].

Appelbaum, Richard P., David Smith, and Brad Christerson. 1994. "Commodity Chains and Industrial Restructuring in the Pacific Rim: Garment Trade and Manufacturing." In *Commodity Chains and Global Capitalism,* ed. Gary Gereffi and Miguel Korzeniewicz, 187–204. Westport, Conn.: Greenwood.

Aptheker, Bettina. 1989. *Tapestries of Life: Women's Work, Women's Consciousness and the Meaning of Daily Experience.* Amherst: University of Massachusetts Press.

Aung-Thwin, Maureen, and Thant Myint-U. 1992. "The Burmese Ways to Socialism." *Third World Quarterly* 13:1: 67–75.

Bercovitch, Sacvan. 1978. *The American Jeremiad.* Madison: University of Wisconsin Press.

Berlant, Lauren. 1998. "Poor Eliza." *American Literature* 70: 3 (September): 635–68.

——. 1997. *The Queen of America Goes to Washington City: Essays on Sex and Citizenship.* Durham: Duke University Press.

Bhabha, Homi K. 1994. *The Location of Culture.* London: Routledge.

Boose, Lynda. 1993. "Techno-Muscularity and the 'Boy-Eternal': From the Quagmire to the Gulf." In *Cultures of United States Imperialism,* ed. Amy Kaplan and Donald E. Pease, 581–616. Durham: Duke University Press.

Bourne, Jenny. 1987. "Homelands of the Mind: Jewish Feminism and Identity Politics." *Race and Class* 29:1: 1–24.

Bronfen, Elisabeth. 1992. *Over Her Dead Body: Death, Femininity, and the Aesthetic*. New York: Routledge.

Brown, David. 1985. "Crisis and Ethnicity: Legitimacy in Plural Societies." *Third World Quarterly* 7:4: 988–1008.

Brown, Wendy. 1991. "Deregulating Women: The Trials of Freedom Under a Thousand Points of Light." *Sub/Versions: Feminist Studies Work-in-Progress*. U.C. Santa Cruz (Winter): 1–8.

———. 1995. *States of Injury: Power and Freedom in Late Modernity*. Princeton: Princeton University Press.

Butler, Judith. 1993. *Bodies that Matter: On the Discursive Limits of "Sex."* New York: Routledge.

———. 1994. "Contingent Foundations: Feminism and the Question of 'Postmodernism.'" In *Feminists Theorize the Political*, ed. Judith Butler and Joan W. Scott, 3–21. New York: Routledge.

———. 1990. *Gender Trouble: Feminism and the Subversion of Identity*. New York: Routledge.

Campomanes, Oscar V. 1992. "Filipinos in the United States and Their Literature of Exile." In *Reading the Literatures of Asian America*, ed. Shirley Geok-lin Lim and Amy Ling, 49–78. Philadelphia: Temple University Press.

Carby, Hazel V. 1992. "The Multicultural Wars." *Radical History Review* 54: 7–18.

Chan, Sucheng. 1991. *Asian Americans: An Interpretive History*. Boston: Twayne.

———. 1990. "Commentary." *Amerasia Journal* 16: 2.

Cheng, Lucie. 1984. "Asian American Women and Feminism." *Sojourner Collective*. New York.

Cheong, Fiona. 1991. *The Scent of the Gods*. New York: W. W. Norton.

Chin, Frank, et al., eds. 1974. *Aiiieeeee!: An Anthology of Asian-American Writers* Washington, D.C.: Howard University Press.

———. 1991. "Come All Ye Asian American Writers of the Real and the Fake." In *The Big Aiiieeeee! An Anthology of Chinese American and Japanese American Literature*, ed. Jeffrey Paul Chan, Frank Chin, Lawson Fusao Inada, and Shawn Wong, 1–92. New York: Penguin.

——— and Jeffrey Paul Chan. 1972. "Racist Love." In *Seeing Through Shuck*, ed. Richard Kostelanetz, 65–79. New York: Ballantine.

——— (Jeffrey Leong). 1978. "Song of the Monogram Warner Bros. Chink: News to Raise the Dead." *Y'Bird Magazine* 1:133.

Chodorow, Nancy. 1974. "Family Structure and Feminine Personality." In *Woman, Culture and Society*, ed. Michelle Rosaldo and Louise Lamphere. Stanford: Stanford University Press.

Chong, Denise. 1994. *The Concubine's Children*. New York: Penguin.

Chow, Rey. 1991. "Violence in the Other Country: China as Crisis, Spectacle, and Woman." In *Third World Women and the Politics of Feminism*, ed. Chandra Talpade Mohanty, Ann Russo, and Lourdes Torres, 81–100. Bloomington: Indiana University Press.

———. 1993. *Writing Diaspora: Tactics of Intervention in Contemporary Cultural Studies*. Bloomington: Indiana University Press.

Chua Beng-Huat. 1994. "Arrested Development: Democratisation in Singapore." *Third World Quarterly* 15:4: 655–68.

Chua, C. Lok. "Constructing an Asian American Protagonist: Popular Culture, Bricolage, and Wendy Law-Yone's *Irrawaddy Tango*." Unpublished manuscript.

Clifford, James. 1997. *Routes: Travel and Translation in the Late Twentieth Century*. Cambridge, Mass.: Harvard University Press.

Creef, Elena Tajima. *Re/Orientations: Imaging Japanese America in 20th Century American Visual Culture*. Unpublished manuscript.

Crow Dog, Mary. 1990. *Lakota Woman*. New York: HarperCollins.

Dirlik, Arif. 1994. "The Postcolonial Aura: Third World Criticism in the Age of Global Capitalism." *Critical Inquiry* 20 (Winter): 328–56.

Doane, Mary Ann. 1982. "Film and the Masquerade: Theorising the Female Spectator." *Screen* 23: 79–82.

duCille, Ann. 1994. "The Occult of True Black Womanhood: Critical Demeanor and Black Feminist Studies." *Signs* 19:3 (Spring): 591–629.

Enloe, Cynthia. 1990. *Bananas, Beaches, and Bases: Making Feminist Sense of International Politics*. Berkeley: University of California Press.

Fanon, Frantz. 1991. *Black Skin, White Masks*. Trans. Charles Lam Markmann. New York: Grove Weidenfeld.

Fischer, Michael M. J. 1986. "Ethnicity and the Post-Modern Arts of Memory." In *Writing Culture: The Poetics and Politics of Ethnography*, ed. James Clifford and George E. Marcus, 194–233. Berkeley: University of California Press.

Fong, Giselle. 1990. "Corrosion." In *Making Face, Making Soul: Haciendo Caras: Creative and Critical Perspectives by Women of Color*, ed. Gloria Anzaldúa, 117. San Francisco: Aunt Lute.

Fong, Katheryn M. 1978. "Feminism Is Fine, But What's It Done for Asia America?" *Bridge: An Asian American Perspective* (Winter): n.p.

Foucault, Michel. 1979. *Discipline and Punish: The Birth of the Prison*. New York: Vintage.

———. 1980. *Power/Knowledge: Selected Interviews and Other Writings 1972–1977*. Ed. Colin Gordon. New York: Pantheon.

Fredholm, Michael. 1993. *Burma: Ethnicity and Insurgency*. Westport, Conn.: Praeger.

Fuss, Diana. 1995. *Identification Papers*. New York: Routledge.

Garcia, Alma M. 1990. "The Development of Chicana Feminist Discourse." In *Unequal Sisters: A Multi-cultural Reader in U.S. Women's History*, ed. Ellen Carol DuBois and Vicki L. Ruiz, 418–31. New York: Routledge.

Gatens, Moira. 1997. "Corporeal Representation in/and the Body Politic." In *Writing on the Body: Female Embodiment and Feminist Theory*, ed. Katie Conboy, Nadia Medina, and Sara Stanbury, 81–89. New York: Columbia University Press.

Gates, Henry Louis, Jr. 1993. "Beyond the Culture Wars: Identities in Dialogue." *Profession* 93: 6–11.

——— and Kwame Anthony Appiah. 1992. "Editor's Introduction: Multiplying Identities." *Critical Inquiry* 18 (Summer): 627.

Gates, Henry Louis, Jr. 1986. "Writing, 'Race' and the Difference It Makes." In *"Race," Writing and Difference*, ed. Henry Louis Gates Jr., 1–20. Chicago: University of Chicago Press.

Gereffi, Gary. 1994. "The Organization of Buyer-Driven Global Commodity Chains: How U.S. Retailers Shape Overseas Production Networks." In *Commodity Chains and Global Capitalism*, ed. Gary Gereffi and Miguel Korzeniewicz, 95–122. Westport, Conn.: Greenwood.

Gilliam, Angela. 1991. "Women's Equality and National Liberation." In *Third World Women and the Politics of Feminism*, ed. Chandra Talpade Mohanty, Ann Russo, and Lourdes Torres, 215–36. Bloomington: Indiana University Press.

Gregory, Chester W. 1974. *Women in Defense Work During World War II: An Analysis of the Labor Problem and Women's Rights*. New York: Exposition.

Grosz, Elizabeth. 1989. "Sexual Difference and the Problem of Essentialism." *Inscriptions* 5:1: 86–101.

Hagedorn, Jessica. 1994. "The Exile Within/The Question of Identity." In *The State of Asian America: Activism and Resistance in the 1990's*, ed. Karin Aguilar-San Juan, 173–82. Boston: South End.

Hall, Stuart. 1986. "Gramsci's Relevance for the Study of Race and Ethnicity." In *The Journal of Communication Inquiry* 10:2 (Summer): 5–27.

———. 1991. "The Local and the Global: Globalization and Ethnicity." In *Culture, Globalization and the World-System*, ed. Anthony D. King, 19–39. London: Macmillan.

Hara, Marie. 1994. *Bananaheart and Other Stories*. Honolulu: Bamboo Ridge.

Harlow, Barbara. 1987. *Resistance Literature*. New York: Methuen.

Hayslip, Le Ly, with James Hayslip. 1993. *Child of War, Woman of Peace*. New York: Doubleday.

———, with Jay Wurts. 1989. *When Heaven and Earth Changed Places: A Vietnamese Woman's Journey from War to Peace*. New York: Penguin.

Heng, Geraldine. 1997. "'A Great Way to Fly': Nationalism, the State, and the Varieties of Third-World Feminism." In *Feminist Genealogies, Colonial Legacies, Democratic Futures*, ed. M. Jacqui Alexander and Chandra Talpade Mohanty, 30–45. New York: Routledge.

———, and Janadas Devan. 1992. "State Fatherhood: The Politics of Nationalism, Sexuality, and Race in Singapore." In *Nationalisms and Sexualities*, ed. Andrew Parker, Mary Russo, Doris Sommer, and Patricia Yaeger, 343–64. New York: Routledge.

Hennessy, Rosemary. 1993. *Materialist Feminism and the Politics of Discourse*. New York: Routledge.

Herr, Michael. 1977. *Dispatches*. New York: Knopf.

Hesford, Wendy S., and Wendy Kozol. Forthcoming. *Haunting Violations: Feminist Criticism and the Crisis of the "Real."* Urbana: University of Illinois Press.

Hirst, Paul, and Grahame Thompson. 1995. "Globalization and the Future of the Nation State." *Economy and Society* 24:3 (August): 408–42.

hooks, bell. 1992. *Black Looks: Race and Representation*. Boston: South End.

————. 1989. *Talking Back*. Boston: South End.

Houston, Jeanne Wakatsuki. 1980. "Beyond Manzanar: A Personal View of Asian American Womanhood." In *Asian Americans: Social and Psychological Perspectives*, ed. Russell Endo, Stanley Sue, and Nathanial Wagner, 17–25. Ben Lomond, Calif.: Science and Behavior Books, vol. 2.

————. 1993. "Colors." *New England Review* 15:3 (Summer): 57–73.

———— and James D. Houston. 1973. *Farewell to Manzanar*. New York: Bantam.

Hwang, David Henry. 1988. *M. Butterfly*. New York: Plume.

Irigaray, Luce. 1985 [1977]. *This Sex Which is Not One*. Trans. Catherine Porter with Carolyn Burke. Ithaca, N.Y.: Cornell University Press.

Iyer, Pico. 1988. *Videonight in Kathmandu and Other Reports from the Not-So-Far-East*. New York: Vintage.

Jameson, Fredric. 1981. *The Political Unconscious: Narrative as a Socially Symbolic Act*. Ithaca, N.Y.: Cornell University Press.

————. 1986. "Third World Literature in the Era of Multinational Capitalism." *Social Text* 15 (Fall): 65–87.

Jayawardena, Kumari. 1986. *Feminism and Nationalism in the Third World*. London: Zed.

Jeffords, Susan. 1989. *The Remasculinization of America: Gender and the Vietnam War*. Bloomington: Indiana University Press.

Johnson, Barbara, ed. 1993. *Freedom and Interpretation: The Oxford Amnesty Lectures 1992*. New York: HarperCollins.

Jones, Ann. 1994. *Next Time, She'll Be Dead, Battering and How to Stop It*. Boston: Beacon.

Kabeer, Nalila. 1994. *Reversed Realities: Gender Hierarchies in Development Thought*. London: Verso.

Kadohata, Cynthia. 1989. *The Floating World*. New York: Ballantine.

Kamani, Ginu. 1995. *Junglee Girl*. San Francisco: Aunt Lute.

Kandiyoti, Deniz. 1994. "Identity and its Discontents: Women and the Nation." In *Colonial Discourse and Post-Colonial Theory*, ed. Patrick Williams and Laura Chrisman, 376–91. New York: Columbia University Press.

Kaplan, Carla. 1996. *The Erotics of Talk: Women's Writing and Feminist Paradigms*. New York: Oxford University Press.

Kim, Elaine. 1984. *Asian American Literature: An Introduction to the Writings and Their Social Context*. Philadelphia: Temple University Press.

————. 1990. " 'Such Opposite Creatures': Men and Women in Asian American Literature." *Michigan Quarterly Review* (Winter): 68–93.

Kim, Ronyoung [Gloria Hahn]. 1986. *Clay Walls*. New York: Permanent.

Kingston, Maxine Hong. 1989. *The Woman Warrior*. Alfred A. Knopf, 1976. Reprint. New York: Vintage.

Koshy, Susan. "The Fiction of Asian American Literature." *Yale Journal of Criticism* 9:2 (1996): 315–46.

Kozol, Wendy. Forthcoming. "Relocating Citizenship and Authenticity in Photographs of Japanese Americans During World War II." In *Haunting Violations: Feminist Criticism and the Crisis of the "Real,"* ed. Wendy S. Hesford and Wendy Kozol. 215–50. Urbana: University of Illinois Press.

Kreager, Philip. 1991. "Aung San Suu Kyi and the Peaceful Struggle for Human Rights in Burma." In *Freedom from Fear*, ed. Michael Aris, 284–325. New York: Penguin.

Laguardia, Dolores, and Hans P. Guth, eds. 1993. *American Voices: Multicultural Literacy and Critical Thinking*. Mountain View, Calif.: Mayfield.

Law-Yone, Wendy. 1993. *Irrawaddy Tango*. New York: Knopf.

———. 1989. "Life in the Hills." *Atlantic* (December): 24–36.

———. 1994. "The Year of the Pigeon." In *Without a Guide: Contemporary Women's Travel Adventures*, ed. Katherine Govier, 41–60. Toronto: Macfarlane, Walter and Ross.

Lee, Helie. 1996. *Still Life with Rice: A Young American Woman Discovers the Life and Legacy of Her Korean Grandmother*. New York: Scribner.

Lee, Rachel. 1995. "Claiming Land, Claiming Voice, Claiming Canon: Institutionalized Challenges in Kingston's *China Men* and *The Woman Warrior*." In *ReViewing Asian America: Locating Diversity*, ed. Wendy L. Ng, Soo-Young Chin, James Moy, and Gary Okihiro, 147–59. Pullman: Washington State University Press.

Lee, Sky. 1990. *Disappearing Moon Cafe*. Seattle: The Seal Press.

———. 1990. "Yelling It: Women and Anger Across Cultures." In *Telling It: Women and Language Across Cultures*, ed. The Telling It Book Collective: Sky Lee, Lee Maracle, Daphne Marlatt, Betsy Warland. Vancouver: Press Gang.

Levins Morales, Aurora. 1981. ". . . And Even Fidel Can't Change That!" In *This Bridge Called My Back: Writings by Radical Women of Color*, ed. Cherríe Moraga and Gloria Anzaldúa, 53–56. New York: Kitchen Table: Women of Color Press.

Lim, Shirley Geok-lin. 1996. *Among the White Moon Faces: An Asian-American Memoir of Homelands*. New York: The Feminist Press.

———. 1989. "The English-Language Writer in Singapore." In *The Management of Success: The Moulding of Modern Singapore*, ed. K. S. Sandhu and P. Wheatley, 523–43. Singapore: Institute of Southeast Asian Studies.

Louie, Andrea. 1995. *Moon Cakes*. New York: Ballantine.

Lowe, Lisa. 1991. "Heterogeneity, Hybridity, Multiplicity: Marking Asian American Difference." *Diaspora* 1:1: 24–44.

———. 1996. *Immigrant Acts: On Asian American Cultural Politics*. Durham: Duke University Press.

———. 1994. "Unfaithful to the Original: The Subject of Dictee." In *Writing Self/Writing Nation: Essays on Theresa Hak Kyung Cha's Dictee*, ed. Elaine H. Kim and Norma Alarcon, 35–69. Berkeley: Third Woman Press.

Lum McCunn, Ruthanne. 1981. *Thousand Pieces of Gold: A Biographical Novel*. New York: Dell.

Mani, Lata. 1989. "Multiple Mediations: Feminist Scholarship in the Age of Multinational Reception." *Inscriptions* 5:1: 1–23.

Marcus, Jane. 1988. "Daughters of Anger/Material Girls: Con/textualizing Feminist Criticism." *Women's Studies* 15: 281–308.

Meer, Ameena. 1994. *Bombay Talkie*. London: High Risk Books/Serpent's Tail.

Milkman, Ruth. 1987. *Gender at Work: The Dynamics of Job Segregation by Sex during World War II*. Urbana: University of Illinois Press.

Mirikitani, Janice. 1978. *Awake in the River*. San Francisco: Isthmus.

———. 1987. *Shedding Silence*. Berkeley: Celestial Arts.

Miyoshi, Masao. 1993. "A Borderless World? From Colonialism to Transnationalism and the Decline of the Nation-State." *Critical Inquiry* 19 (Summer): 726–51.

Mohanty, Chandra Talpade. 1991. "Introduction: Cartographies of Struggle: Third World Women and the Politics of Feminism." In *Third World Women and the Politics of Feminism*, ed. Chandra Talpade Mohanty, Ann Russo, and Lourdes Torres, 1–47. Bloomington: Indiana University Press.

Moraga, Cherríe, and Gloria Anzaldúa, eds. 1981. *This Bridge Called My Back: Writings by Radical Women of Color*. Latham, N.Y.: Kitchen Table Press.

Morrison, Toni. 1993. *Playing in the Dark: Whiteness and the Literary Imagination*. New York: Random House.

Mukherjee, Bharati. 1981. "An Invisible Woman." *Saturday Night* (March): 36–40.

———. 1989. *Jasmine*. New York: Ballantine.

———. 1993. "Love Me or Leave Me." In *Visions of America: Personal Narratives from the Promised Land*, ed. Wesley Brown and Amy Ling, 187–94. New York: Persea.

———. 1988. *The Middleman and Other Stories*. New York: Ballantine.

Mura, David. 1993. "No-No Boys: Re-X-Amining Japanese Americans." *New England Review* 15:3 (Summer): 143–65.

Nagata, Donna K., and Yuzuru J. Takeshita. 1998. "Coping and Resilience Across Generations: Japanese Americans and the World War II Internment." *Psychoanalytic Review*, 85:4 (1998): 587–613.

Nguyen, Viet Thanh. 1997. "Representing Reconciliation: Le Ly Hayslip and the Victimized Body." *Positions: East Asia Cultures Critique* 5:2: 605–42.

Noh, Eliza. 1997. "'Amazing Grace, Come Sit on My Face,' or Christian Ecumenical Representations of the Asian Sex Tour Industry." *Positions: East Asia Cultures Critique* 5:2: 439–65.

Odzer, Cleo. 1994. *Patpong Sisters: An American Woman's View of the Bangkok Sex World*. New York: Blue Moon Books.

Omi, Michael, and Howard Winant. 1986. *Racial Formation in the United States, from the 1960's to the 1980's*. New York: Routledge and Kegan Paul.

Ong, Aiwah. 1988. "Colonialism and Modernity: Feminist Re-presentations of Women in Non-Western Societies." *Inscriptions* 3:4: 79–93. University of California, Santa Cruz, Center for Cultural Studies.

Ono, Yoko. 1993. *Family Album June 15–August 30*. Berlin: Stiftung Starke.

———. 1970. *Grapefruit*. Wunternaum Press, 1964. Reprint, New York: Simon and Schuster.

Palumbo-Liu, David. 1995. "Introduction." In *The Ethnic Canon: Histories, Institutions, and Interventions*, ed. David Palumbo-Liu, 1–27. Minneapolis: University of Minnesota Press.

Pateman, Carole. 1988. *The Sexual Contract*. Stanford: Stanford University Press.

Peterson, V. Spike. 1996. "The Politics of Identification in the Context of Globalization," *Women's Studies International* 19:2: 5–15.

Peterson, V. Spike. 1995. "The Politics of Identity and Gendered Nationalism."
In *Foreign Policy Analysis: Contiguity and Change in Its Second Generation*,
ed. Laura Neack, Jeanne A. K. Hey, and Patrick Haney, 167–86. Englewood
Cliffs, N.J.: Prentice Hall.

Qadir, Shahid, Christopher Clapham, and Barry Gills. 1993. "Sustainable
Democracy: Formalism vs. Substance." *Third World Quarterly* 14:3: 415–
22.

Riviere, Joan. 1986 [1929]. "Womanliness as a Masquerade." In *Formations of
Fantasy*, ed. Victor Burgin, James Donald, and Cora Kaplan, 35–44. London:
Methuen.

Rogin, Michael. 1996. *Blackface, White Noise: Jewish Immigrants in the Hollywood Melting Pot*. Berkeley: University of California Press.

———. 1992. "Blackface, White Noise: The Jewish Jazz Singer Finds His Voice."
Critical Inquiry 18 (Spring): 416–53.

Romero, Mary. 1985. "A Comparison between Strategies Used on Prisoners of
War and Battered Wives." *Sex Roles* 13:9/10: 537–47.

Rorty, Richard. 1997. "Justice as a Larger Loyalty." In *Cosmopolitics: Thinking
and Feeling Beyond the Nation*, ed. Pheng Cheah and Bruce Robbins, 45–58.
Minneapolis: University of Minnesota Press.

Rowe, John Carlos. 1989. "'Bringing it all back home': American Recyclings of
the Vietnam War." In *The Violence of Representation: Literature and the History of Violence*, ed. Nancy Armstrong and Len Tennenhouse, 197–218. New
York: Routledge.

Rubin, Gayle S. 1993. "Thinking Sex: Notes for a Radical Theory of the Politics
of Sexuality." In *The Lesbian and Gay Studies Reader*, ed. Henry Abelove,
Michele Aina Barale, and David M. Halperin, 3–44. New York: Routledge.

———. 1975. "Traffic in Women: Notes on the 'Political Economy' of Sex." In
Toward an Anthropology of Women, ed. Rayna Reiter, 157–210. New York:
Monthly Review Press.

Russell, Diana. 1982. *Rape in Marriage*. New York: Macmillan.

Said, Edward. 1984. "The Mind of Winter: Reflections on Life in Exile." *Harpers*
(September): 49–55.

———. 1993. "Nationalism, Human Rights, and Interpretation." In *Freedom
and Interpretation: The Oxford Amnesty Lectures 1992*, ed. Barbara Johnson,
175–205. New York: HarperCollins.

———. 1979. *Orientalism*. New York: Vintage.

San Juan, E., Jr. 1991. "Beyond Identity Politics: The Predicament of the Asian
American Writer in Late Capitalism." *American Literary History* 3:3 (Fall):
542–65.

Scarry, Elaine. 1985. *The Body in Pain: The Making and Unmaking of the World*.
New York: Oxford University of California Press.

Schueller, Malini Johar. 1992. *The Politics of Voice: Liberalism and Social Criticism from Franklin to Kingston*. Albany: SUNY Press.

Scott, Joan W. 1992. "Experience." In *Feminists Theorize the Political*, ed. Judith
Butler and Joan W. Scott, 22–40. New York: Routledge.

Sedgwick, Eve Kosofsky. 1990. *Epistemology of the Closet*. Berkeley: University
of California Press.

Sesser, Stan. 1989. "A Rich Country Gone Wrong." *New Yorker*, 9 October: 55–96.

Silverstein, Josef. 1980. *Burmese Politics: The Dilemma of National Unity*. New Brunswick, N.J.: Rutgers University Press.

Smith, Barbara. 1982. "Toward a Black Feminist Criticism." In *All the Women Are White, All the Blacks Are Men, But Some of Us Are Brave: Black Women's Studies*, ed. Gloria T. Hull, Patricia Bell Scott, and Barbara Smith, 157–75. New York: The Feminist Press.

Song, Cathy. 1983. *Picture Bride*. New Haven: Yale University Press.

Spivak, Gayatri. 1988. "Can the Subaltern Speak?" In *Marxism and the Interpretation of Culture*, ed. Cary Nelson and Lawrence Grossberg. 271–313. Urbana: University of Illinois Press.

———. 1988. *In Other Worlds: Essays in Cultural Politics*. New York: Routledge.

———. 1993. *Outside in the Teaching Machine*. New York: Routledge.

Sturken, Marita. 1991. "The Wall, the Screen, and the Image: The Vietnam Veterans Memorial." *Representations* 35 (Summer): 118–42.

Su, Karen. 1994. "Jade Snow Wong's Badge of Distinction in the 1990's." *Critical Mass: A Journal of Asian American Cultural Criticism*. U.C. Berkeley 2:1 (Winter): 3–52.

Sundquist, Eric J. 1993. *To Wake the Nations: Race in the Making of American Literature*. Cambridge, Mass.: Harvard University Press.

Tajima, Renee E. 1989. "Lotus Blossoms Don't Bleed: Images of Asian Women." In *Making Waves: An Anthology of Writing by and about Asian American Women*, ed. Asian Women United, 308–17. Boston: Beacon.

Takaki, Ronald. 1989. *Strangers from a Different Shore: A History of Asian Americans*. New York: Penguin.

Tan, Amy. 1989. *The Joy Luck Club*. New York: Ballantine.

Tate, Claudia. 1992. *Domestic Allegories of Political Desire: The Black Heroine's Text at the Turn of the Century*. New York: Oxford University Press.

Taylor, Diane. 1997. *Disappearing Acts: Spectacles of Gender and Nationalism in Argentina's "Dirty War."* Durham: Duke University Press.

Telemaque, Eleanor Wong. 1978. *It's Crazy to Stay Chinese in Minnesota*. Nashville: Thomas Nelson.

Tifft, Larry L. 1993. *Battering of Women: The Failure of Intervention and the Case for Prevention*. Boulder, Colo.: Westview.

Trimmer, Joseph F. 1994. "Heaven and Earth: The Making of a Cross-Cultural Autobiography." *CultureFront* (Summer): 33–36, 79.

Trinh, T. Minh-ha. 1989. *Woman, Native, Other: Writing Postcoloniality and Feminism*. Bloomington: Indiana University Press.

Tru'o'ng, Monique T. D. 1997. "Vietnamese American Literature." In *An Interethnic Companion to Asian American Literature*, ed. King-kok Cheung, 219–46. Cambridge: Cambridge University Press.

Turner, Bryan S. 1990. "Outline of a Theory of Citizenship." *Sociology* 24:2 (May): 189–217.

Wade, Robert. 1996. "Globalization and Its Limits: Reports of the Death of the National Economy are Greatly Exaggerated." In *National Diversity and*

Global Capitalism, ed. Suzanne Berger and Ronald Dore, 60–88. Ithaca, N.Y.: Cornell University Press.

Walker, Lenore E. 1979. *The Battered Woman*. New York: HarperPerennial.

Wallace, Michele. 1982. "A Black Feminist's Search for Sisterhood." In *All the Women Are White, All the Blacks Are Men, But Some of Us Are Brave: Black Women's Studies*, ed. Gloria T. Hull, Patricia Bell Scott, and Barbara Smith. New York: The Feminist Press.

Wallerstein, Immanuel. 1995. "The Construction of Peoplehood: Racism, Nationalism, Ethnicity." Editions La Découverte, 1988. Reprint. *Race, Nation, Class: Ambiguous Identities*, by Etienne Balibar and Immanuel Wallerstein, trans. Chris Turner. London: Verso.

———. 1991. *Geopolitics and Geoculture: Essays on the Changing World-system*. Cambridge: Cambridge University Press.

Weglyn, Michi. 1976. *Years of Infamy: The Untold Story of America's Concentration Camps*. New York: William Morrow.

Weiss, Linda. 1997. "Globalization and the Myth of the Powerless State." *New Left Review* 225: 3–27.

West, Lois. 1992. "Feminist Nationalist Social Movements: Beyond Universalism and Towards a Gendered Cultural Relativism." *Women's Studies International* 15:5/6: 563–79.

White, Hayden. 1973. *Metahistory: The Historical Imagination in Nineteenth-Century Europe*. Baltimore: Johns Hopkins University Press.

Wiegman, Robyn. 1995. *American Anatomies: Theorizing Race and Gender*. Durham: Duke University Press.

Wong, Jade Snow. 1989. *Fifth Chinese Daughter*. Seattle: University of Washington Press.

———. 1951. "Growing Up Between the Old World and the New." *The Hornbook Magazine* 27 (December).

———. 1975. *No Chinese Stranger*. New York: Harper & Row.

Wong, Nellie. 1984. *The Death of Long Steam Lady*. Los Angeles: West End.

———. 1977. *Dreams in Harrison Railroad Park*. Berkeley: Kelsey St. Press.

Wong, Sau-ling Cynthia. 1995a. "Denationalization Reconsidered: Asian American Cultural Criticism at a Theoretical Crossroads." *Amerasia Journal* 21:1/2: 1–27.

———. 1993. *Reading Asian American Literature: From Necessity to Extravagance*. Princeton: Princeton University Press.

———. 1995b. "'Sugar Sisterhood': Situating the Amy Tan Phenomenon." In *The Ethnic Canon: Histories, Institutions, and Interventions*, ed. David Palumbo-Liu, 174–210. Minneapolis: University of Minnesota Press.

Wong, Shawn. 1995. *American Knees*. New York: Simon and Schuster.

———. 1993. "Literary Scholarship in the 1990s." In *Bearing Dreams, Shaping Visions: Asian Pacific American Perspectives*, ed. Linda Revilla, Gail M. Nomura, Shawn Wong, and Shirley Hune. Pullman: Washington State University Press.

Wong, Shelley Sunn. 1994. "Unnaming the Same: Theresa Hak Kyung Cha's *Dictee*." In *Writing Self, Writing Nation: A Collection of Essays on Dictee*, ed. Elaine H. Kim and Norma Alarcon, 103–40. Berkeley: Third Woman Press.

Wong, Su-Ling, and E. H. Cressy. 1952. *Daughter of Confucius: A Personal History*. New York: Farrar.

Woo, Merle. 1981. "Letter to Ma." In *This Bridge Called My Back: Writings by Radical Women of Color*, ed. Cherríe Moraga and Gloria Anzaldúa, 140–47. New York: Kitchen Table: Women of Color Press.

Woolf, Virginia. 1938. *Three Guineas*. London: Hogarth.

Yamada, Mitsuye. 1982. *Camp Notes and Other Poems*. Shameless Hussy Press, 1976. Reprint Latham, N.Y.: Kitchen Table: Woman of Color Press.

———. 1981. "Invisibility is an Unnatural Disaster: Reflections of an Asian American Woman." In *This Bridge Called My Back: Writings by Radical Women of Color*, ed. Cherríe Moraga and Gloria Anzaldúa, 35–40. Latham, N.Y.: Kitchen Table: Women of Color Press.

Yamamoto, Traise. 1999. *Masking Selves, Making Subjects: Japanese American Women, Identity, and the Body*. Berkeley: University of California Press.

Young, Iris Marion. 1987. "Impartiality and the Civic Public: Some Implications of Feminist Critiques of Moral and Political Theory." In *Feminism as Critique: On the Politics of Gender*, ed. Seyla Benhabib and Drucilla Cornell, 37–76. Minneapolis: University of Minnesota Press.

———. 1990. *Throwing Like a Girl and Other Essays in Feminist Philosophy and Social Theory*. Bloomington: Indiana University Press.

Yung, Judy. 1990. "The Social Awakening of Chinese American Women as Reported in *Chung Sai Yat Po*, 1900–1911." In *Unequal Sisters: A Multi-cultural Reader in U.S. Women's History*, ed. Ellen Carol DuBois and Vicki L. Ruiz, 195–207. New York: Routledge.

Yuval-Davis, Nira. 1991. "The Citizenship Debate: Women, Ethnic Processes and the State." *Feminist Review* 39 (Winter): 58–68.

———. 1997. *Gender and Nation*. London: Sage.

Index